THE GREEN
NEW DEAL
FROM BELOW

THE GREEN
NEW DEAL
FROM BELOW

HOW ORDINARY PEOPLE
ARE BUILDING A JUST
AND CLIMATE-SAFE ECONOMY

Jeremy Brecher

Publication was supported by a grant from the Howard
D. and Marjorie I. Brooks Fund for Progressive
Thought.

Library of Congress Cataloging-in-Publication Data
Names: Brecher, Jeremy, author.
Title: The green new deal from below : how ordinary
people are building a just and climate-safe economy
/ Jeremy Brecher.
Description: Urbana : University of Illinois Press,
[2024] | Includes bibliographical references and
index.
Identifiers: LCCN 2024020317 (print) | LCCN
2024020318 (ebook) | ISBN 9780252046186 (cloth ;
alk. paper) | ISBN 9780252088278 (paperback ; alk.
paper) | ISBN 9780252047459 (ebook)
Subjects: LCSH: Environmental policy—Economic
aspects—United States. | Sustainable development—
United States. | Economic development—
Environmental aspects—United States. | Social
justice—United States.
Classification: LCC HC110.E5 B698 2024 (print) |
LCC HC110.E5 (ebook) | DDC 333.70973—dc23/
eng/202405
LC record available at https://lccn.loc.gov/2024020317
LC ebook record available at https://lccn.loc.
gov/2024020318

CONTENTS

ACKNOWLEDGMENTS

I would like to thank all my friends and coworkers at the Labor Network for Sustainability, who have contributed to making this book possible and who are helping create a Green New Deal from Below.

Thanks once again to Jill Cutler, who has uncomplainingly served as my "in-house editor" through more versions of this material than I would care to count.

Thanks to Becky Glass, who provided invaluable editorial assistance along the way.

Thanks to Jamie Cantoni, who has contributed to the making of this book in innumerable ways, and has also helped create conditions that have facilitated its writing.

Thanks to Todd E. Vachon, who has been an exemplary ally in developing the vision of the Green New Deal from Below.

Thanks to Ming Chu Yuen for much help along the way.

Thanks to all who have read parts of the material for this book at various stages.

Thanks to Data for Progress for permission to use their charts.

Thanks to Greenpeace, the Connecticut Roundtable on Climate and Jobs, and Mustafa Salahudden for permission to use photographs.

Special thanks to Iris Dement for her inspiration and for permission to quote from her anthem "Workin' on a World."

This book is dedicated to all those who are building the Green New Deal. They are indeed "workin' on a world."

INTRODUCTION
SHIFTING THE SENSE OF WHAT IS POSSIBLE

The Green New Deal is a visionary program designed to protect the earth's climate while creating good jobs, reducing injustice, and eliminating poverty. Its core principle is to unite the necessity for climate protection with the goals of full employment and social justice.

The Green New Deal erupted into public attention as a proposal for national legislation, and the struggle to embody it in national legislation is ongoing. But there has also emerged a little-noticed wave of initiatives from community groups, unions, city and state governments, tribes, and other nonfederal actors designed to contribute to the climate protection and social justice goals of the Green New Deal. Rep. Alexandria Ocasio-Cortez (AOC), who helped initiate the campaign for a Green New Deal, has called it "a Green New Deal from Below."[1]

The purpose of this book is to provide an overview of Green New Deal from Below initiatives in many different arenas and locations. These initiatives encompass a broad range of the programs already under way and in development. The projects of Green New Dealers recounted here should provide inspiration for thousands more that can create the foundation for local, national, and even global mobilization—and reconstruction.

THE NEW DEAL AND THE GREEN NEW DEAL

In 1933, in the depths of the worst economic depression the United States has ever known, newly elected president Franklin D. Roosevelt launched the New Deal, a set of government programs to provide employment and social security, reform tax policies and business practices, and stimulate economic recovery. It included the building of homes, hospitals, school,

"Make Detroit the Engine of the Green New Deal!" July 31, 2019. Photo by Paul Becker, Wikimedia commons.

roads, dams, and electrical grids, as well as restoration of millions of acres of degraded farm and forest land. The New Deal put millions of people to work and created a new policy framework for American democracy. It became the touchstone of US politics for the rest of the decade, galvanizing efforts for democratic social change while provoking wrathful condemnation from defenders of the status quo.

The New Deal was a cluster of social experiments whose wide-ranging programs were primarily designed to counter various aspects of the Great Depression. These programs included public employment (Works Progress Administration and Civilian Conservation Corps); farm price supports (Agricultural Adjustment Act); environmental restoration (reforestation and land conservation); labor rights (Wagner Act); minimum wages and standards (National Recovery Act and Fair Labor Standards Act); cooperative enterprises (Works Progress Administration support for self-help); public infrastructure development (Tennessee Valley Authority and rural electrification); subsidies for basic necessities (food commodity programs and the Federal Housing Act); construction of schools, parks, and housing (Civil Works Administration); and income maintenance (Social Security Act).

The New Deal of the 1930s was not a single program or piece of legislation—it was a whole era of turmoil in which contesting forces tried to meet a devasting crisis and shape the future of American society. Besides its famous "alphabet soup" of federal agencies, the New Deal was part of a process of social change that included experimentation at a state, regional, and local level; organization among labor, unemployed, urban, elderly, and other grassroots constituencies; and lively debate on future possibilities that went far beyond the policies actually adopted.

Eighty-five years later, the New Deal still haunted the American imagination—and became the symbol for a new effort to address the emerging crises of climate, inequality, injustice, and job degradation. In the week following the 2018 midterm elections, a group of 150 protesters led by young people with the Sunrise Movement occupied the office of likely Democratic House Majority Leader Nancy Pelosi, urging her to support a "Green New Deal." Newly elected House Rep. Alexandria Ocasio-Cortez (D-NY) joined the protest with a resolution in hand to establish a Select Committee for a Green New Deal. It drew on the heritage of the original New Deal to call for a "new national, social, industrial, and economic mobilization on a scale not seen since World War II and the New Deal." It also drew on proposals that were widespread a decade earlier for a Global Green New Deal to counter both climate change and the Great Recession. From its inception it represented a confluence of "outsider" social movements and "insider" elected representatives.

The proposal quickly amassed support among congressional representatives, progressive organizations, and young people across the country. A poll released December 14, 2018, by the Yale Program on Climate Change Communication found that 40 percent of registered voters "strongly support" and 41 percent "somewhat support" the general concepts behind a Green New Deal.[2] A poll by Data for Progress (shown below) in early 2024—five years after the introduction of the original Green New Deal resolution—found that "the Green New Deal is still incredibly popular."[3]

The Green New Deal Agenda and Accompanying Bills Are Widely Popular

Respondents received a series of questions that described the Green New Deal agenda and specific bills that have been proposed by lawmakers in recent sessions of Congress. After reviewing a description, respondents were then asked whether they support or oppose the policy.

	Strongly support	Somewhat support	Don't know	Somewhat oppose	Strongly oppose	Support	Oppose	Net
Green New Deal for Health	33%	35%	8%	9%	14%	68	23	+45
Green New Deal for Public Schools	34%	34%	7%	10%	15%	68	25	+43
Green New Deal for Public Housing	34%	33%	8%	10%	15%	67	25	+42
Green New Deal	31%	34%	9%	9%	16%	65	25	+40
Green New Deal for Cities	29%	34%	9%	13%	15%	63	28	+35

0% 25% 50% 75% 100%

January 26–27, 2024 survey of 1,216 U.S. likely voters   ⊞ DATA FOR **PROGRESS**

The original 2018 Green New Deal resolution submitted by Representative Ocasio-Cortez (AOC) called for a ten-year mobilization to achieve 100 percent of national power generation from renewable sources; a national "smart grid"; energy efficiency upgrades for every residential and industrial building; decarbonizing manufacturing, agriculture, transportation, and other infrastructure; and helping other countries achieve carbon-neutral economies and a global Green New Deal. It proposed a job guarantee to assure a living wage job to every person who wanted one, mitigation of income and wealth inequality, basic income programs, and universal health care. The resolution advocated innovative financial structures including cooperative and public ownership and public banks. Since that time, a wide-ranging discussion has extended and fleshed out the vision of the Green New Deal to include an even broader range of proposals to address climate, jobs, and justice.

At its core, the Green New Deal would work toward saving the climate by meeting scientific targets for the reduction of greenhouse gases. It would seek to end the epidemic of poverty by mitigating deeply entrenched racial, regional, and gender-based inequalities in income and wealth and distributing federal aid and other investment equitably to historically impoverished and marginalized communities. And it would provide good jobs, constructing a just and climate-safe economy.

A wide swath of public interest organizations soon endorsed the Green New Deal; it also instantly became a prime whipping boy for the Right. Its core ideas were embodied in legislation introduced by Ocasio-Cortez and Sen. Edwin Markey, which divided the Democratic party into pro- and anti-Green New Deal factions. Democratic presidential candidate Joe Biden convened a unity task force that included Sen. Bernie Sanders, AOC, and the head of Sunrise, which recommended a plan for "combatting the climate crisis and pursuing environmental justice" that incorporated many elements of the Green New Deal but eschewed the name. Biden called his program Build Back Better, and after the 2020 elections, this became the nomenclature of choice for Democratic party and allied climate, jobs, and justice programs. A broad coalition of organizations called the Green New Deal Network, for example, developed and promoted an extensive legislative program, described on its website as "in line with the Green New Deal vision," which it dubbed the THRIVE Agenda.[4] Supported by more than 100 members of Congress and 280 organizations, the THRIVE Act was introduced in Congress in the fall of 2020.

In August 2022, Congress passed President Biden's Inflation Reduction Act, which includes many important elements of the Green New Deal. It provides the largest climate protection investment ever made. The act will create an estimated 1 to 1.5 million jobs annually for a ten-year period. It includes modest but significant funding to address pollution in frontline communities. But the power of the fossil fuel industry and its allies was still enough to gut important parts of a Green New Deal program for climate, jobs, and justice—and to add provisions that actually promote climate change and environmental injustice.

The legislation includes only a fraction of the investment necessary to meet the 2015 Paris Agreement's climate goals and prevent the worst consequences of global warming. It allows much of its funding to be squandered on unproven technologies that claim to reduce greenhouse gas emissions but whose primary effect may simply be to enable the continued burning of fossil fuels—and to enrich their promoters. It allows *increased* extraction of fossil fuels, especially on federal lands. It allows massive drilling and pipeline construction that will turn areas like the Gulf Coast, Appalachia, and Alaska into de facto "sacrifice zones" where expanded fossil fuel infrastructure will devastate the environment—and the people. It does not guarantee that the jobs it creates will be good jobs. It makes few "just transition" provisions for workers and communities whose livelihoods may be threatened by the changes it will fund. It lacks the visionary quality of the Green New Deal while falling far short of its specific policies.

The Green New Deal was displaced from the central role in political and media attention it had gained by three forces. The excoriating attacks of the political Right, supported by the fossil fuel industry, helped publicize but also stigmatize the Green New Deal, leading to a loss of its initial support among Republicans and some independents. Joe Biden's substituting "Build Back Better" for the "Green New Deal" coopted much of its program while reducing its profile in the public arena. The legislative struggles over Biden's Build Back Better programs lacked the transformational dimension of the Green New Deal.[5]

The Green New Deal still embodies the aspirations of a wide swath of the American people for a transformation that will address climate, jobs, and justice. A poll by Data for Progress found "The Green New Deal is incredibly popular."[6] In early 2022, Data for Progress conducted polling on six core Green New Deal bills. Even with high costs disclosed, every bill has majority support from every demographic polled other than Republicans. That means that men, women, voters over and under forty-five all strongly supported every bill, as did Black, white, and Latinx voters, and urban, rural, and suburban voters. Black voters supported every core piece of GND legislation by at least +60 percentage points. The Green New Deal for Cities, which would fund climate projects in every city or county, enjoyed support from rural voters by an +35-point margin. Republicans support the Green New Deal for Schools by a 4-point margin. All bills enjoyed some GOP voter support while they receive zero GOP support in Congress.

Despite this wide popular support, the Green New Deal has been largely stymied by a national political system corrupted by fossil fuel interests, deadlocked by Republican intransigence, and intimidated by right-wing abuse—and because many though not all national-level Democratic party politicians have shut up about it.

THE GREEN NEW DEAL—FROM BELOW

The Green New Deal was a proposal for national mobilization, and national legislation has remained an essential element. How much of the national Green New Deal program will actually be passed now or in the future remains uncertain.

But meanwhile, there are thousands of efforts to realize the goals of the Green New Deal at community, municipal, county, state, tribal, industry, and sectoral levels. While these cannot substitute for a national program, they can contribute enormously to the Green New Deal's goals of climate protection, jobs, and economic justice. Indeed, they may well turn out to be the tip of the Green New Deal spear, developing in the vacuum left by the limitations of national programs.

These may appear to be isolated, unconnected efforts, but in fact they represent a concerted force with common goals, strategies, and modes of action—a veritable Green New Deal from Below. The Green New Deal from Below is a unique political formation, neither a political party or lobby nor a civil society organization, not exclusively an electoral machine nor exclusively a direct-action movement. While it embodies thousands of initiatives in hundreds of cities, states, unions, communities, universities, and other institutions it is not a set of unrelated bits and pieces. To deny the Green New Deal from Below is an entity is like seeing the steeple, the doors, the cross, the altar, and the stones of a church but maintaining there is no church—only these disparate elements.

The Green New Deal from Below embodies a strategy known in military terminology as "outflanking." While Green New Deal programs have been largely blocked at the federal level, its proponents have moved to hundreds of arenas at state, local, and civil society levels. Its efforts are linked into what has been called the "Lilliput strategy," in which power results not from control of one dominant power center, but rather from the linking and distributed coordination of myriad dispersed forces.

The unifying concept of the many Green New Deal from Below initiatives is to meet the urgent need for climate protection in ways that address the needs of working people and disadvantaged constituencies. This provides a framework for moving beyond piecemeal policies to a set of integrated strategies for social change. For example, it integrates the need to protect the climate with the need for good jobs. It similarly integrates the need for climate protection with the need to reduce the current concentration of carbon pollution, such as fossil fuel power plants, in impoverished neighborhoods of color.

This integration of programs and policies goes hand in hand with the integration of previously isolated or antagonistic constituencies. The Green New Deals from Below described in this book are almost all the product of coalitions in which diverse participants join together around common interests and a common program. Coalition participants often include neighborhood and community groups, unions and other labor organizations, ethnic and racial organizations, political leaders and activists, government officials and staff members, youth and senior groups, and religious congregations, as well as environmental, climate, and climate justice organizations.

The way the Green New Deals from Below implement their objectives is strikingly different from dominant principles of public policy over recent decades—often referred to as "neoliberalism"—that defined private enterprises as the only appropriate vehicles for realizing social objectives and condemned governmental policies that pursued means or ends other than facilitating the accumulation of private wealth. Rather than simply offering financial incentives for desired behavior, Green New Deal programs involve public planning, investment, and strict criteria for realizing public goals. Implementation is not limited to private corporations but involves direct government programs, public banks, coops, and other alternatives to private profit-driven corporations. Finding resources often involves "Robin Hood" strategies like fees for fossil fuel pollution and taxes on large corporations.

The climate protection policies of Green New Deals from Below aim to reduce greenhouse gas emissions at the rapid pace that climate science has determined is necessary. They focus on the effective strategies promoted by climate scientists: expand renewable energy; use energy more efficiently; and rapidly eliminate the burning of fossil fuels. They have generally eschewed such unproven, dangerous, and/or far more costly approaches as capturing greenhouse gases after they have been produced, adding hydrogen to the fossil fuel mix, and expanding the use of nuclear energy.

The Green New Deal from Below is what is sometimes called a hybrid movement, one that operates both inside and outside the dominant political framework. It includes established and aspiring elected officials, party leaders, government bureaucrats, and electoral activists. It also includes communities, ethnic groups, labor organizations, and a great range of other constituencies existing in civil society. It pursues its objectives through a combination of conventional political methods like supporting candidates, proposing and lobbying for legislation, and educating and persuading the public; and direct-action methods like occupying the offices of politicians, blocking the building of fossil fuel pipelines, and participating in and supporting strikes that aim for a just transition to a climate-safe economy. Green New Deals simultaneously act within, alongside, and against the institutions and personnel of the political system.

Green New Deal from Below actions are almost always conducted by coalitions of very diverse constituencies. The Green New Deal for Education brings together teachers, other school staff, students, parents, construction worker unions, and racial justice advocates to fight for investment in healthy schools free from fossil fuel pollution. Similarly, state coalitions have brought together unions, climate-impacted communities, discriminated-against racial and ethnic groups, and climate and climate justice advocates around legislation phasing out fossil fuels in ways that will create good jobs, support community development, eliminate environmental injustices, and build climate-friendly housing and transit.

Green New Deal from Below actions aim to make concrete changes that make a difference in people's daily lives—whether that be through shutting down a polluting coal-fired power plant in an asthma-stricken community or providing free transit or free bicycles for young people. They aim to educate and inspire; for example, free transit and free bicycles not only reduce vehicle pollution but let young people discover for themselves alternatives to cars for getting around. They aim to shift the balance of power away from fossil fuel polluters, exploitative corporations, and the wealth-bloated 1 percent and toward exploited workers, discriminated-against constituencies and communities, and other non-elites. And, as a necessary means to all these ends, they aim to expand democracy and counter our national trend toward autocracy and plutocracy.

The Green New Deals have powerful opponents. They range from fossil fuel companies striving to maintain a business strategy that means "game over" for a decent human life and natural environment to wealthy individuals and institutions striving to maintain and expand an unjust share of the good things of the earth. While the Green New Deal from Below has had some notable successes—many of them recounted in this book—there is no guarantee that it will ultimately prevail.

Green New Deal initiatives at local and state levels can play a crucial role in realizing both the climate and the justice goals of the Green New Deal. They can build a constituency supporting a national Green New Deal. They can serve as testing grounds that provide a "proof of concept" for the Green New Deal. They can provide building blocks that can be linked together to form a Green New Deal that is more effective because it has strong local roots. Programs "from below" can reach out and coordinate with each other. They can also be coordinated with national level planning and investment; some national Green New Deal proposals lay out policies and institutions through which such coordination can be promoted. Realizing Green New Deal goals requires a federal and even a global role, but the Green New Deal from Below is starting right at home.

The greatest success of the Green New Deal from Below may be to expand the limits of the possible. It thereby empowers people to fight for the things they need but which have long seemed beyond their reach. To paraphrase Boston's Green New Deal mayor Michelle Wu, it has shifted "the sense of what was possible."

BOOK OUTLINE

Chapters 1 and 2 of this book examine Green New Deals in the cities and in the states. Chapters 3 and 4 present the central role of organized labor and frontline communities in the Green New Deal from Below. Chapters 5, 6, and 7 describe how the Green New Deal from Below is building a climate-safe economy through renewable energy production, energy efficiency, and phasing out fossil fuel extraction and burning. Chapter 8 looks at Green New Deal programs in transportation, one of the crucial areas for climate, jobs, and justice. Chapters 9 and 10 describe how local and state Green New Deals are protecting workers and communities who might otherwise be harmed by the transition to a climate-safe economy. Chapter 11 lays out Green New Deal jobs programs, jobs corps, and legislation designed to reverse the burgeoning degradation of work. The conclusion interprets the Green New Deal from Below as a political strategy for integrating programs and people to realize climate, jobs, and justice. While the chapters have been framed to present a comprehensive view of the Green New Deal from Below, the different strands of the story are inherently intertwined and so the subjects covered in the chapters inevitably overlap.

This book is designed to provide an overview of the Green New Deal from Below as a whole while also presenting a wide range of examples. These examples are presented in varying depth to allow broad coverage while also showing in detail how Green New Deals from Below actually work on the ground. Different accounts deliberately focus on different aspects of the story, such as historical background, political context, organizational matrices, coalition structure, policy choices, and political power.

Some of the examples presented in this book are explicitly self-described as Green New Deal programs; others don't use the label but seek the same goals and apply similar principles. These examples are by no means exhaustive—they are just a small selection of the activities under way or being initiated. Nor is there any pretense that any of them represent perfect realization of Green New Deal objectives—they are limited both by the inevitable problems of innovation conducted by imperfect human beings in the face of massive and destructive opposition, and by the absence of a concerted national program. But to a remarkable extent they are realizing core goals of the Green New Deal by reducing fossil fuel pollution, creating jobs, and reducing injustice. They are offered as inspiring examples of the possibilities for popular action and the potentials for achieving both climate and justice objectives.

This book was started in the fall of 2021 and finalized in the fall of 2023. Many of the stories it tells were in mid-career, their ultimate outcomes still hanging in the balance. That is also true of the Green New Deal from Below as a whole. Is it a brilliant flame that may simply burn out? Will it continue as one but not a decisive element in a society and a world hurtling toward midnight? Or will it prove to be the start of a turn away from catastrophe and toward security and justice? The answer will largely depend on what people decide to do with the possibilities opened up by the Green New Deal from Below.

Some of the efforts described in this book have already met rebuff or rollback. Culver City, California, for example, replaced car lanes with bike lanes on some of its roads in 2021, but in 2023 it converted bike lanes back to car lanes.

But new and expanded Green New Deal–style initiatives are also occurring all the time. In April 2023, for example, Brandon Johnson, a union organizer, was elected mayor on a "Green New Deal for Chicago" platform and immediately initiated the Chicago Green New Deal. In May 2023 the New York state legislature passed the Build Public Renewables Act to start investing in renewable energy and requiring state-owned properties to run on renewable energy by 2030. The Educators Climate Action Network (ECAN), representing American Federation of Teachers and

National Education Association local unions across the country, launched a campaign for a Green New Deal for Schools. And in September 2023 the United Auto Workers union struck the Big Three auto companies demanding a "just transition" to carbon-free electric vehicles—and won their core just-transition demands, laying the basis for a transformation of the US auto industry.

The world historian Arnold Toynbee once delineated how great civilizational changes occur. Existing leaders of existing institutions face new challenges—but fail to change to meet them. Their civilizations thereby become vulnerable to collapse. In such a setting, however, a creative minority may arise that proposes—and begins to implement—new solutions. Surely climate change represents such a civilizational challenge, and just as surely our existing institutions and their leaders are failing to make the changes it requires. But at the grassroots a creative minority is at work establishing new solutions that are reconstructing society on new principles. Their work is manifested in the Green New Deal from Below.

To realize its potential, the Green New Deal must be more than a collection of federal programs; it must be a society-wide effort, a popular mobilization. The original New Deal of the Great Depression was just that. Millions of people in thousands of communities pitched in to undertake local initiatives. These initiatives often reached out to each other locally, regionally, and nationally, both assisting and demanding change at the top. Meanwhile, the national New Deal encouraged and supported these local initiatives. The result was the New Deal as a social movement that went beyond the vision of many of its national leaders to implement democratic grassroots change to meet the desperate needs of its participants.

That is the promise of the Green New Deal from Below. To see in detail how Green New Deals from Below are achieving all this "on the ground," read on!

1

THE GREEN NEW DEAL IN THE CITIES

The Green New Deal has been largely blocked at the national level, but it is thriving in communities, cities, and states. Some of the most impressive implementations of its principles and policies are occurring at a municipal level. In cities throughout the United States, new political formations, often but not always under the banner of the Green New Deal, are creating a new form of urban politics. They pursue the Green New Deal's core objectives of fighting climate change in ways that produce good jobs and increase equality based on coalitions of activists from impoverished neighborhoods, disempowered racial and ethnic groups, organized labor, and advocates for the environment. These coalitions engage widespread democratic mobilization. In this chapter I examine Green New Deal–style programs developing in Boston, Los Angeles, and Seattle, and review other programs and policies being adopted in cities around the country that use climate protection as a vehicle for creating jobs and challenging injustice.

BOSTON'S GREEN NEW DEAL

According to a 2020 report, if global warming is not abated Boston could have forty days above 90 degrees Fahrenheit annually by 2030. By 2070 it could have ninety such high-heat days—virtually the entire summer—and thirty days reaching or exceeding 100 degrees.[1]

Boston has the nation's third highest rate of displacement of longstanding minority communities by gentrification.[2] A nationwide survey shows that Black people consider Boston the least welcoming of eight major American cities. Only 4 percent of households earning $75,000 or more across Greater Boston are African American.[3]

Green New Deal Press Conference, Seattle City Council, August 6, 2019. Wikimedia commons.

In April 2019, shortly after Rep. Alexandria Ocasio-Cortez and Sen. Ed Markey submitted their Green New Deal resolution to Congress, the Boston City Council passed 9–3 a resolution supporting it. Lead sponsor City Councilor Michelle Wu said, "The climate crisis is here now. We see it in Boston every single year."[4]

Wu also posed a question to the Boston climate community: "What could the city do in the vacuum of federal leadership?"[5] Her answer came in the form of the report "Planning for a Boston Green New Deal and Just Recovery,"[6] which took eighteen months to develop through local conversations and consultations with experts. Drawing on plans and programs from Seattle, Los Angeles, New York, Austin, Minneapolis, Madison, and Long Beach, the report called for carbon neutrality by 2040, 100 percent sustainable electricity by 2035, net-zero municipal buildings by 2024, expanding the city's tree canopy, and establishing a youth Urban Climate Corps. It also included a "Blue New Deal" to connect local fishers to Boston restaurants and food distributors.[7]

The plan emphasized the justice dimension of the Green New Deal. Brad Campbell, president of the Conservation Law Foundation, said, "It really covers a broader range of issues and much more explicitly ties the climate crisis to social justice issues." Nina Schlegel, a Boston climate activist on Wu's staff, said, we want "policy change that also dismantles and rectifies past injustices." That means "looking at housing and displacement and looking at the proliferation of luxury development." It means "looking at unequal access to transit, and where our heat islands are located." The plan proposed comprehensive rezoning to increase neighborhood density, building inexpensive cooperative housing, adding parks, free-to-ride electric buses, and intersecting bike lanes and car-free walking districts. The plan included a "justice audit" of city programs and spending. Green bonds and taxes on predatory landlords would help fund it.[8]

The Boston Green New Deal built on more than a decade of research and grassroots organizing around climate and justice issues. It was also the program for Wu's anticipated run for mayor of Boston.

The daughter of Taiwanese immigrants, Wu was the first nonwhite woman to serve as Boston City Council president. She presents her concerns about both climate and social justice based on her personal experience. Climate change is "very personal"; we need to "draw people in by focusing on how every single person is deeply impacted." She tells people, "I'm a mom, and I have two boys, they're 3 and 5. I want more than a coin flip's chance for my two boys to be able to live on this planet and enjoy it."

A poll by Demos shortly before the election found strong support among Boston voters for a Green New Deal agenda that would invest in green energy and promote clean air and water for residents. Boston voters supported a Green New Deal agenda by more than a 60-point margin—including Democrats by a more than an 85-point margin and independents by more than a 34-point margin (see graphic on the next page).[9]

Wu explained her electoral strategy in an interview in *The Nation*:

> In my time in City Hall, it has been less about shifting the odds of who can win and more about shifting the sense of what was possible. In Boston, from the very beginning of our campaign, my team and I decided we would run on big ideas and deep organizing, and focus more on building community anywhere we went rather than trying to corral the numbers for a specific day and leave it there. So we ran a campaign that put our resources toward distributed [grassroots] organizing and multilingual outreach. We had neighborhood organizing teams across every neighborhood in our city, and we had launched a campaign almost 14 months before Election Day, but many of our volunteers and neighborhood leaders were first-time campaign volunteers. We were lightly supporting and checking in with everyone, but our teams were running independently and designing their own activities.[10]

On election day Wu won 64 percent of the vote.

Boston Voters Strongly Support The City Pursuing a Green New Deal Agenda

Do you support or oppose the Boston City Council pursuing a Green New Deal Agenda, by which the council would pursue policies to invest in green energy and promote clean air and water for city residents?

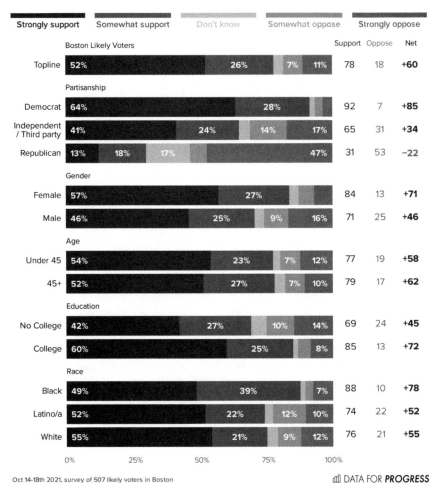

	Support	Oppose	Net
Boston Likely Voters			
Topline	78	18	**+60**
Partisanship			
Democrat	92	7	**+85**
Independent / Third party	65	31	**+34**
Republican	31	53	**−22**
Gender			
Female	84	13	**+71**
Male	71	25	**+46**
Age			
Under 45	77	19	**+58**
45+	79	17	**+62**
Education			
No College	69	24	**+45**
College	85	13	**+72**
Race			
Black	88	10	**+78**
Latino/a	74	22	**+52**
White	76	21	**+55**

Oct 14-18th 2021, survey of 507 likely voters in Boston   DATA FOR **PROGRESS**

THE BOSTON GREEN NEW DEAL HITS THE GROUND RUNNING

Like Franklin Roosevelt's original New Deal, the Boston Green New Deal jump-started with a rapid cascade of new legislation and new programs, starting on the first day of the mayor's administration with transit.

The cost of public transportation has been a class issue in Boston for a long time. A song written for the 1949 Boston mayoral campaign called

"The MTA"—originally banned on Boston radio and a decade later a national top hit for the Kingston Trio—proclaimed:

> You citizens of Boston don't you think it's a scandal
> How the people have to pay and pay?
> Fight the fare increase!

A central plank of the Boston Green New Deal—embodying both climate and justice objectives—was free public transportation, aka "Free the T." On her first day in office, Mayor Wu announced a pilot fare-free bus program, which set aside $8 million for lines serving environmental justice communities.

Two weeks later Mayor Wu announced a new fleet utilization policy to deploy electric vehicles for the city and add seventy-eight EV charging stations by the end of 2022. The city also partnered with two community organizations to launch a community-based EV car share service in Roxbury called Good2Go, which makes available EV cars for as little as $5 an hour.[11] The city subsequently launched an electric school bus pilot program, replacing twenty diesel buses with electric ones as a first step toward full electrification of the school bus fleet by 2030. The city also launched an electric vehicle "train the trainer" program under which the city's central fleet management team will train students and city fleet managers in electric vehicle maintenance.[12]

Right after Mayor Wu's inauguration the Boston City Council unanimously voted to divest Boston's $1.3 billion trust funds from fossil fuels, tobacco, and private prisons. Signing the ordinance as her first in office, Wu said, "In this closing window of time to act, Boston must lead by taking every possible step for climate justice. Divesting from harmful industries to invest in sustainable and healthy jobs is not only the pathway to a green and resilient future; it's also the most responsible stewardship of taxpayer dollars." She called it a "big step forward towards a Boston Green New Deal."[13]

The Boston Green New Deal moved rapidly to address the needs of historically poor and discriminated-against communities. In April Mayor Wu announced a Heat Plan focused on five environmental justice "hot spot" communities: Chinatown, Dorchester, East Boston, Mattapan, and Roxbury. The Heat Plan is a component of Climate Ready Boston, the city's initiative to prepare for the near- and long-term effects of climate change, including sea-level rise, coastal storms, extreme precipitation, and extreme heat.

Climate Ready Boston was based on an analysis showing that historically redlined areas are 7.5°F hotter in the day, have 40 percent less tree canopy, and have 20 percent less parkland than areas designated as "A: Best." The Heat Plan is coordinated with an Urban Forest Plan, which provides nature-based cooling solutions like protecting existing trees and planting new ones. The city also launched a Boston Extreme Temperatures Response Task Force to deal with heat emergencies and distributed thirty pop-up cooling kits, including a hose, misters, and a tent, to community organizations planning summer events.[14]

In May, the city launched a "Solarize Eastie" pilot program to expand neighborhood solar panel installation and onsite battery storage to the environmental justice community of East Boston. The program uses a group-buying model to reduce energy costs by aggregating demand and securing a discounted price per watt. Boston's chief of Environment, Energy, and Open Space, the Rev. Mariama White-Hammond, commented that such programs "allow us to bring energy benefits to environmental justice communities while helping us achieve our collective goal of decarbonization."[15]

A few months later the city announced another component of Climate Ready Boston designed to protect East Boston and Charlestown from coastal flooding caused by sea-level rise and storm surge. The plan utilizes nature-based solutions aimed to preserve the essential functions and historic character of the East Boston and Charlestown waterfronts while undoing the harm done by past actions that put the communities at risk.[16]

Early in 2022 the Office of Budget Management, the Boston City Council, and the mayor began a series of listening sessions and a survey in twelve languages to help draw up the next city budget. More than a thousand residents directly engaged in the process. The budget, unveiled in April, included such items as:

- $206 million for housing stability, affordable homeownership, and financial assistance to first-generation homebuyers
- $34 million for economic opportunity and inclusion, to grow BIPOC-owned businesses, further invest in Main Street business districts, expand tuition-free community college and workforce training programs, and create a commercial rental rebate program to support small business recovery and build wealth in Boston neighborhoods
- $31.5 million for climate-focused investments, including expanding the Green Youth Jobs program, creating walking and biking infrastructure, growing and preserving the urban tree canopy, strengthening local food systems, and supporting electrification of the city vehicle and school bus fleet
- $20 million for transformative arts and culture investments that will facilitate placemaking and strengthen both downtown and

neighborhood communities (Community arts and culture programs were among the most visible expressions of the original New Deal of the 1930s.)

The budget works in concert with $350 million in federal funding from the American Rescue Plan Act (ARPA) "to accelerate a Green New Deal for Boston."[17]

A month after releasing the budget, Boston announced a Green New Deal for Boston public schools. It included $2 billion to launch fourteen new construction or major renovation projects and accelerate ongoing district-wide improvements, including energy and water efficiency upgrades, the installation of solar panels, renovations to bathrooms and kitchens, schoolyard improvements, and the installation of air conditioners and water fountains. Jessica Tang, president of the Boston Teachers Union, said, "The BTU is thrilled to hear the announcement of much-needed upgrades to school facilities through a Green New Deal for Boston Public Schools."[18]

A critical part of Boston's Green New Deal strategy is to use the city's procurement powers to reshape its economy. The city moved to establish a Contractor Opportunity Fund and to expand access to city contracts for minority- and women-owned business enterprises. And it is seeking to address the effects of discrimination in its procurement process on minority-owned and women-owned businesses.

In 2022 the Boston public schools began providing free breakfast and lunch to its students regardless of income. In May 2022 the City of Boston and school system announced that City Fresh, a Roxbury-based employee- and Black-owned food service company, will provide breakfast, lunch, after-school meals, fresh snacks, and summer meals for the 50,000 students in the Boston public schools. All meals will be freshly made in City Fresh's Roxbury production facility with nutritious ingredients, including locally sourced food. Boston School Superintendent Brenda Cassellius said, "Our new partnership with City Fresh ensures Boston Public Schools students and staff have access to a wide range of culturally relevant, nutritious foods and keeps City dollars in our neighborhoods by supporting a black-owned business that represents the heart and soul of Roxbury." The program implements a City Council ordinance passed in 2019 setting goals for Boston's Good Food Purchasing Program, the local embodiment of a national program designed to align city food procurement with the goals of racial equity, environmental sustainability, and local economic development.[19]

Worker empowerment is an often underemphasized aspect of the Green New Deal. Toward the end of her first year as mayor, Michelle Wu established a Boston Cabinet for Worker Empowerment. While its mandate is so far rather vague, its focus includes "regulating, overseeing, and improving workplace conditions and health for workers" and "expanding economic opportunity for workers through access to quality jobs, skills trainings, and career pipelines."[20] The city also established a Chief People Officer Operations Cabinet to oversee programs for city employees, including mental health supports and employee transit benefits.[21]

From the outset, the Boston Green New Deal focused on a Youth Green Jobs program. According to Mayor Wu, "Boston's Youth Green Jobs Corps acts as a roadmap to provide livable wages, good benefits, and strong worker protections for our young people and returning citizens." The Green Jobs Corps is an "earn and learn" program that pays workers to participate in hands-on training while providing them with career readiness support and connections to employers in green industries. Priority populations include returning citizens released from incarceration, court-involved residents, youth who have experienced homelessness or housing instability, young people who have been in foster care, and other marginalized youth.

Dubbed PowerCorpsBOS, the program was inspired by the Philadelphia PowerCorpsPHL and supported by city funds and $9 million from ARPA. The Reverend White-Hammond said, "The green jobs program serves the dual purpose of creating job opportunities for our young adults while protecting our city from the ravages of climate change and enhancing quality of life for all residents."[22]

In December 2022 Boston graduated the first PowerCorpsBOS cohort. The twenty-one graduates had spent six months learning about green industries and skill sets, such as native and invasive plant identification, environmental conservation, parks maintenance, general labor operations, OSHA safety certification, career readiness, and resumé writing and interviewing. According to a city press release, PowerCorpsBOS "assisted 87 acres of public land, removed 284 bags of invasive material, worked with 18 service project partners, planted 61 trees, underwent 16 hours of tree climbing training, earned three college credits from UMass Mount Ida in Arboriculture, talked to 68 employees in private and public industry, worked with four different city departments, pruned 32 trees, attended an International Society of Arboriculture New England chapter conference, participated in 12 hours of mock interviews, and completed 16 hours of financial literacy courses."[23]

In Boston as in many other cities, urban planning and development (aka "urban renewal") has been a key force in destroying communities and segregating cities by race and class—effects that have been difficult for even progressive city administrations to reverse. According to Mayor

Wu, the purpose of Boston's redevelopment agency from the time it was established seventy years ago was to "clear the way for new development, even if that meant displacing tens of thousands of working class, immigrant, and Black and brown residents."

The original Boston Green New Deal plan had proposed comprehensive rezoning to address displacement and luxury development. In her first State of the City report a year after her inauguration, Mayor Wu announced a dramatic step: shutting down the Boston Planning and Development Agency and replacing it with a new City Planning and Design Department. The agency's urban renewal mission of eradicating so-called "blight and urban decay" would be replaced with a mission to ensure "resiliency, affordability, and equity."[24] This would "restore planning as a central function of City government" rather than leaving it in the hands of private developers and a semi-autonomous urban development agency.

RACING STEP BY STEP

While Mayor Wu strove to fully utilize the powers and visibility of a big-city mayor, the Boston Green New Deal drew on decades of work by community, labor, and other civic organizations and issue advocates. Many of these forces were brought together in the Boston Green New Deal Coalition, which holds monthly meetings to report on and mobilize support for Green New Deal programs.[25]

Although a review of the first year of the Boston Green New Deal reveals dozens of programs initiated at rapid-fire speed, Mayor Wu herself was frustrated by what she considered its slow start and limited achievements. On the first anniversary of her inauguration, she complained to a radio interviewer that the slow-moving searches for top leaders to fill crucial cabinet posts and establishing new collective bargaining agreements with the city's unions had commanded a large portion of her time.[26]

While the original Boston Green New Deal plan laid out big-picture climate and social justice objectives and broad policies to realize them, Mayor Wu's actions in her first year were primarily aimed at achieving immediate gains that would affect a wide range of constituencies and sectors and create momentum for realizing more. This required understanding the powers and limits of municipal government and what impact they have on ordinary people. She told an interviewer,

> City government is where a Green New Deal means doubling the number of street trees, so we are absorbing storm water, cleaning our air, and bringing beauty to our communities. It means converting our school bus fleet over to electric, which will not only get harmful pollution out of the lungs

of our kids and out of our neighborhoods, but also tap into mobile charging stations that large electric buses can become in times of power outages.

For every big issue, we have a way to take immediate action at the city level. When we talk about our economic recovery and closing the racial wealth gap, we are focused immediately on how we're spending nearly $700 million every year of city contracting dollars through our procurement system, making sure those dollars are going to Black and brown businesses, to local Boston entrepreneurs, to keep dollars circulating within our neighborhoods. There's always a way to make an impact, day by day, at the city level.

The interlocking crises of the pandemic, climate change, and our day-to-day economic situation and racial injustices mean that if you're truly meeting people where they are, you have to move at the speed of families rather than the speed of government.

By combining urgency with small steps forward, the Boston Green New Deal aims to help lay the groundwork not only for local but also for national transformation. According to Wu, "We can each be a proof point for how big change can happen day by day. And we can create the momentum for state and federal government to really show that we can put forward big changes that deliver immediate impact and draw more people into government."[27]

THE LOS ANGELES GREEN NEW DEAL

Los Angeles is the second largest city in the United States with nearly 4 million residents. It has long been known as the "smog capital of America."

In 2019 Los Angeles launched the Los Angeles Green New Deal. According to Mayor Eric Garcetti, the plan was based on four key principles: A commitment to the Paris Climate Agreement, a responsibility to deliver environmental justice and equity through an inclusive economy guided by the communities themselves, a duty to ensure that every Angeleno has the ability to join the green economy, and a resolve to demonstrate the art of the possible and lead the way.[28] The plan called for "five zeroes":

Zero Carbon Grid: 100 percent carbon-free electricity by 2035
Zero Carbon Buildings: 100 percent net-zero carbon new buildings by 2030 and all buildings by 2050
Zero Carbon Transportation: 80 percent zero emission vehicles in the city by 2035 and 100 percent by 2050
Zero Waste: 95 percent landfill diversion rate by 2035 and 100 percent by 2050
Zero Wasted Water: 100 percent of wastewater recycled by 2035

To lead the mobilization LA's Green New Deal created a Climate Emergency Commission, an Office of the Climate Emergency Mobilization Director, and a Jobs Cabinet.[29] Echoing national Green New Deal proposals, it promised to "improve air and water quality, reduce the energy burden of low-income households, address food deserts, provide economic opportunity in green jobs, build greater access to open space—and correct long-running environmental injustice across our city."[30]

The Los Angeles Green New Deal was one of the first municipal climate action plans designed to meet the international Paris Agreement limits on global warming and achieve carbon neutrality by 2050. The plan laid out 445 initiatives estimated to create 300,000 green jobs by 2035 and 400,000 by 2050.[31]

At the end of May 2022, the city released its third annual progress report on the LA Green New Deal.[32] It found that LA:

- Has met or is on track to meet 60 percent of its ninety-seven Green New Deal goals for 2021
- Generates 36 percent lower emissions than in 1990
- Meets 43 percent of its energy needs with renewables like wind and solar
- Will generate 97 percent of energy with renewables by 2030
- Is ahead of schedule on EV charger installations, cool roof and cool pavement installations
- Is behind schedule on waste reduction and tree planting[33]

Early in 2022 the Los Angeles City Council established a moratorium on oil drilling, approved $110 million in the city budget to decarbonize nine city properties, and created a new Climate Emergency Mobilization Office. In December 2022 the City Council passed and outgoing mayor Eric Garcetti signed a series of ordinances to phase out oil drilling, prohibit natural gas in new construction, and outlaw Styrofoam and single-use plastics.[34]

Buildings account for 43 percent of greenhouse gas emissions in Los Angeles. An ordinance passed 12–0 by the City Council in December 2022 requires new buildings to be all-electric. Starting in April 2023, new buildings are prohibited from having combustion equipment, gas piping, or fuel gas for purposes such as space and water heating, cooking, and drying clothes. Electricity must be the sole source of energy for all lighting, appliances, and equipment.

The ordinance was developed by the city in partnership with Leap LA, a coalition of community groups and environmental justice advocates, and received strong support from organizations representing frontline communities. Gloria Medina, executive director of SCOPE LA, said community members in South Los Angeles made an effort to learn about decarbonization and the impacts of poor climate on their health. "It is about Black, Brown and Indigenous community members at the forefront," Medina said of the ordinance. "This is their win." Frontline communities have been raising concerns "for a long time," according to Nancy Halpern Ibrahim, executive director of Esperanza Community Housing. Those concerns have "only recently" been "heeded by our systems and politicians," she said in a statement. "We want to be clear that this was only possible because of the leadership of front-line communities." Chelsea Kirk, a policy analyst at Strategic Actions for a Just Economy, said, "We think this is a super important, logical first step that allows us to make progress in our net-zero carbon goals as outlined in the Green New Deal." Retrofitting older buildings represents the logical next step, which will require protection for renters and an increase in production of renewable energy. According to Councilwoman Nithya Raman, "We are in a good position to be able to discuss those issues in detail, with the safeguards that we need to ensure that renters are not bearing the burden of retrofitting costs."[35]

THE SEATTLE GREEN NEW DEAL

Seattle represents a model of a municipal Green New Deal very different from Boston or Los Angeles. The initiative for the program came primarily from a coalition of activists, especially in poor communities, rather than from mayors and mayoral candidates. The program is paid for by a special tax on big business, voted by the city council. A Green New Deal Oversight Board with strong representation from climate-impacted communities makes recommendations for how to use the funds.

Syris Valentine, cochair and youth representative on the Green New Deal Oversight Board, described its origin and development.[36] Shortly after the Sunrise Movement's 2018 sit-in in House Speaker Nancy Pelosi's office demanding a Green New Deal, members of the climate group 350 Seattle met over dinner to discuss the difficult task of pushing for national policy change from the local level. Someone asked, "What would it look like to have a Green New Deal for Seattle?" That kicked off a weeks-long discussion that included Indigenous-led and frontline-focused organizations along with environmental NGOs.[37]

In June 2019 following the wave of Sunrise Movement youth-led action for a national Green New Deal, 350 Seattle and Got Green, an environmental justice organization based in Seattle's South End, teamed up to

launch a campaign for a local Green New Deal. The emerging coalition
dubbed itself Seattle for a Green New Deal, "a people-powered movement demanding that the City of Seattle create its own Green New Deal
to eliminate climate pollution by 2030."[38]

> Together, we mobilized over 10,000 people in the first 3 months of the
> campaign: we held community events; canvassed dozens of Seattle
> neighborhoods, and organized a game-changing candidate forum (7 of
> 9 City Council seats were up that year!). And as all that organizing was
> underway, 350 Seattle and Got Green worked with a broad coalition
> of environmental justice groups and City Council champions to cre-
> ate Seattle's Green New Deal resolution. This coalition included Got
> Green, Puget Sound Sage, Mazaska Talks, Chinese Information Services,
> Duwamish River Community Coalition, Transit Riders Union, Sierra
> Club, and Emerald Cities Collaborative.[39]

The Green New Deal for Seattle was endorsed by over 200 organizations,
including labor unions, advocates from low-income communities and communities of color, tribal nations, faith leaders, healthcare providers, businesses, environmental advocates, and clean energy experts. One hundred
people delivered a letter to the mayor demanding the city eliminate all
emissions by 2030. In August a jam-packed city council meeting passed
a Green New Deal resolution committing to the 2030 goal, affirming the
importance of a just transition, and outlining strategies to become carbon-
free in an equitable way.[40] In September the city council established the
Green New Deal Oversight Board comprised of nineteen individuals, many
connected to groups disproportionately affected by climate breakdown.

Faced with the COVID pandemic, in 2020 the Seattle city council
passed a progressive payroll tax called JumpStart Seattle. It provided
emergency pandemic funding for a year, then directed its funds to support affordable housing, small businesses, equitable development, and
the Green New Deal. Businesses with at least $7 million in annual payroll
were taxed 0.7 percent to 2.4 percent on salaries and wages spent on
Seattle employees who make at least $150,000 per year, with tiers for
various payroll and salary amounts. For example, a company with an $8
million payroll and one employee making $180,000 would pay a tax of
0.7 percent on $180,000—or $1,260. The 2.4 percent rate applied to sala-
ries of at least $400,000 at companies with at least $1 billion in annual
payroll—notably Amazon. The tax applies to about 800 businesses and
raises about $200 million per year.

There was a political backstory to JumpStart Seattle. In 2018 the city had
passed a per-employee "head tax" on large corporations—but repealed it less

than a month later under pressure from Amazon and other businesses. Labor was split on the tax, with unionized service workers backing it and construction workers opposing it. In 2019 five city council candidates defeated five business-backed candidates. A "Tax Amazon" campaign threatened to take a big business tax to the voters. The JumpStart Seattle tax plan differed from the previously defeated "head tax" proposal by exempting lower-paying jobs at local businesses. As University of Washington professor Jason Vigdor explains, "Politics is about coalition building, and two years ago Amazon was able to construct a coalition. But there aren't a lot of people working for Bartell Drugs making $150,000. The way this tax has been structured distributes the burden of the tax to the businesses with a greater capacity to pay." JumpStart Seattle was opposed by the Seattle Metropolitan Chamber of Commerce, the Downtown Seattle Association, and a number of neighborhood business associations. It received united backing from organized labor. It passed the city council 7–2.[41]

When the Green New Deal Oversight Board convened in late 2021, it conducted surveys and listening sessions on how to spend Green New Deal funds. It distilled proposals into fifteen recommendations to the mayor and city council, including investing in climate resilience, electrifying city vehicles, and supporting tribal sustainability projects.[42]

Unfortunately, the city thereupon diverted much of the revenue from JumpStart to its general fund. The Green New Deal Oversight Board pushed back, urging the city to put guardrails around JumpStart. After the board summoned community members to attend the city council's budget meetings, the council proposed budget amendments more in line with the Green New Deal Board's recommendations. Based on the board's proposals, in September 2022 the city passed $6.5 million in Green New Deal Opportunity Fund investments to accelerate the city's efforts to reduce greenhouse gas emissions, build community resilience to climate change, and increase net-zero affordable housing.[43]

By 2023 the board had shaped the investment of $27 million for climate resilience in frontline communities, electrification of multifamily affordable housing, and help for low-income homeowners to transition to electric heating.[44] Seattle's Environmental Justice Fund provided $750,000 to the Beacon Hill Council, Black Farmer's Collective, El Centro de la Raza, Environmental Coalition of South Seattle (ECOSS), FEED Seven Generations, Rainier Avenue Radio, Restaurant 2 Garden, Somali Community Services of Seattle, Sound Generations, South Seattle Emerald, United Indians of All Tribes Foundation, Wa Na Wari, and the Wing Luke Memorial Foundation.[45]

Activists involved with the Seattle Green New Deal have reflected on the experience. Syris Valentine says, "This wouldn't have happened without a strong grassroots campaign." Jess Wallach of Seattle 350, also a member of the Oversight Board, describes the recipe for organizers' rapid success: equal parts building robust relationships among community partners, maintaining public pressure on city officials, and forging an alliance with a supportive city council member. Taken together, these actions created a strong "inside-outside game."

Debolina Banerjee, Green New Deal Oversight Board member and Puget Sound Sage policy analyst, observes, "We didn't organize with labor early enough." Unions felt like they were being asked to support something they didn't help shape. Eventually, the coalition won labor support, but it cost time, energy, and effort that could have been saved by reaching out at the start.

Matt Remle, another Oversight Board member and cofounder of the Indigenous rights organization Mazaska Talks, says the coalition avoided tokenizing by coordinating with representatives from environmental justice organizations and giving them the gavel—not just a seat at the table. While working with then-council member Mike O'Brien's office to craft the resolution and ordinance, frontline voices were prioritized in defining agendas and goals as well as directing the shape the legislation would take. In the end, frontline communities won eight of the nineteen seats on the Oversight Board.

Receiving an award to Seattle from the global climate group C40 Cities, Seattle Mayor Bruce Harrell articulated the meaning of the Green New Deal in American cities: "Effective climate justice work requires true collaboration with those most impacted by economic, racial, and environmental injustice. It's about people, connection, and partnership. Seattle's Green New Deal centers our most impacted communities and brings forward meaningful solutions to meet the scale of the climate crisis."[46]

MILES TO GO BEFORE WE SLEEP

Cities have enormous opportunities to establish Green New Deal–type programs—and an enormous need to do so. Worldwide, cities produce more than 70 percent of carbon emissions. US cities are marked by extremes of climate change vulnerability and extremes of wealth and poverty. The Green New Deals in Boston, Los Angeles, and Seattle show that cities have the potential to realize much of the Green New Deal program of creating jobs and equity by protecting the climate.

Unfortunately, in many cities that capacity is not being used. Each year the research organization the American Council for an Energy Efficient Economy issues a "City Clean Energy Scorecard," which has become a principal resource for tracking clean energy plans, policies, and progress in large US cities. Its 2021 report found that, of the 100 cities surveyed, 63 had adopted a community-wide greenhouse gas (GHG) goal; 38 had released enough data to assess progress toward their goals; and only 19 cities are on track to achieve their near-term GHG goals. Of the 177 new clean energy actions the scorecard reviewed, 38 percent related to adoption of a clean energy plan, partnership, goal, or governmental procedure. Thirty-four percent were designed to improve energy efficiency of buildings. Twenty-eight percent promoted clean energy infrastructure. Less than 20 percent were equity-driven initiatives.

The scorecard identified leading cities across five policy areas:

Community-wide initiatives: Seattle, San Jose, Denver, and Washington, DC, have set GHG reduction goals; adopted strategies to mitigate the heat island effect; and pursued community engagement with historically marginalized groups.

Buildings: Denver, New York, and Seattle have established stringent building energy codes and requirements for energy performance in large existing buildings.

Transportation: San Francisco, Washington, DC, and Boston have instituted location efficiency strategies, more efficient modes of transportation, transit and electric vehicle infrastructure investments, and used transportation planning to reduce the isolation of historically marginalized communities.

Energy and water: Boston and San Jose have effective energy efficiency programs, programs to decarbonize the electric grid and reduce GHG emissions, and programs to simultaneously save water and energy.

Local government operations: Boston, Orlando, Portland, and San Francisco are substantially reducing local government GHG emissions through investments in energy-efficient municipal vehicle fleets, renewable energy systems, and complete municipal building retrofits.[47]

The scorecard incorporated justice-oriented policies, such as requiring equity assessments for city policies and budgets, providing support for owners of affordable housing to achieve energy performance standards, funding subsidized access to public transportation for low-income communities, and creating utility-administered energy efficiency programs for low-income customers.[48]

The Green New Deals in Boston, Los Angeles, and Seattle provide a wholistic approach that addresses all of these policy areas as elements of a coordinated strategy of transformation. They show what is needed—and what is possible.

2

THE GREEN NEW DEAL IN THE STATES

States have the power to implement much of the Green New Deal—and some states are using that power. States regulate electric generation, local distribution of electricity, and siting decisions. They set the parameters for urban planning and public transit. Most states have adopted renewable portfolio standards that require utilities to use a certain percentage of electricity from renewable sources. Many have adopted policies for energy storage, electric vehicles, energy efficiency standards for appliances and buildings, low carbon fuel standards, and emissions fees and taxes. And some are combining such climate protection policies with strategies to create good jobs and overcome longstanding economic and social injustices.

There are organizing efforts for programs that embody the principles of the Green New Deal in every one of the fifty states. In many states some of these policies have already been established and are starting to be implemented. This is largely a result of popular pressure and organization. It also results from politicians trying to appeal to concerned electorates. These victories have typically been produced by coalitions whose objectives combine climate, jobs, and justice.[1]

HAWAII: "A POSTCARD FROM THE FUTURE"

In 2015 Hawaii became the first US state to pass a law requiring that all electricity come from renewable energy sources. In 2020, after years of pressure from environmental advocates, the legislature banned the use of coal for producing electricity, effective the end of 2021.[2] On September 1, 2022, Hawaii closed its only coal-fired power plant as a step toward its goal of 100 percent renewable energy by 2045.[3]

Los Angeles skyline with smog and smoke. Photo by Chris M, Adobe Stock.

Hawaii Electric, an investor-owned utility that supplies all the electricity on Oahu and most in the rest of Hawaii, already produces more than 30 percent of its electricity from renewable sources. Hawaii has fourteen major solar, battery, or geothermal projects scheduled for completion by 2024. It is emphasizing projects that include battery storage. For example, Mililani Solar 1, Oahu's largest solar and storage project, can deliver its 30 megawatts to a battery array that can hold 156 megawatt-hours to use at night. In addition to providing power at demand peaks, the battery will help maintain the stability of the grid by preventing shutdowns and providing rapid restarts. The estimated cost of Mililani's power is one-third the current cost of electricity produced by burning oil.[4]

Hawaii long encouraged the development of rooftop solar energy through net metering, a system that pays people with solar collectors to export their extra energy to the grid. But in 2015, with rooftop solar growing rapidly, the utilities and regulators abolished net metering and ended the incentives, severely limiting new solar installations. As the deadline for closing the last coal plant approached in 2021, however, fear of a power shortage emerged. In response, Gov. David Ige launched the Powering Past Coal Task Force to ensure a smooth grid transition.[5] While in many locations utilities and rooftop installers each try to limit the other's development, in the face of impending shortages Hawaii Electric and rooftop solar installers teamed up to support a plan to pay households an upfront cash bonus plus a monthly credit on their bills for adding a battery to their rooftop solar so they can export power to the grid during two hours of peak demand every evening. The result will be a system that expands rooftop, community, and utility-scale solar at the same time.[6]

AES Corporation, which ran the now closed coal-fired power plant, says there were forty full-time employees working there. The company claims it has provided them training for its solar and battery facilities and helped the majority of them to transition to renewable energy positions.[7] Others will work with other companies in the same industrial park; several thermal power plants, for example, use directly transferable skills.[8]

One impediment to the development of solar energy is Hawaii's shortage of land. Many potential sites are located in communities where plantation workers used to live—and those communities often resist imposed development. Renewable energy developer Noelani Kalipi notes that "Hawaii has a long history of developers coming in and promising the world." Successful solar development requires connecting with communities and actually grappling with the issues that residents raise. Building trust as a responsible partner for the community takes time and money. "Money talks, but money doesn't always win."[9]

The conversion to renewable energy also has support among Indigenous Hawaiians. At the ground-breaking ceremony for the Mililani Solar 1 battery storage project, Kahu Kordell Kekoa, a Hawaiian spiritual leader, said, "Today, we're going to turn the dirt. But the turning of the dirt is not just for this place; it's for what will come out of this place. Our children will never know what this looked like. In fact, they won't even know what a coal station looked like. And what a blessing that is."[10]

The shutting down of coal and the ramping up of renewable energy is only one aspect of Hawaii's Green New Deal–style policies, summed up in its official "Legal and Statutory Sustainability Targets."[11] Targets include:

- *Locally produced food*: Double local food production to provide 30 percent of food served in public schools by 2030; 42 percent of all produce purchased by government departments local by 2045
- *Energy efficiency portfolio standards*: Reduce 4,300 gigawatt hours of electricity use by 2030
- *Renewable portfolio standard*: 40 percent of net electricity renewable by 2030; 70 percent by 2040; 100 percent by 2045
- *Net-zero energy use*: All schools net-zero renewable energy by 2035
- *Clean transportation*: State fleet zero-emission vehicles by 2030

A "Green New Deal" bill proposed in the 2021 Hawaii legislature recognized that the work done so far is only a beginning. "Lest Hawaii lose its leadership position in meeting the future of labor, justice, and equity, the legislature embraces Aloha 'Aina [Native Hawaiian expression literally meaning "love of the land"] as a green new deal to decarbonize Hawaii's systems of food, energy, and transportation, and to sequester carbon through systems of agriculture, waste management, and ecosystem restoration."[12]

ILLINOIS

In 2016 Illinois passed a widely touted Future Energy Jobs Act (FEJA). It set a target of 25 percent renewable energy by 2025; allocated $5 billion for energy efficiency; and provided access to solar energy and job training in low-income and environmental justice communities. The campaign for the law was largely led by the Illinois Clean Jobs Coalition, which included the state's major environmental groups along with hundreds of environmental justice, community, labor, faith, and public health organizations. But according to in-depth reporting by political scientist and activist Sarah Spengeman, the law was largely written by "energy industry insiders and policy experts" with little opportunity for "workers or marginalized populations" to "identify their needs or voice concerns."[13]

The legislation sparked a boom in solar energy, but according to Spengeman it failed to achieve its job quality and economic justice goals. It "failed to include labor standards protecting clean energy workers" or "a just transition plan for displaced fossil fuel workers." It also neglected to "fund outreach or programs to ensure any newly created capital would benefit those historically excluded from opportunities for wealth creation."

According to Illinois AFL-CIO Secretary-Treasurer Pat Devaney, "We don't have to speculate about what would happen without labor standards; we have a case study in FEJA." The law had "no labor standards" and "what we saw throughout all sectors of renewable energy development" was "out-of-state contractors bringing in out-of-state workers, with no benefit to the Illinois workforce or union workforce."[14]

In 2018 the Illinois Clean Jobs Coalition decided to draft a new bill—this time through a highly participatory process dubbed "Listen, Lead, Share"—that would result in a law "written by communities for communities." The coalition set broad goals: 100 percent clean energy, clean transportation, job creation, and a just transition. Then the group launched hundreds of community "listening sessions" in all fifty-nine state legislative districts with emphasis on environmental justice and community-based organizations. A quarter of a million dollars was provided to dozens of small organizations to support their capacity to participate. Thousands of people gave their input. The listening sessions were held in religious congregations, school gymnasiums, and recreation centers, ranging from small focus groups of five people to full auditoriums. They "sought out people's real challenges and worries for the clean energy transition" and gathered ideas for "solutions, programs, and investments" to ensure that "the transition's benefits were felt equally."

After the bill was drafted, the Clean Jobs Coalition held two more rounds of listening sessions to be sure it corresponded to what the grass-roots wanted. This had the additional benefit of recruiting informed and committed support.

Meanwhile, Illinois labor unions established a separate Climate Jobs Illinois coalition, which campaigned for its own Clean Union Jobs Act. It required employers receiving state aid to pay the region's prevailing wage, agree to remain neutral in the face of any unionization drives, follow fair-bidder standards, and negotiate project labor agreements.[15]

The negotiations between these two coalitions and numerous other players were arduous and long. Agreement had to be reached on legislation that would meet the differing requirements of both coalitions. For example, prevailing wage requirements were a central demand of the unions that made up the Climate Jobs Illinois coalition. But many in the Clean Jobs Coalition feared that the burden of administering those requirements would put small, especially minority, contractors at a disadvantage. The final version of the act read, "To address administrative barriers for small clean energy businesses, the Department of Labor will assist contractors with prevailing wage payroll administrative burdens."

After many such creative compromises, the Illinois legislature passed the Climate and Equitable Jobs Act, incorporating large parts of both coali-tions' bills. It sharply reduces carbon emissions while advancing equity, justice, and quality jobs. Journalist Liza Featherstone calls the legislation a "Green New Deal" for Illinois.[16]

The act commits Illinois to zero-carbon electricity by 2045 and a net-zero carbon economy by 2050. Its renewable portfolio standard will require 40 percent renewable electricity by 2030 and 50 percent by 2040. Renewable energy subsidies will double to $580 million per year, with nearly one-third of the funds designated for community-based and brownfield solar projects. Rooftop solar funding for low-income home-owners and renters, public buildings, and environmental justice nonprofits will increase from $10 million to $50 million a year. All private coal- and oil-fired power plants must reach zero emissions—tantamount to retire-ment—by 2030; municipally owned power plants must reduce emissions 45 percent by 2035 and 100 percent by 2045. Private natural gas plants must freeze their emissions immediately and shut down by 2045. Nuclear power plants were provided a subsidy and permitted to remain open for the next five years. A "green bank" called the Illinois Finance Authority Climate Bank will provide seed funding and seek private investment for green projects. Every five years state agencies must report on progress toward renewable energy goals.

The act set a goal of one million electric vehicles on the road by 2030. It provides rebates of $4,000 per vehicle for electric cars and light trucks. The state will rebate up to 80 percent of the costs of electric vehicle infrastructure for projects that pay prevailing wages. Forty-five percent will go to low-income and marginalized communities.

The act closely integrates justice provisions with its climate policies. For example:

- The first fossil fuel plants to be shut down will be those nearest to low-income and marginalized communities.
- The law requires diversity reporting for renewable projects and for the entire renewable energy industry.
- It allocates $80 million for Clean Jobs Workforce Network Hubs run by local organizations in thirteen of the state's low-income communities to deliver outreach, recruitment, training, and placement for climate jobs.
- It provides travel stipends, work clothes, tools, and childcare for training and incubator program participants.
- A program will train people currently in prison and place them in clean energy jobs upon release.
- A Clean Energy Jobs and Justice Fund will underwrite projects in low-income and marginalized communities.
- $35 million a year is allocated for a clean energy incubator program for small energy businesses.

Many of these proposals emerged from the listening sessions organized by the Clean Jobs Coalition.

The act also integrates the main labor rights and standards policies advocated by the Climate Jobs Illinois coalition into its climate provisions. Utility-scale solar and wind projects must establish project labor agreements. All nonresidential projects must pay prevailing wages. The act is estimated to create 50,000 construction jobs over the next ten years.

Recognizing that the transition to a climate-safe economy may produce dislocation and hardship, the act provides protection and support for workers and communities who it may affect adversely. It requires companies shutting down fossil fuel plants to inform affected communities two years in advance. In addition, the act provides reinvestment in adversely affected communities, committing $47 million annually to convert coal power plants to solar farms or energy storage facilities, $40 million per year to compensate communities for lost property taxes, and economic development and job training in communities where mines or power plants are closed. Finally, the legislation establishes a "Displaced Energy Workers Bill of Rights," which allocates $40 million to create renewable energy jobs for laid-off workers.

The act also promotes democratic control and accountability. For example, it establishes new ethical standards for utilities and creates a Public Utility Ethics and Compliance Monitor to enforce them. And it requires utilities to fund the participation of nonprofit representatives in regulatory proceedings.

Climate journalist David Roberts says the act's "comprehensive package of labor, diversity, and equity standards" embodies "the most stringent labor and equity requirements of any state clean energy program." The bill passed in part because "every group gave a little to get a lot." He especially singles out the Illinois environmental justice community, which used "three years of relentless grassroots organizing" to build "an incredible political force" and "without which the bill couldn't have passed and wouldn't have been as equity-focused."

The impact of the Climate and Equitable Jobs Act was rapidly visible on the ground. According to the Illinois Solar Energy Industries Association, five months after the passage of the act solar businesses had installed enough renewable energy to power 30,000 homes, an increase due in large part to the act. The solar industry expected to increase its Illinois workforce by almost 50 percent in 2022. The industry said it was supporting diversity, equity, and inclusion by "recruiting from solar job training programs, creating internal committees focused on diversity, and hiring consultants and recruiters to guide their diversity efforts."[17]

CALIFORNIA: CLIMATE CATASTROPHE—AND CLIMATE PROTECTION

California is the world's fifth largest economy. Climate change has led to unprecedented heat, drought, storms, wildfires, and other extreme weather conditions that have devasted many parts of the state. Partially as a result, 80 percent of Californians consider climate change "a serious concern" and 60 percent want to see state-led climate action.

In 1988, just as scientists were confirming the threat of climate change, California mandated an inventory of greenhouse gas emissions. In 2002 it passed vehicle emission standards far exceeding those set by the federal government. In 2006 it passed AB 32, the Global Warming Solutions Act, which required that greenhouse gas emissions be reduced back to 1990 levels by 2020 and established a cap-and-trade program. Subsequent legislation required emissions be cut to 40 percent below 1990 levels and mandated 60 percent of all electricity from renewable sources by 2030 and 100 percent by 2045.[18]

As the deadline for legislation approached on the last evening of August 2022, the California legislature passed five laws embodying major climate protection and justice measures:[19]

Restrictions on oil and gas drilling: New oil and gas wells must be set back at least 3,200 feet from homes, schools, and hospitals. Existing wells within the protected zone must meet strict pollution controls, monitor toxic leaks and emissions, install alarm systems, and limit noise, light, dust, and vapors. The bill was labeled a "job killer" by the state Chamber of Commerce and faced fierce lobbying from oil and gas companies and some trade unions.

Renewable energy: California had already mandated that 60 percent of its electricity must come from noncarbon sources like solar and wind power by 2030 and 100 percent by 2045. Noncarbon energy will in addition need to be sufficient to accommodate an expected 68 percent increase in energy use by 2045. New legislation requires reaching interim benchmarks: 90 percent by 2035 and 95 percent by 2040. All state agencies must source their energy from 100 percent renewable sources by 2035. Another bill to raise overall greenhouse gas emission goals from 40 percent to 55 percent below 1990 levels by 2030 lost by 4 votes; the state is already struggling to reach the 40 percent goal.

Cutting emissions: In 2018 then-governor Jerry Brown signed an executive order requiring the state to be carbon neutral by 2045. New legislation wrote that goal into law. It also required an 85 percent reduction in GHG emissions from all sources in the state—designed to ensure that carbon neutrality is mostly achieved by lowering emissions, not by taking carbon out of the air. It allows the remaining reductions to be met by planting trees or such currently unproven technologies as direct air carbon capture.

Extending Diablo Canyon: The deadline for shutting down the Diablo Canyon nuclear reactors, which provide 9 percent of California's electricity, was extended for five years and their operator given a $1.4 billion loan to help prevent a shortfall of electrical supply.

Carbon capture: Legislation directs the California Air Resources Board to set regulations for carbon capture, utilization, and storage projects at oil refineries and other polluting industries. It bans carbon capture from being used to extract more oil—currently its major commercial use. Other legislation requires the state to set targets for removing carbon from the atmosphere with nature-based methods, such as planting trees, restoring wetlands, and scaling up public landscaping and urban forestry projects. What programs will emerge from this process remain to be seen.

Most of these policies were opposed by a coalition of business groups, including the California Business Roundtable and California Chamber of Commerce. They were joined by most building trade unions in a formal alliance called Common Ground, which had helped kill previous climate legislation.[20] Common Ground describes itself as "part of a joint labor management committee between the State Building and Construction Trades Council of California and the Western State's Petroleum Association."[21] Kevin Slagle, a spokesperson for the oil industry trade group Western States Petroleum Association, characterized the state's proposed GHG reduction standard as "an extraordinarily aggressive goal that would require large-scale transformation of California's entire economy." Such opposition was overcome in part by Gov. Gavin Newsom's last-minute decision to support the climate bills after staying quiet and not backing them until mid-August.

The end-of-session climate legislation came on top of other climate moves by California government during 2022:

Food recycling: In January California instituted the largest mandatory residential food waste recycling program in the United States to cut down the state's methane emissions. Californians will toss excess food into green waste bins rather than the trash. Municipalities will then turn the food waste into compost or biogas. The state must cut organic waste in landfills by 75 percent from 2014 levels by 2025. Grocery stores must donate edible food that otherwise would be thrown away to food banks or similar organizations.

Beyond fracking and oil extraction: After years of pressure from environmental justice, public health, labor, and climate organizations across California, in April Governor Newsom announced a ban on new fracking projects by 2024 and directed the California Air Resources Board to analyze pathways to phase out oil extraction across the state by no later than 2045. According to Collin Rees of Oil Change International, this made California the highest-producing jurisdiction in the world to commit to a phase-out of oil extraction.[22] It "sets a vision for a managed decline of fossil fuel extraction," although it is not realizing that vision "on a timeline necessary to stave off even the worst impacts of climate change."

Banning sale of gasoline cars: In August, the California Air Resources Board approved a plan to phase out the sale of gas-powered cars over the next thirteen years in America's largest auto market. The new rule would require zero-emission vehicles to reach 35 percent of sales by 2026, 68 percent by 2030 and 100 percent by 2035.[23] In 2021, only 12 percent of new cars sold in California were zero-emission.

Offshore wind: In August, the California Energy Commission adopted a report setting goals for offshore wind of 2,000–5,000 megawatts by 2030 and 25,000 by 2045—enough electricity to power 25 million homes. The report was developed in coordination with federal, state, and local agencies and stakeholders including tribal governments, fisheries, and other ocean users. Renovations to prepare for offshore wind construction are already under way at the Port of Humboldt Bay.[24]

Community solar: Legislation passed in August is likely to unleash a rapid expansion of community solar as a result of a new compensation system. Payment for energy delivered to the grid will now be based on its value at the time it is delivered. This means that community solar projects that are built with battery storage will receive the higher price paid at times of peak demand. The law passed by a broad majority and was backed by solar developers, environmental justice organizations, consumer advocates, the homebuilding industry, and utility workers. At least 51 percent of subscribers to a project will have to be low-income. Workers must be paid at least prevailing wages.[25]

According to Governor Newsom, the new laws will create 4 million jobs.[26]

In its 2022 budget, California put a significant amount of money where the state's mouth was. The budget had a nearly $100 billion operating surplus, primarily due to its high tax rates on its wealthiest residents; the top 1 percent of earners paid nearly half of personal income-tax collections.[27] The budget included $54 billion in climate spending over five years:

- $6.1 billion for electric vehicles, including money to buy new battery-powered school buses
- $14.8 billion for transit, rail, and port projects
- $8 billion to clean up and stabilize the electric grid
- $2.7 billion to reduce wildfire risks
- $2.8 billion in water programs to deal with drought

At the outset of 2023 Governor Newsom proposed to cut $6 billion from the climate budget he had proposed just months before. Faced with a $22 billion budget deficit, he proposed line-item cuts for electric vehicles, clean energy, wildfire prevention, and programs to help low-income residents cope with extreme weather. Other cuts came in programs that would restore wetlands and protect cities from coastal storm surges. Some of the cuts may be restored by funds from the federal Inflation Reduction Act or from an improved budget situation. Months of negotiations were expected before release of a revised budget for legislative action.[28]

While California's climate initiatives received national attention, the state also passed extraordinary labor and social justice policies, making the whole climate-labor-justice package a substantial down payment on a Green New Deal for the state. Programs included:

Car-free tax credit: $1,000 refundable tax credit to low-income Californians who don't own cars. The legislation, the first of its kind in the country, is designed as a reward and an incentive for living car-free.

Free school meals: In August California established a Universal Meals Program to provide nutritious free meals to all 6 million public school students—the first state to do so.[29] When the program started at Foussat Elementary School in Oceanside, a teacher noticed immediately that "The kids are eating way more and they're more focused, eager to learn and they're just happier."[30]

Labor rights: California fast-food workers have held more than 300 strikes over abusive conditions. The Fast Foods Accountability and Standards Recovery Act provides bargaining rights to the state's more than half-a-million fast-food workers. It establishes a fast-food council made up of workers, franchise owners, and franchising companies like McDonald's that will negotiate employee wages, hours, and working conditions. Industry groups rapidly began organizing a referendum to overturn the law.[31] Another new law allows farmworkers to vote to unionize by mail rather than just in person. The United Farm Workers union held a 335-mile march from Delano to Sacramento in support of the bill. Governor Newsom initially opposed the bill but at the last minute decided to sign it.[32]

Housing: Legislation will allow developers to circumvent certain permitting processes in order to build affordable and market-rate housing on underutilized commercial space, described by housing advocates as "monumental" steps to address California's housing shortage. Other bills will turn underutilized state office buildings into affordable housing; encourage denser housing in cities; and eliminate requirements for parking in new homes built near bus stops or train stations. A constitutional amendment will be placed on the 2024 ballot that will repeal a requirement that publicly funded affordable housing projects receive voter approval.[33]

Early in 2022 the California Air Resources Board (CARB), which sets climate and air pollution policy in the state, proposed a plan to reduce greenhouse gas emissions by 40 percent below 1990 levels by 2030. The draft plan was widely criticized as inadequate to address the climate crisis, and Governor Newsome asked the agency to be more aggressive. In November CARB issued the final draft plan—designed to reduce emissions by 48 percent by 2030. It incorporates the extensive climate legislation passed in 2022. It commits to build no more natural gas plants. The state estimates it would cut air pollution by 71 percent and save Californians $200 billion each year in healthcare costs due to pollution, while creating 4 million new jobs.

Newsome describes it as "the most ambitious set of climate goals of any jurisdiction in the world" which will spur an "economic transformation akin to the industrial revolution."[34]

Extensive as these Green New Deal–style programs may be, they are unlikely to be adequate to fully meet the need either for climate protection or for social justice. Nor is it certain what kinds of sanctions there may be for failing to implement policies or realize targets. There will remain work to be done to ensure the programs are adequate to the need and that they are realized in fact.

California still has plenty of room for additional Green New Deal–style programs. Ellie Cohen, CEO of the policy nonprofit the Climate Center, and UC Berkeley professor Dan Kammen have argued that California's 2030 target should be at least 55 percent below 1990 levels and that it should not rely on "failed and expensive" carbon capture technologies.[35] And a proposal from the Green New Deal California Coalition for a "Justice40" policy that would have required California to invest at least 40 percent of federal climate and infrastructure funding in communities that have been historically neglected by discriminatory and racist policies was defeated in the legislature.[36]

LABORATORIES OF THE GREEN NEW DEAL

Justice Louis Brandeis famously called the states laboratories of democracy. Today they are serving as laboratories of the Green New Deal.

Many states in addition to the three I have described in this chapter are implementing Green New Deal–style plans for expanding jobs and justice by reducing greenhouse gas emissions to protect the climate. For example:

New York: The 2019 New York Climate Leadership and Protection Act requires net-zero carbon emissions by 2050. It includes a Just Transition Working Group to address workforce development and job creation and a Climate Justice Working Group to address the needs of low-income and minority communities.[37] A draft report laying out detailed strategies for reaching these goals was issued January 1, 2022.[38]

Mississippi: In July 2022 Mississippi passed a set of rules subsidizing rooftop solar, including rebates for low- and middle-income customers, incentives for school solarization, and net metering. Keith Johnston, a senior attorney at the Southern Environmental Law Center, said Mississippi is encouraging rooftop solar because "it benefits low, moderate income households, and it benefits customers generally and the grid generally."[39]

Maine: In 2019 Maine passed legislation that increased its renewable portfolio standard to 80 percent by 2030 and set a goal of 100 percent by 2050. It also passed a Green New Deal Act that provides solar installations on newly built schools and requires construction of grid-scale power generation to employ people from an apprenticeship program.

State initiatives include an impressive range of Green New Deal policies. On the climate side these include shutting down fossil fuel facilities, building new fossil-free energy systems, and forms of energy efficiency ranging from low-emission building standards to electrification of vehicles. Expanded labor rights and standards include requirements for prevailing wages, project labor agreements, and employer neutrality on union representation. Policies to counter historical injustices range from recruitment, training, and job ladders for workers from discriminated-against demographics to priority for closing power plants in highly polluted climate justice communities. Just transition measures include investment in communities impacted by climate policies, transition assistance for workers, and requiring employers to provide preferential employment opportunities for affected employees. Associated social welfare measures have ranged from free meals for all public school students to low-emission, low-income housing to job training centers in low-income neighborhoods.

Of course, not all "Green New Deal states" have adopted all of these policies, and some states have actively rejected them. Alabama, for example, deliberately discourages solar installations by allowing its largest utility, Alabama Power, to charge a fee averaging $27 a month for customers with rooftop solar. (Not surprisingly, Alabama rates forty-ninth among US states in solar installations.)[40] Alabama, Arkansas, Georgia, Indiana, Kansas, Kentucky, Louisiana, Mississippi, Missouri, Montana, Nebraska, Ohio, Oklahoma, South Carolina, Texas, Utah, and West Virginia have gone so far as to sue the federal government for allowing California to ban the sale of new gasoline-powered cars.[41]

There are also constitutional limitations on what states can do. For example, national transportation and grid designs are difficult for states to determine, even when they cooperate across state boundaries. And almost all states are blocked by their own constitutions from the kind of deficit spending that multiplies the financial power of the federal government.

While the powers states can exercise in our federal system may appear constitutionally limited, in fact those limits are highly flexible, and states can engage in many kinds of radical action if there is a supportive political context. Before and during the New Deal states established their own bank deposit insurance systems, created publicly owned utilities, imposed mortgage moratoriums, and banned injunctions against strikes.[42] These programs might have seemed beyond the jurisdiction of states just a few years earlier. Similarly, Green New Deal from Below programs can be creative in utilizing all the potential powers of state government.

The political dynamics that lie behind these state results vary considerably. In Hawaii, a broad consensus supported the transition away from fossil fuel energy, and the main concern was how to mesh fossil fuel cutbacks with the necessary expansion of renewable energy. In Illinois, environmental justice, labor, renewable energy, and utility interests battled over the content of a climate protection bill. The positive outcome resulted from the eventual decision of pro-climate protection forces to support each other's programs and from the utility industry's sidelining as a result of scandals that marginalized it and some of its leading political supporters.[43] In California, devastating effects of climate change multiplied popular support for strong action; a large short-term budget surplus facilitated massive climate spending; and the last minute-decision of the governor to back a raft of legislative climate initiatives swung the balance to passage.

Climate protection efforts by states reach beyond the geographical boundaries of the United States. When President Donald Trump announced US withdrawal from the Paris Climate Agreement, the governors of New York and California initiated the US Climate Alliance and pledged to comply with the Paris Agreement. The alliance now includes twenty-four states that are committed to:

- Reducing collective net GHG emissions relative to 2005 levels by at least 26–28 percent by 2025 and 50–52 percent by 2030
- Collectively achieving overall net-zero GHG emissions as soon as practicable, and no later than 2050
- Centering equity, environmental justice, and a just economic transition in their efforts to achieve their climate goals and create high-quality jobs

California, Maine, Massachusetts, Oregon, Rhode Island, and Washington are also part of the global Under2 Coalition, which brings together over 270 subnational governments representing 1.75 billion people and 50 percent of the global economy committed to climate protection policies.[44]

Creating a just, prosperous, and climate safe economy requires multiple changes in every aspect of society. The Green New Deal involves just such a comprehensive transformation. The range of programs and policies emerging in Green New Deal–style programs at the state level are beginning for the first time to embody such breadth and complexity of change. If all the elements in the state Green New Deal–type actions were brought to scale and spread to other states and other levels of government, it would be the basis for a transition to climate safety, good jobs for all, and a far fairer, more equal society.

3

UNIONS MAKING A GREEN NEW DEAL

While unions have been divided on the Green New Deal as a federal policy platform, many national and local unions have initiated projects that embody the principles and goals of the Green New Deal in their own industries and locations. Indeed, some unions have been implementing the principles of the Green New Deal since long before the Green New Deal hit the headlines, developing projects that help protect the climate while creating good jobs and reducing racial, economic, and social injustice.[1]

Even some of the unions that have been most dubious about climate protection policies are getting on the clean energy jobs bandwagon. The United Mine Workers of America (UMWA) announced in March 2022 that it will partner with energy startup SPARKZ to build an electric battery factory in West Virginia that will employ 350 workers. The UMWA will recruit and train dislocated miners to be the factory's first production workers. According to UMWA International Secretary-Treasurer Brian Sanson, "We need good, union jobs in the coalfields no matter what industry they are in. This is a start toward putting the tens of thousands of already-dislocated coal miners to work in decent jobs in the communities where they live."[2]

ELECTRICAL WORKERS FIGHT FOR CLIMATE, JOBS, AND JUSTICE

What does it look like when a local union engages with the Green New Deal goals of jobs and justice through climate protection? International Brotherhood of Electrical Workers (IBEW) Local 569 in California's San Diego and Imperial Counties provides one answer.

Detroit demonstration for a Green New Deal, July 31, 2019. Photo by Paul Becker, Wikimedia commons.

The Salton Sea area at the southern end of California is a hotspot for geothermal energy. It also covers one of the world's largest deposits of lithium—a critical component for lithium batteries and solar energy. With the necessity to replace fossil fuels in order to protect the climate, mining the "Lithium Valley" for lithium and geothermal heat is projected to produce thousands of jobs in Imperial County, one of California's most impoverished regions. An extraction prototype has already begun. But whether those jobs will be good jobs and who will get them remain open questions.

One of the groups trying to answer those questions is IBEW Local 569. It represents over 3,600 union electricians, power professionals, and other workers in San Diego and Imperial County.[3] In 1999 it was one of the first IBEW locals in the nation to start training on solar technologies.[4] From there, its training programs grew to include energy efficiency, electric vehicle charging infrastructure, and energy storage. The union office was a test site for a utility program that installs electric vehicle charging stations at workplaces around San Diego County. IBEW members installed the charging units and can power up their plug-in electric vehicles at the union hall. These green technologies are helping to reduce greenhouse gas emissions and creating jobs for Local 569's membership.[5] The local even hired an environmental organizer to be a member of its staff—perhaps the first in the country to do so.

With industry partners, IBEW 569 owns and operates the San Diego and Imperial Electrical Training Centers, which provide state-approved electrical apprenticeships with good wages, family healthcare, retirement benefits, and college credits. The union's apprenticeship program recruits from the local community, including high schools and veteran programs, and is currently training more than 550 apprentices.[6] Trained workers are critical to the Green New Deal goals of climate protection combined with good jobs and justice on the job.

The electricians in Local 569 play a key role in reaching the city of San Diego's goal of 100 percent clean energy by 2035.[7] These clean energy programs at the same time provide good jobs for local electrical workers. IBEW 569 members have logged millions of work hours building more than a gigawatt of solar and wind projects, installing more than 10,000 rooftop solar installations, building hundreds of electric vehicle charging stations, and constructing some of the largest energy storage projects in the western United States.

In addition to creating jobs for the existing IBEW workforce, renewable energy projects have also created new pathways into union careers for residents in Imperial County, one of the most disadvantaged areas in California. After investing in an electrical apprenticeship training facility, Local 569 brought hundreds of local residents into the IBEW who were able to build renewable energy projects in their local community while receiving training, good wages and benefits, and a voice on the job through union representation. Thanks to recruitment, apprenticeship, and local hire polices, Imperial County now has 65–90 percent local hire for community residents on renewable energy projects.[8]

Local 569 is also playing a role in shaping San Diego's policies to protect the climate, provide good union jobs, and address the needs of disadvantaged communities—the basic goals of the Green New Deal. The union has advocated local hire agreements, joint labor-management apprenticeship partnering, workforce safety standards and certifications, and responsible contractor criteria to create family-sustaining green jobs that provide upward mobility and career opportunities.[9] And it has fought to include the following requirements for every energy provider in San Diego's 100 percent Renewable Energy Program Implementation Plan:[10]

Energy identification: Inform utility customers of the percentage of renewable, greenhouse gas–free electricity offered. Power may be labeled as "clean" or "green" if it comes from renewable energy generated from solar, wind, or geothermal.

Exclude Renewable Energy Certificates: Provide renewable energy from sources customers can trust while creating union jobs in the community for local workers. Renewable Energy Certificates (RECs), which allow companies to meet environmental requirements by buying certificates instead of cutting emissions or increasing renewable energy, must not be marketed as "clean" or "green" so as not to mislead the public.[11]

Communication to consumers: Send at least three written notices to potential customers, and each notice will include a description of the percentage of the power mix that comes from California solar, wind, geothermal, small hydroelectric, or other state-certified green power sources.

Union jobs: Procure power from union-generated sources; employ unionized customer service representatives; sign project labor agreements on each power generation project; sign project labor agreements on energy efficiency projects/programs; agree in writing to neutrality in the event employees or subcontractor employees wish to unionize.

Community benefits: Sign community benefits agreements to include local projects and local hiring and prioritize projects, programs, and actions to reduce emissions in disadvantaged communities.

Local project build-out: Emphasize development of new renewable resources from proven developers in San Diego and adjacent counties and strictly limit the use of nonrenewable energy sources.

Energy efficiency: Develop a resource plan that integrates supply-side resources with programs that will help customers reduce their energy costs through improved energy efficiency and other demand-side measures.

Assess workforce impacts: Determine if the program will 1) result in negative impacts for employees of the incumbent utility (including layoffs, work hour reductions, etc.) and 2) if the wages, fringe benefits, and job protections are similar to those offered by the utility to employees in comparable job classifications.

Local 569 is trying to incorporate these principles into city and county climate action plans and in the Regional Decarbonization Framework. And it is working with several coalitions to shape the new Regional Transportation Plan to include more investment in building mass transit hubs, electrifying transit with zero-emission EV buses, and developing multiunit affordable housing along transit corridors.

Will these Green New Deal principles be applied in the new Lithium Valley mining-and-geothermal industry? Local 569's Environmental Organizer Cristin Marquez says the union wants to make sure there are high-road, high-wage jobs and that those jobs are available to the people of high-unemployment Imperial County. IBEW 569 has more than 250 electricians and many more apprentices ready to work in Imperial Valley. The union has been presenting its program to the Lithium Valley Commission and other governmental bodies that will determine the shape of the industry. If it can incorporate its principles and policies into the lithium industry, that will mean a new building block for a climate-safe economy and a transformation for one of the most impoverished areas in California.

GREEN LABORERS

The Laborers International Union of North America (known as LIUNA or simply the Laborers') has a reputation as one of the unions most hostile to the movement against fossil fuel infrastructure. LIUNA has said the Green New Deal "threatens to destroy workers' livelihoods" and "increase divisions and inequality."[12] During the fight over the Keystone XL Pipeline its president Terry O'Sullivan was widely known for his attacks on "delusional environmentalists" and their supporters within labor. The LIUNA website is proudly plastered with pictures and descriptions of fossil fuel projects ranging from the Dakota Access Pipeline to the Maine Natural Gas Pipeline that the union's members have helped to construct.[13] But right alongside these projects the website is also proudly plastered with pictures of climate-protecting renewable energy, energy-efficiency, and energy-use-reduction projects that LIUNA members have constructed. For example:

- LIUNA local 271 members helped build Deep Water Wind, the nation's first offshore 30-megawatt wind farm in the waters off Rhode Island. The $451 million project created 80–100 good jobs and reduced dependence on foreign sources of energy.
- LIUNA members were vital to the construction of the $1 billion Central Light Rail Transit project, which connects St. Paul to downtown Minneapolis. It includes 9.8 miles of underground track and twenty-three stations. In 2016, the green lines provided approximately 12.7 million rides.
- LIUNA members are building many solar power plants in California, including the Mojave Solar Plant. The project received $1.2 billion in funding from the federal government and created 830 construction jobs and 70 permanent operation jobs as well

as thousands of indirect jobs. The plant is expected to generate 617,000 megawatts of power annually, enough to power more than 88,000 households.

• In Boston, LIUNA Local 7 members assisted in a $63 million project to rebuild and improve public housing with energy efficiency and renewable energy measures that will save the Housing Authority over $56 million annually. The project created more than 600 local jobs.

These green projects don't make up for the climate-destroying projects LIUNA members work on or the union's unremitting hostility toward those who oppose them. But it does show that the direct interest of workers in climate protection and a Green New Deal is so powerful that even the unions that fight climate protection measures also have to recognize their members' interest in advancing them.

MINNEAPOLIS JANITORS STRIKE FOR A GREEN TRAINING FUND

On February 27, 2020, thousands of Minneapolis cleaning workers walked off their jobs and struck their downtown commercial high-rises. Among their key demands was that their employers take action on climate change. It was one of the first—perhaps the very first—union-sanctioned strike in the United States for climate protection demands. The janitors are members of Service Employees International Union (SEIU) Local 26. They are employed by over a dozen different subcontractors to clean corporate buildings like IDS, Capella Tower, EcoLab, U.S. Bank, Wells Fargo, United Health Group, Ameriprise, and many more across the Twin Cities. The workers are overwhelmingly immigrants and people of color.

According to participants, Local 26's concern with climate goes back at least to 2009. Many people both on staff and in the leadership of the union care about climate and the environment, concerns that came up frequently in conversations. Climate was a popular issue that resonated for the union's members. Many of the immigrant members were well aware of the impact of climate change on their homelands. Elsa Guaman, a janitor at ABM who cleans the United Health Group headquarters, said,

> We are people from the countryside in Ecuador, and when I was young it was a fertile place. But then the droughts began, and the land didn't produce anymore. As people who lived on what we took from the earth, we had to leave. We were not alone; millions of people from the areas near my village left too, in one of the biggest migrations ever out of South America. Now I clean buildings that are some of the biggest polluters in Minnesota, which furthers the same problem that made me immigrate.

This must be addressed. I think if we win green cleaning, we can send a message.[14]

But what could their union do about climate change besides put out statements and support other organizations? They learned a partial answer from California janitors who had won demands for "green cleaning." Local 26 included green cleaning demands in their 2009 negotiations. They won contract language establishing in each company an ad hoc committee of union and company representatives. The committee members would "review the use of green chemicals." The contract language recognized company responsibility for a safe and healthy workplace and "the use of materials that contribute to a healthy and sustainable ecological environment." The employer would provide training to employees on the "use, mixing, and storage" of cleaning chemicals. The employer "shall make every effort to use only green, sustainable cleaning products where possible."

The janitors continued trying to strengthen the environmental language in subsequent contracts. In 2019, the union presented a demand for green technician janitorial training. It brought in janitors from California who already won a green training fund. According to Local 26's bargaining update for its members, "Our members are uniquely positioned to help lead the change we all need, in helping to convert to clean energy in this especially important sector. Top-down policies won't work if the people who will be responsible for implementing these changes on a day-to-day basis don't have a voice." One key is training for front line janitors, as green technicians, so that they have the skills. Local 26 demanded a "training program for Green Technicians (including $0.20 differential) and expanded use of green cleaning." The union also proposed to create a "table" with building owners and community groups focused on climate to develop "bold solutions." They would include "GREEN NEW DEAL" policies, getting Minnesota to 100 percent renewable energy, reducing waste, and closing the HERC incinerator that burns trash from downtown office buildings and pollutes nearby neighborhoods.[15]

On February 27 the janitors walked out for a planned one-day warning strike. They set up picket lines outside the downtown buildings. Then they were joined by youth climate strikers and other supporters in a march through downtown. Former local 26 staffer Steve Payne said,

I don't know that I've ever seen a more powerful union action. There were at least a couple hundred environmental allies that joined the picket lines—which is really impressive. The chants shifted from English to Spanish to Somali, people were dancing to hip hop and Latino music.

> It was a great mixing of all the parts of our movement we need: white
> middle-class environmental activists, young diverse climate strikers,
> low-wage immigrant workers—all fighting for the same set of demands.

After their one-day warning strike, the janitors went back to work as
planned. Then they announced they would strike again—whereupon, after
a marathon twenty-two-hour bargaining session, they won a contract that
included funding for a labor-management cooperation fund for a green
education initiative as well as significant wage increases, sick days, and
other demands. The janitors approved the new contract unanimously.[16]

Minneapolis janitors have started taking classes paid for by the new
labor-management fund. Thanks to the fund they receive their regular
pay while taking classes. As a prelude to the green education initiative,
in 2021 the first class of fifteen janitors graduated from English language
classes.[17]

A GREEN NEW DEAL FOR SOMERVILLE

Somerville, Massachusetts, is an inner suburb of Boston and the most
densely populated city in New England with 81,000 residents. It was long
an industrial center inhabited by repeated waves of immigrants, but it has
increasingly become a bedroom community for Boston and Cambridge.

Somerville is currently being transformed by the extension of the Boston
Metropolitan Transit Authority subway system's Green Line throughout
the city, bringing transit access to 80 percent of Somerville residents. Over
5 million square feet of new development is in the works.[18]

Somerville's long-term mayor supported development but not union
labor for either city employees or for construction, much of which, to the
dismay of building trades unions, was done non-union. In 2017, Bernie
Sanders's supporters in Our Revolution won a progressive majority on the
board of aldermen (now city council). Seeing a shift in the political winds,
the head of the greater Boston Building Trades, Brian Doherty, and other
union leaders, decided the time was ripe to establish a community-labor
coalition to demand a new orientation for development. According to
Doherty,

> What we've experienced in Somerville is income inequality in real time.
> Developers coming into this city to our back yard, where our friends and
> families live, exploiting it to make as much money as they can to fill the
> coffers of rich people. Developers come into our town and say, we need
> breaks. We need to undermine workers rights. We need to undermine
> environmental protections. We can't do affordable housing.

People who care about environmental justice, housing stability, workers rights and giving people a fair day's pay for a fair day's work: We have to stand up collectively as partners.[19]

The building trades partnered with Our Revolution Somerville for a breakfast kickoff on December 16, 2017, where coalition leaders met with the city council to describe their respective issues. Early participants included:

AFSCME Local 274
Building and Construction Trades Council of the Metropolitan
    District
Community Labor United
Firefighters Local 76
Good Jobs Somerville
Good Jobs, Strong Communities Coalition
Greater Boston Labor Council
IUPAT DC 35
MassCOSH
Mass Senior Action Council—Cambridge/Somerville
New England Joint Board UNITE HERE
New England Regional Council of Carpenters
Our Revolution—Somerville
SEIU Fireman & Oilers Local 3
SEIU Local 509
SEIU Local 888
Somerville Municipal Employees Association
Teamsters Local 25
Teamsters Local 122
The Welcome Project—Somerville[20]

The first focus of the newly formed Somerville Stands Together (SST) coalition was a $2 billion project being developed in Union Square in anticipation of the subway expansion. The coalition, backed by unions of municipal workers, firefighters, and hotel and restaurant workers and by immigrant organizers mobilized for a project labor agreement that would provide union conditions for Union Square construction and operation. Meanwhile, a Union Square neighborhood organization called Union United, anchored by organizers from the Somerville Community Corporation, successfully campaigned for a community benefits agreement with the developer, USQ. Although SST did not win a project labor agreement, labor rights and local hire language was included in the community benefits agreement. Contractors are required to use their "best efforts" to ensure that "at least 20% of its workforce are qualified Somerville residents; 20% of its workforce are qualified minorities; and 8% of its workforce are qualified women."[21]

Initially there were no environmental groups in SST. But in 2018 some activists in 350MA and the Climate Coalition of Somerville decided to reach out to community and labor constituencies and started attending SST's monthly meetings. They were welcomed and began occasionally pointing out ways that SST programs might be mutually reinforcing with climate and environmental objectives. An SST leader pointed out that "this all ties together." The head of the municipal workers union hosted a local cable TV show on labor, climate, and the Green New Deal with Joe Uehlein of the Labor Network for Sustainability, which led to the holding of a Labor-Climate Summit in September 2020.

The City of Somerville had established its "Somerville Climate Forward" action plan in 2018. It presented a comprehensive set of programs for climate protection, but it had two limitations. It called for the city to become carbon-neutral, but it had only a 2050 target, no interim targets, and no program to implement or enforce compliance. And it did little to address labor or justice concerns. An SST working group met through the spring and summer of 2021, dissected the plan, and developed a revision dubbed the "Somerville Climate Further Forward Plan." It moved up the target for carbon neutrality from 2050 to 2035, established interim benchmarks, delineated labor standards, and incorporated plans to meet equity goals. It called for economic development "to not only achieve climate mitigation and adaptation goals, but also to create jobs with prevailing wages and benefits for all workers, create a public transportation system that benefits lower income neighborhoods, and build and upgrade housing for all community residents."[22]

In anticipation of the bipartisan American Rescue Plan Act and American Infrastructure and Jobs Act, a second SST working group developed a program for "shovel-ready" projects for federal funding that would meet SST's goals. The working groups developed a Somerville Green New Deal statement that set out four goals for the city: Increase economic, social, and racial equity; target projects to meet city carbon neutrality by 2035; adopt model project labor standards; and build Workforce of the Future.[23]

In August 2021, SST gave a PowerPoint presentation of its recommendations at two pre-election forums. All candidates for mayor and for city council attended the forums—and all endorsed the SST proposals. The mayor who was elected had worked with SST on the Climate Further Forward plan.

Nearly $72 million is now on its way to Somerville under the American Rescue Plan. A substantially larger pot of money will be coming under the federal Infrastructure and Jobs Act, and more is expected from state programs as well. A city committee that is determining American Rescue Plan allocations has set aside $18 million for projects proposed by community groups. SST has asked that its role should not be proposing particular projects, but advising on how to make the process inclusive and make sure that projects address Green New Deal goals.

SST leaders say they have achieved a coalition perspective, with labor, community, and climate organizations joined together around what have become common concerns. Despite their successes, they are well aware that realizing their goals will take many more struggles. They are currently developing their next set of objectives and campaigns. The new climate benchmarks need to be incorporated into city plans. SST has a "local hire" committee working to make sure the local hire language in the Union Square Community Benefits Agreement gets implemented. It recently ran a community seminar on community benefit agreements in preparation for upcoming campaigns to include them in the many new development projects springing up around the Green Line. More broadly, Somerville's Green New Deal advocates say the city needs to implement a new approach to development, one that requires union labor and prioritizes women and people of color.

SST aims for nothing less than what it calls a "Green New Deal for Somerville." It sees an opportunity to realize several essential goals at the same time. "We can renew the city's built environment in a way that forsakes dependence on fossil fuels that damage the environment to reliance on renewable energy sources that save the environment. And doing this will create many new, well-paying jobs that can raise the living standards of all the city's residents and promote social, economic, and racial equality. The city can become a model of a local Green New Deal, that can be emulated by other cities across the state and the country."[24]

UNIVERSITY UNIONS MAKING A GREEN NEW DEAL

Colleges and universities have become major centers for action on climate change. At the same time, they have become a major focus for union organizing and activism. Now these two strands are beginning to converge. Rutgers, the State University of New Jersey, provides a case in point.

Faculty and graduate student employees at Rutgers belong to one union, the Rutgers American Association of University Professors–American Federation of Teachers (AAUP-AFT). Among its members are longtime climate activists and an impressively large number of climate scientists. The union became increasingly involved in climate action, participating in the 2017 March for Science, the Jersey Renews Coalition, and the Labor Network for Sustainability's Labor Convergence on Climate Change. In its 2018 postdoc negotiations the union unsuccessfully demanded formation of joint labor-management-community committees on greenhouse gas emissions reduction.

The union's concern found expression in a long and detailed resolution "In Support of the Green New Deal, Student Climate Strikes, and a Climate Action Plan for Rutgers University," adopted in March of 2020. It said in part,

> Every amount of greenhouse gas emitted into the atmosphere worsens the developing global climate crisis, leading to real and increasingly measurable risks to human and ecosystem health, to the economy, and to global security.
>
> Stabilizing the global climate requires net-zero global carbon dioxide (CO_2) emissions, meaning any residual emissions must be offset by verifiable efforts to accelerate the natural removal of CO_2 from the atmosphere, as well as major reductions in the emissions of other greenhouse gases.
>
> Meeting the international climate targets laid out in the Paris Agreement requires an urgent global transition from a trajectory of rising greenhouse gas emissions to one of falling greenhouse gas emissions, including the cessation of construction of new fossil-fuel infrastructure.
>
> New Jersey is particularly exposed to sea-level rise associated with warming oceans and melting glaciers, leading to substantially increased exposure to tidal flooding and the impacts of storms, such as Hurricane Sandy.
>
> Rutgers University, on its campus and in its facilities around the state, is exposed to numerous climate change-intensified hazards, including heat waves, rain-driven flooding, and coastal flooding; and Rutgers AAUP-AFT members are exposed to these climate-related hazards in their workplaces and communities.[25]

The resolution supported the 2019 Green New Deal Resolution sponsored by Rep. Alexandria Ocasio-Cortez and Sen. Ed Markey and its proposals for "net-zero greenhouse gas emissions through a fair and just transition for workers and vulnerable communities"; "millions of good, high-wage jobs"; "investments in U.S. infrastructure, industry, and society"; "clean air and water, climate resiliency, sustainable livelihoods, and access to nature"; "justice and equity for frontline communities"; and "transparent consultation collaboration, and partnership with frontline and vulnerable communities, labor unions, worker cooperatives, civil society groups, Academia, and business."

The AAUP-AFT resolution demanded that Rutgers University, "through bargaining and other means," develop a climate action plan that will achieve "carbon neutrality in all University operations by 2030."

The resolution supported global student strikes for climate action, student calls for divestment of university funds from fossil fuels companies, and AFT endorsement only for political candidates who support the Green New Deal or an equivalent program.

The Rutgers AAUP-AFT, along with other locals, pushed for the national AFT to take a strong stand on climate. In July 2020 the national AFT convention adopted a resolution backing the Green New Deal.[26] It said that the labor movement must be at the center of shaping climate policies, "including tax-base support for impacted communities, wage replacement and parity for affected workers," along with retirement protections and job and training guarantees. It called for funding Green New Deal programs through progressive taxes on the rich, including a billionaire net worth tax, and reductions in Defense Department spending that is not related to veterans. During the floor debate, delegates adopted an amendment endorsing a "national green schools campaign" calling for retrofitting and installation of solar panels at public schools across the nation. The resolution declares that the AFT will work to "ensure that no worker is left behind."

David Hughes, past president of AAUP-AFT Rutgers, who helped draft the resolution, said, "Our government has got to respect science and protect us." The Rutgers local thereupon went on to help found the Educators Climate Action Network, which brings together members of both the AFT and the National Education Association from around the country to campaign for a Green New Deal for Education.

Following years of campaigning for divestment from fossil fuels, in September 2019 700 students, faculty, staff, and community members mobilized for a divestment rally and march through the streets of New Brunswick in coordination with the Global Climate Strike.[27] Then a student coalition formally called on Rutgers to divest from fossil fuel companies. In October 2020, the Rutgers University Student Assembly announced that an overwhelming 90 percent of students voted in a referendum to support fossil fuel divestment and investments in clean energy. The Rutgers AAUP-AFT executive committee in December 2020 called on Rutgers to "immediately begin selling all its holdings in firms that extract, produce, refine, sell, store, or transport oil, gas, or coal." Finally in March 2021 the Rutgers Board of Governors and Board of Trustees voted to divest from fossil fuels.

AAUP-AFT's David Hughes portrayed divestment as a steppingstone toward a broader vision of decarbonization at Rutgers. The union "wants all of Rutgers' electricity to come from solar panels, installed over parking lots, on roofs, and off campus if necessary. . . . The university could not only generate its own electricity carbon-free but supply power to cooperatives of residents near its campuses in Camden, Newark, and New Brunswick. Having greened its portfolio, Rutgers is now in a position to green its campuses. The university needs to go the full mile now and become a campus driven by renewable energy while supplying affordable, resilient, carbon-free power to vulnerable communities."[28] This was in effect a call for the university to become an "anchor institution" for a Green New Deal in the many communities surrounding its campuses.

The impact of the divestment decision went beyond Rutgers. American Federation of Teachers President Randi Weingarten noted, "The university community at Rutgers has shown that when people come together around an issue like climate sustainability, change is possible. Hopefully the work Rutgers is doing on fossil fuel divestment will set a standard for other institutions." A resolution at the 2022 AFT convention urged that its members' retirement funds be removed from "all corporations or other entities that extract, transport, trade, or otherwise contribute to the production of coal, oil, and gas—and to reinvest those funds in projects that benefit displaced workers and frontline communities in the state or region of the AFT members."[29]

In October 2022, Rutgers University students, faculty, graduate workers, and staff joined for a "Day of Action for Climate Justice and a Better Rutgers" including speak-outs, rallies, and marches for climate justice and fair contracts for the university's 19,000 union employees. Rebecca Givan, president of Rutgers AAUP-AFT, said,

> Our different organizations and unions all chose this day to send a message to the Rutgers administration and to political officeholders, so we're working together to support each other. Students have been organizing for climate justice measures, and they need to be heard. The contracts for our unions at Rutgers expired nearly three months ago—we need the administration to act on our proposals with the same urgency we feel.

The day of action started with a demonstration calling on New Jersey governor Phil Murphy to veto proposals for seven major fossil fuel projects. Next, a rally on campus called on the university to start bargaining with its workers for a fair contract. Then climate justice activists led a march to New Brunswick City Hall calling for city-level climate reforms: expand and add city bike lanes; build green affordable housing with solar-ready rooftops; oppose a gas power plant in Woodbridge, New Jersey; and install community gardens in each neighborhood. "The day of action and the list of demands that were presented," said AAUP-AFT Climate Justice Committee Chair Todd Vachon, "were co-created by members of the union working in partnership with student and community activists." Our union "believes strongly in bargaining for the common good as an effective means of building power by forging deep relationships with our communities and students and fighting together with shared purpose."

In 2023 the Rutgers AAUP-AFT initiated a series of "Freedom Schools" in the tradition of "Ella Baker, the Student Nonviolent Coordinating Committee, and the 1960s civil rights movement"—for example, one on "What Is Climate Justice, and Why Are Unions Integral to It?" The goal of the Freedom School is to be a "virtual classroom and discussion space for union members, students, and the community to develop leadership and political consciousness for a new generation."[30] The union partnered with student and community groups in a successful "No LNG Bomb Trains" campaign in Camden and is working with a similar coalition to stop construction of a new fossil fuel power plant in Woodbridge. And it is working with community and environmental justice groups toward developing community solar and resilience hubs in Camden.

Four years after its original bargaining demand, the Rutgers AAUP-AFT won a joint labor-management-community committee on greenhouse gas emissions reduction. The committee met quarterly until the historic strike in April of 2023. Union climate activists hope to reopen this regular meeting space as an arena to pursue their "broader vision of decarbonization at Rutgers."

UNIONS RESHAPING STATES FOR CLIMATE, JOBS, AND JUSTICE

State governments have been a major focus of union action for Green New Deal–type programs. While such state programs have received wide publicity, the role of unions in promoting them has seen less attention. States where labor and allies won major labor-climate legislation in 2021 include:

Connecticut

Unions and environmental groups passed strong labor and equity standards for renewable energy projects through the state legislature. According to the bill's promoter, the Connecticut Roundtable on Climate and Jobs—an alliance of labor, community, environmental, religious, and social justice groups dedicated to combating climate change, creating jobs, and

promoting racial, economic, and environmental justice—the legislation
will contribute to:

> *Workforce development*: by helping working-class families in Con-
> necticut access clean technology careers by requiring developers to
> partner with approved in-state apprenticeship and pre-apprentice-
> ship programs. Currently, renewable energy developers regularly
> hire out-of-state workers.
> *Prevailing wage*: by preventing state procurements and other large
> state-funded projects from driving down the market value of labor.
> Prevailing wage will be required for utility-scale or grid-con-
> nected projects that are assisted by the state (excludes residential
> installations).
> *Community Benefits Agreement*: will ensure that host communities
> of renewable energy projects receive real benefits from renewable
> energy projects by requiring developers to negotiate community
> benefits agreements. This codifies the industry best practice for
> community outreach.[31]

New York

Unions and allies were prime movers for the 2018 Climate Leadership and
Community Protection Act. It required 100 percent carbon-free electricity by 2040 and economy-wide net-zero carbon emissions by 2050. The
act calls for disadvantaged communities to receive 40 percent of spending on clean energy and energy efficiency programs; housing; workforce
development; pollution reduction; low-income energy assistance; and
energy, transportation, and economic development.[32] Following on from
this legislation, in its 2021 budget New York State included new renewable-
energy job standards. The legislation requires prevailing wage and project
labor agreements for construction on renewable-energy projects and labor
peace agreements for operations and maintenance work.[33]

Maine

Unions pushed Maine lawmakers to require a project labor agreement on
the state's first offshore wind project, which means that the Maine workers
constructing massive turbines to supply clean energy throughout the state
will be paid family-sustaining wages with strong labor protections. Now
a dozen unions and labor federations have organized the Maine Labor
Climate Council, which seeks to "develop the labor movement's vision for
how to tackle the twin crises of climate change and inequality in a way that

creates good Maine union jobs, reduces carbon emissions and economic inequality, and provides a seat at the table for workers and unions in this process." The new council issued a report spelling out how to implement these objectives. It proposes to electrify all state and local vehicles, including school and city buses, by 2040; build a high-speed rail corridor from Bangor to Boston with connections to Lewiston/Auburn; do deep energy-efficiency retrofits and install solar on all K–12 public schools and publicly owned buildings by 2035; and install 3 gigawatts of renewable energy by 2030 and upgrade Maine's energy transmission and storage capacity.[34] It is promoting further legislation "to reduce carbon emissions, tackle racial and economic inequality, and create good union jobs."[35]

Illinois

Organized labor played a special role in passage of the 2021 Climate and Equitable Jobs Act, discussed in chapter 2. The legislation was the product of a multiyear effort and months of negotiations between the environmental/climate/faith/environmental justice-based Clean Energy Jobs Coalition, the renewable developers' Path to 100 Coalition, and the newly formed labor coalition Climate Jobs Illinois.

Climate Jobs Illinois represents much of the Illinois labor movement. Its executive committee includes Chicago Regional Council of Carpenters; Illinois Education Association; Illinois Federation of Teachers; International Association of Bridge, Structural, Ornamental and Reinforcing Iron Workers Union; International Association of Heat and Frost Insulators and Allied Workers; International Brotherhood of Electrical Workers (IBEW) State Council; IBEW Local 134; International Union of Operating Engineers Local 150; Laborers International Union of North America Great Lakes Region, Laborers International Union of North America Midwest Region; Service Employees International Union State Council; and United Auto Workers Region 4.

The new law will set the state on a path to a carbon-free power sector by 2045 with the strongest in the nation labor and equity standards. The bill will slash emissions, create thousands of new clean energy union jobs, expand union apprenticeships for Black and Latinx communities, increase energy efficiency for public schools, and safeguard the jobs of thousands of union workers at the state's nuclear plants. It also contains a transition program for families and communities currently reliant on jobs in the fossil fuel industry.

According to Climate Jobs Illinois, the law "sets the strongest clean energy labor standards in the country" and "promises to raise the bar for

other states seeking to enact new labor and employment policies for building and maintaining clean energy developments." Pat Devaney, secretary-
treasurer of the Illinois AFL-CIO, said, "We have a lot of jobs in the energy
sector and particularly in fossil fuel generation, so for us to come forward
with a proactive plan [for transitioning] from fossil generation to clean
energy, I think, really says a lot about labor's commitment to combating
climate change."[36] Unions and their allies are pushing similar legislation
for climate, jobs, and justice in many other states as well.

ON MANY FRONTS

These examples only scratch the surface of union involvement with Green
New Deals from below. Here are a few more:

Loggers preserving the forest: In the 1980s and 1990s the International
Woodworkers Association, representing woodworking and forestry workers, fought a contentious battle with environmentalists over logging in
the Pacific Northwest. But the union, now the Woodworkers Department
of the International Association of Machinists and Aerospace Workers
(IAM), has switched to promoting forest preservation as a key element
of sustainable jobs as well as climate protection.[37]

A union creating a "climate justice agenda" for its employer: The CUNY
Professional Staff Congress—the American Federation of Teachers Local
2334—represents the 30,000 full- and part-time faculty and professional
staff at the City University of New York. In December 2021, 150 members
met to develop a "Climate Justice Agenda for CUNY." The conference
was organized by the union's Environmental Justice Working Group,
which started in 2016 and has been active in city- and state-wide climate
coalitions. The conference identified climate protection demands for the
university, including transformation of its food service, environmental
education across the curriculum, community collaborations, infrastructure improvements, and divestment of university funds from fossil fuel
holdings. The Professional Staff Congress is now campaigning for these
objectives both on individual campuses and CUNY-wide.[38]

Cleaning up the L.A. port: An alliance of unions, environmentalists, and
community groups supported by the Teamsters successfully combatted
severe pollution in the Port of Los Angeles. The alliance developed a plan
to restructure work relations in the port to provide the self-employed,
largely immigrant Latinx truck drivers regular jobs with employers who
would be responsible for providing low-emission trucks. Their plan for
decasualizing the workforce was going forward until a court ruled that

the workers were independent contractors and therefore not eligible for union representation. Workers responded with a series of strikes and a subsequent court decision found that the drivers are workers whose labor rights must be respected.[39]

There are scores of other examples. A September 2021 study by the Center for American Progress listed dozens of Green New Deal programs promoted by unions at state and local levels.[40] The National Nurses United is campaigning for climate-safe hospitals—it has also provided medical care for many climate demonstrators brutalized by violent opponents. The AFT and NEA have worked with construction unions to campaign for green, carbon-free schools. SEIU property management Local 32BJ in the New York metropolitan area runs a "Green Supers Program" to provide a professional building service workforce capable of reducing energy use, conserving water, saving money, and providing cleaner and healthier buildings to live in.[41]

The United Association (UA), Steelworkers (USW), and other unions are conducting extensive training for workers in the wind power industry. The Utility Workers Union is campaigning and training for reconstruction and public ownership of the electrical grid.[42]

DIG WHERE YOU STAND

Workers and unions are among those who have the most to gain by climate protection that produces good jobs and greater equality. That's why unions in the most diverse industries and occupations are creating their own Green New Deal–type programs in localities around the country. Whether or not their participants call them the "Green New Deal," they embody the Green New Deal's fundamental principles.

The unions and workers involved range across the entire workforce. The occupations involved run from loggers to professors and from port truck drivers to nurses. The initiatives range from local and single-employer projects to programs for multistate regions. They are training the workers who are essential to building the new economy. They are fighting for policies that increase jobs and justice by protecting the climate. And they are actually creating the products and services that are necessary for a prosperous climate-safe future.

Workers are essential to fixing our economy because they have the skills and knowledge to actually build the Green New Deal. They are showing that we can start achieving Green New Deal goals from climate-safe energy to good jobs to a more equal society right now. And they represent an organized force that can press for the interests of ordinary people in both the economic and the political arena.

Workers are creating their own Green New Deal programs because they need a Green New Deal for survival and a decent future. They are showing that they don't have to wait to start addressing the problems we face. Unions, labor councils, and other worker organizations can start addressing them right now—in fact, they are already doing so. The next step could be to recognize and celebrate this growing wave of constructive activity. To start sharing with each other what workers are doing and what we can learn from it—and ultimately to combine them to create labor's own Green New Deal from Below.

4

CLIMATE JUSTICE FROM BELOW

Although the Green New Deal is often thought of as a program for climate and jobs, justice has been a central element from its very beginning. The initial Green New Deal resolution proposed by Rep. Alexandria Ocasio-Cortez included as a core aim to "promote justice and equity by preventing current and repairing historic oppression to frontline communities." That included:

- providing resources, training, and high-quality education, including higher education, to all members of our society, with a focus on frontline communities, so they may be full and equal participants in Green New Deal projects;
- directing investments to spur economic development, as well as deepen and diversify industry in local and regional economies and build wealth and community ownership, prioritizing high-quality job creation and economic, social, and environmental benefits in frontline communities and deindustrialized communities that may otherwise struggle with the transition;
- ensuring democratic and participatory processes that are inclusive of and led by frontline communities and workers to plan, implement, and administer Green New Deal projects at the local level;
- obtaining the voluntary, prior, and informed consent of Indigenous peoples for all decisions that affect them, honoring all treaties with Indigenous peoples, and protecting and enforcing the sovereignty and land rights of all Indigenous peoples.[1]

Virtually all Green New Deal from Below–style programs include a strong social justice component. This chapter concentrates on some examples that have emerged from and primarily represent the demands of people of color and frontline communities.

Office of Indian Energy director Wahleah Johns joins the tribal leader caucus at the 2022 Tribal Clean Energy Summit in Washington, DC. Photo by Donica Payne, Wikimedia commons.

THE SUN ALSO RISES AT SUNSET PARK

On October 29, 2009, Superstorm Sandy devasted poor, low-lying neighborhoods of New York City. As official relief agencies like FEMA and the Red Cross floundered, a citywide network of mutual-aid volunteers mobilized through Occupy Wall Street.[2] Calling itself Occupy Sandy Relief, hundreds of volunteers quickly improvised systems of assistance for people in hard-hit neighborhoods who were being neglected by conventional aid efforts. I visited the aging Saint Jacobi Church in the Sunset Park neighborhood of South Brooklyn where thousands of pounds of donated clothes, heaters, and generators were being loaded up in cars to be taken out to the Rockaways, Staten Island, and other hard-hit locations.[3]

A few weeks later I was invited to take part in a small discussion in Sunset Park about how to head off the city's plan to use the disaster to pursue massive development that would displace the people of the neighborhood, and how instead to develop and promote reconstruction plans that emerged from the neighborhood and represented its interests. Two months after Sandy, a community organization named UPROSE convened a meeting in Sunset Park to engage with community members about their experiences during and after the storm. Sharing stories of neighbors

helping neighbors led participants to declare, "We are the first respond-
ers!" They began to come up with community resiliency strategies and to
identify opportunities for climate adaptation projects in their own homes
and neighborhood blocks. The meeting attendees asked UPROSE to put
their ideas into a plan for action. The result was the Sunset Park Climate
Justice Center.[4]

UPROSE had started in 1966 as a service agency, the United Puerto
Rican Organization of Sunset Park, but later changed its name and its
focus to grassroots community organizing to empower the predominantly
low-income Latinx and Asian residents to fight for neighborhood development that benefits local people. It campaigned against lead paint, fought
an expansion of the Gowanus Expressway, and helped kill a proposal to
build a massive power plant on a floating barge off Sunset Park. UPROSE
engaged in constructive initiatives as well. When Sunset Park residents
dreamed of a waterside park, UPROSE helped organize a campaign that
resulted in 2014 in turning a contaminated brownfield and illegal dumping
ground into the Bush Terminal Piers Park. The park features a bike path,
soccer field, a bird sanctuary, and benches for viewing the water. Sunset
Park youth helped design the park.

The new Sunset Park Climate Justice Center had as its goals:

- To build the capacity of Sunset Park's indigenous leaders and local
  businesses to effectively respond to future severe weather events,
  coordinate the allocation of community resources, and mitigate the
  impacts of future severe weather, including the possible release
  of harmful chemicals; such capacity will enable the community to
  care for itself and to enter the future not as passive victim, but as
  active designer and agent.
- To engage community members and local businesses in leadership
  development and in a block-by-block, building-by-building assess-
  ment, mapping, and relationship-building process to create, implement, and manage a truly grassroots-led climate adaptation and
  community resiliency plan.
- To develop the tools and partnerships needed to transition the
  Sunset Park industrial area from a traditional twentieth-century
  industrial operations model into a twenty-first-century climate
  resilient and sustainable industrial area adapted to climate change;
  such a transition will ensure the long-term availability of business
  development and employment opportunities for NYC's largest
  walk-to-work community, Sunset Park.
- To engage community residents and local businesses in the public
  processes (land-use planning, infrastructure design, permitting, etc.)
  required to adapt the community's infrastructure to climate change.

The center began addressing community environmental needs through self-help. Activists spoke to neighbors and landlords about painting rooftops white to reduce heat buildup; building a storm-water collection system to reduce water usage and create a backup in case the water supply is cut off; and testing the suitability of backyard soil for small urban farms. They talked with local businesses ranging from auto shops (the community's biggest industry) to taco and dumpling vendors. At the request of participants at neighborhood meetings, the center set up a system of block captains to prepare for future disasters.

UPROSE and the center ultimately wanted the community to have a voice in the larger decisions affecting it. "You've got an industrial sector that really protected us and kept this a working-class community," said Elizabeth Yeampierre, long-time executive director of UPROSE. The community had previously pushed without success to convert its deteriorating waterfront into a green, sustainable port. It would be energy efficient, sensitive to local ecology, a source of permanent jobs, and designed to manage floods—in effect a local Green New Deal. Developers had instead built Industrial City, an upscale sixteen-building complex. Then developers tried to rezone the area to allow further expansion, displacing longtime residents and driving up rents. UPROSE packed public meetings, held rallies, and lobbied local elected officials. Ultimately the developer withdrew the plan.

In 2018 UPROSE launched Sunset Park Solar, New York City's first community-owned solar cooperative. Partners include the New York City Economic Development Corporation, the woman-owned solar installer 770 Electric, and the consumer-owned cooperative Co-op Power. The solar collectors are installed on the roof of the Brooklyn Army Terminal. They are collectively owned by all energy users who subscribe. It will serve 200 low-income residents.

Meanwhile, UPROSE developed a plan for a South Brooklyn offshore wind assembly and maintenance hub. It sought to preserve the "working waterfront" and create jobs in clean energy manufacturing, part of its vision for a Green Resilient Industrial District, or GRID. Yeampierre says, "We can start using the industrial sector to build for the climate future, for adaptation, mitigation, and resilience."

It's finally happening: In January 2023 the State of New York selected the South Brooklyn Marine Terminal in Sunset Park for a wind turbine assembly and maintenance hub to service Northeast offshore wind projects. Equinor Wind U.S., a key contractor, said the port upgrades will provide 1,500 short-term and 500 long-term jobs locally. It will contract with minority- and women-owned business enterprises for at least 30 percent of its supply chain needs. It will also invest $5 million in an "ecosystem fund" that the city says will "bring more New York City residents into offshore wind careers, propel offshore wind innovation, and support a just transition." Yeampierre said of the long-term advocacy of UPROSE, "This community vision of taking the industrial waterfront so that it could start building for climate adaptation, mitigation, and resilience is not new. These are victories that don't happen overnight."[5]

THE BLUE NEW DEAL

The Shinnecock people have lived on New York's Long Island since the end of the last Ice Age more than 10,000 years ago. In 1640, European settlers signed agreements recognizing Shinnecock rights, including their right to harvest seaweed in the waters adjoining their territory. Seaweed was an important part of the Shinnecock economy, used for insulation, medicine, and fertilizer.

Shinnecock tribal member and attorney Telga Troge helped research early law cases that recognized the Shinnecock's rights. After a long legal struggle, in 2010 the Shinnecock won federal recognition, based in part on their legally recognized seaweed harvesting rights. Troge says that despite their legal rights, the New York State Department of Environment Conservation is notorious for still harassing tribal members who go out fishing. Troge describes how on one side of Shinnecock Hills, "you have billionaire's row where some of the wealthiest people in America have homes"; on the other side you have Shinnecock territory, where "60% of us are living in complete poverty."[6]

In 2019 a film about the Shinnecock's struggle for their rights caught the eye of staff members at GreenWave, a nonprofit that replicates "regenerative ocean farming" and trains and supports local communities around the world to start their own ocean farms. Part of GreenWave's mission is to ensure marginalized communities—including Indigenous peoples with close ties to the ocean—not only benefit from but lead in the burgeoning seaweed industry. GreenWave connected with Becky Genia, a Shinnecock elder and a central figure in the film, to see if any tribal members would be interested in starting a kelp farm.

Tela Troge says GreenWave's model "closely matched our skills, our expertise, our traditional ecological knowledge." She felt that "the act of cultivating seaweed" was "a really powerful way to assert our tribal sovereignty over the water." It also could help counteract the effect of excess nutrient runoff from wealthy nearby estates that was devastating their waters. "Kelp has an incredible ability to sequester carbon, which is one of the problems that we're facing here with ocean acidification. But sugar kelp also thrives on nitrogen, which is perfect because there is an excess of nitrogen in the water." She and five other Indigenous women formed the Shinnecock Kelp Farmers, the first Indigenous-owned seaweed farm on the East Coast, and with support from GreenWave and the neighboring Sisters of St. Joseph retreat built a seed nursery and began cultivating sugar kelp.

GreenWave was founded by Bren Smith, a long-time oysterman whose Thimble Island Ocean Farm lies off Branford, Connecticut, on the other side of Long Island Sound from the Shinnecock territory. After Smith's oystering operation was wiped out by Hurricane Irene and then again by Superstorm Sandy, he developed a system for lowering his fishing lines into the sea when a storm approached, using a rope scaffolding hung from buoys and anchored to the seafloor. When he found his lines were frequently encrusted by mussels and seaweed, he decided to follow nature's example by growing a mix of seaweed and shellfish on his scaffolding—inventing what has come to be known as the polyculture regenerative ocean farming model.

Smith was impressed by the potential ecological benefits of vertical ocean farming. The oysters and other mollusks filtered massive amounts of nitrogen out of the water—including the fertilizer runoff from on-land farming. And kelp can absorb five times more carbon than land-based plants and requires zero inputs—making it "the most sustainable form of food production on the planet." Smith recruited celebrity chefs and major institutional food buyers to start including kelp in their offerings.[7]

Although many investors saw profit opportunities in Smith's innovations and tried to capitalize on them, Smith had a different vision. His nonprofit GreenWave open sourced the farm design, so that anyone with a boat, twenty acres, and $20,000 can start their own farm. In her presidential campaign, Senator Elizabeth Warren introduced a Blue New Deal plan largely based on Smith's vision. Mayor Michelle Wu included the Blue New Deal as part of her Boston Green New Deal.

The six women of Shinnecock Kelp Farmers started by nurturing kelp from microscopic cells to young plants ready to transport into their farm. Then they waded out to attach them to the horizontal ropes of their farm. They returned repeatedly to tend the lines even in the middle of winter. After a few months the kelp was ready for harvest.

The Shinnecock Kelp Farmers' business model is to be Indigenous-led "from seed to sale." While kelp can have many uses, the women see their primary market as a "natural soil amendment," an eco-friendly alternative to conventional fertilizer that can be sold to farms, institutions, golf courses, college campuses, and anyone who is cultivating any type of plants.

The winter of 2022–23 marked the third growing season for the Shinnecock Kelp Farmers. They planted more than 15,000 feet of seeded kelp lines—more than ten times the previous year.[8] Most of what they harvest will be dried and ground down into natural soil amendment. They are negotiating with vineyards, golf courses, and landscaping companies about purchasing their product. One of the farmers noted, "We're always looking to target those large-scale polluters."

In the coming years, the farmers intend to scale-up their production by building a permanent, state-of-the-art nursery at the nearby retreat of the Sisters of St. Joseph's and increasing the number of sites where they farm in adjoining waters. As Troge and her colleagues plan ahead, they're also looking to bring on additional staff to help manage the harvests. They plan to hire from within the Shinnecock community. Troge says, "I'm just really excited about building up to the point to offer people living-wage jobs."

They hope to see wide-scale kelp farming in Long Island Sound that goes beyond Shinnecock. Troge says,

> We can't do this alone. We are a collective of six intergenerational Indigenous women, and we're doing our part, but we need to build a huge network—a huge collective of kelp farmers. We need to get kelp into every single body of water. We need to meaningfully mitigate a lot of the damage that is happening, and we'll only be able to do that if we can get as much kelp into the water as possible. We have a lot of carbon to sequester and we have a whole lot of excess nitrates that we need to remove.
>
> We need to stop the chemical fertilizers and septic systems seeping into the water. For this, the return of land to Indigenous people is really key. We're hoping that because of our rights, our experience, and our traditional ecological knowledge, we can be a little bit ahead of the game and help provide seedlings to those who are interested—once the legislation catches up with the interests of those looking to clean up the water.

Shinnecock Kelp Farmers identifies "addressing the climate crisis" as a core objective. Troge says, "We're constantly battling the threats of the climate crisis. We have been taught by our elders how to survive here, often with very little resources. We're taught how to think of the entire ecosystem anytime that we're taking action. Additionally, we're taught to think seven generations ahead. It's a lot of what drives us in educating and sharing our message, and hopefully getting others engaged in taking action to protect the water now." What they've already done is having an impact. Within their first season, scallops, clams, seahorses, and other species that have experienced precipitous declines in Shinnecock Bay have been sheltering in their kelp lines.

There is a striking convergence between the Shinnecock Kelp Farmers' vision and that of GreenWave. In his book *Eat Like a Fish* Bren Smith lays out "principles of regenerative ocean agriculture" that could well serve as guidelines for a "Blue New Deal," which could be a key element of the Green New Deal from Below. Smith calls for a "circular" economy that coordinates different activities through decentralized networks rather than conventional corporate vertical integration. A key objective is to keep ocean farming affordable, especially for former fishers, Native Americans, and others who have been excluded or extruded from mainstream employment. That means keeping the cost of entry low, limiting the number of acres any one entity can hold, and requiring living wages and employment open to all. Ocean farmers own their businesses, but the ocean remains a commons open for all to boat, fish, and swim.

For an embodiment of the principles of the Green New Deal—creating jobs and countering historic injustices by remediating the climate—Shinnecock Kelp Farmers would be hard to beat.

THE GULF SOUTH FOR A GREEN NEW DEAL

In May 2019 more than eight hundred advocates, farmers, fisherfolk, and community leaders from the Gulf South states gathered in New Orleans to project a shared vision of regional sustainability in response to the global climate crisis. The result was the Gulf South for a Green New Deal Policy Platform.[9]

The policy platform defined the Gulf South as the five states of Texas, Louisiana, Mississippi, Alabama, and Florida. Together they form the world's fifth largest economy. Mississippi, Louisiana, and Alabama have three of the five largest Black populations in the nation; the region includes the territory of more than ten Native American nations. The Gulf South provides three-quarters of the nation's oil and gas. The number of days over 100 degrees in the region is predicted to rise fourfold by 2050.

The policy platform endorsed the core elements of Representative Ocasio-Cortez and Senator Markey's Green New Deal legislation: We are in a climate emergency. Bold national action is necessary. The federal government has a moral obligation "to create a Green New Deal with the promise to create millions of new high-paying jobs and counteract systemic injustices."

The policy platform emphasized the aspects of the Green New Deal that focus on issues of justice. The Green New Deal must "prioritize the needs and voices of those disproportionately impacted by our current social systems: Indigenous Peoples, communities of color, migrant communities, deindustrialized communities, depopulated rural communities, low-income workers, women, elderly, LGBTQ+ people, the unhoused, people with disabilities, youth, and people with criminal records." And it must "provide access to healthcare, affordable housing, public transportation, and economic security, education, worker rights, and ownership."

The policy platform laid out a series of "frontline values" to help shape a Green New Deal and repair historical injustices as part of climate protection, including:

- *Follow Indigenous and frontline leadership.* Their voices must be prioritized. Rights and treaties of tribal nations must be recognized.
- *Build community wealth and health.* Green New Deal jobs must offer living wages and prioritize sustainable practices of farming, "remediating toxic soil and reforesting our degraded land," transitioning energy infrastructure to "renewables like Solar and Wind energy," and preparing vulnerable communities and land for a changing climate while caring for those in need.
- *Advance community and local control.* Shift power "away from large corporations and to local communities." Communities must create and control their own wealth through affordable housing and sustainable homeownership, public control of natural resources, and renewable energy sources.
- *Use an intersectional approach.* Affordable housing, access to healthcare, land sovereignty, and economic justice are necessary elements of "climate resiliency." Eliminating policy barriers to formerly incarcerated, differently abled, trans and queer people is "climate equity."
- *Value all humans equally.* Green New Deal mobilization must ensure the safety, dignity, and self-determination of all workers, and value nonworkers—children, students, unemployed people, elders, and people with disabilities—as worthy of support.

The Gulf South for a Green New Deal has developed a unique structure to connect diverse issues and organizations. It has built state hubs that bring together existing state and local organizations to define state Green New Deal priorities and organize support for action to realize them.[10]

Florida

The Florida Hub of Gulf South for a Green New Deal raised and distributed over $700,000 in 2022 for more than a dozen groups all over the state, such as Lead Coalition of Bay County, La Mesa Boricua de Florida, Coalition of

100 Black Women, and Catalyst Miami.[11] Florida Student Power's "Power University" led an eight-week training for students on political education and participation in democratic processes. The Farmworkers' Association of Florida advocates for farmworkers and their families with the Defending Immigrants' Rights Program. Catalyst Miami's Worker-Owned Enterprises Program is supporting the development of worker cooperatives. SMASH Miami established a Housing and Healing Justice Corps.

Alabama

Energy Alabama launched the "Energy Freedom Campaign" to challenge the state's policies that have made it the lowest producer of renewable energy in the Southeast. Other groups organized to run candidates in local Public Service Commission elections to advocate for electric coops. The Alabama Rivers Alliance followed wastewater infrastructure money to hold the state accountable for getting it to the communities that need it most.

Mississippi

Gulfport's EEECHO is organizing to resist the planned Drax and Enviva biomass facilities as false climate solutions. The Steps Coalition Housing Initiative is working to build affordable housing for Mississippi Gulf Coast residents. Sipp Culture's Community Farm is developing food sovereignty in Utica, Mississippi. Mississippi Rising Coalition's Hub City Mutual Aid Project is developing community gardens aimed at addressing food apartheid.

Louisiana

The Louisiana Just Recovery Network is helping communities impacted by climate disasters to rebuild through the creation of well-paid jobs for local residents. Various member organizations are resisting the development of carbon capture and sequestration facilities across Louisiana. Others have developed solar and storage bills that are moving through the legislature. The Greater New Orleans Housing Alliance's #PutHousingFirst campaign is pushing for the implementation of the city's Ten-Year HousingNOLA Plan.

Texas

The Carrizo/Comecrudo Tribe of Texas is documenting and protecting sacred sites being impacted by the petrochemical buildout, such as Garcia

Pasture. In northeast Houston West Street Recovery is pressuring the state's General Land Office to stop discriminatory climate mitigation funding from Hurricane Harvey. Southern Sector Rising is building a network of air monitors in North Texas called SharedAirDFW to provide Dallas and Fort Worth residents with access to real-time air pollution data. Many groups, including PACAN and the Society of Native Nations, are campaigning to block construction of Energy Transfer's Blue Marlin Pipeline off the coast of Port Arthur, Texas.

Recognizing the common experience of the Gulf South and Appalachia as the objects of extraction and exploitation, a "Gulf to Appalachia People's Movement Assembly" process was recently initiated to form an alliance of the Gulf South for a Green New Deal and similar groups in Appalachia.

The original New Deal of the 1930s, while it provided substantial benefit to people of color, immigrants, and other disadvantaged groups, was notorious for implementing exclusionary racist policies in housing and other spheres that were demanded by federal legislators from the South. Today's Green New Deal, in contrast, was initiated in large part by people of color and other disadvantaged groups. Policies to challenge racial and other injustice are at its core, and frontline communities are central to the coalitions that have been implementing the Green New Deal from Below.

5

CLIMATE-SAFE ENERGY PRODUCTION

The original 2018 Green New Deal resolution submitted by Rep. Alexandria Ocasio-Cortez called for a national ten-year mobilization to achieve 100 percent of national power generation from clean, renewable, and zero-emission energy sources. That would be achieved by "dramatically expanding and up-grading renewable power sources" and "deploying new capacity." The shift to zero-emission energy is an essential component of protecting the climate by reducing greenhouse gas emissions. It also will create millions of jobs and shut down the fossil fuel extraction and generation facilities that threaten the health of people everywhere, and especially in the low-income, discriminated-against communities where such facilities are concentrated.[1]

Meeting the Green New Deal energy production goals requires an unprecedented transformation of the energy system, and that requires national investment and planning. But much of the transformation will actually be composed of local building blocks—and those can begin right now. Indeed, there are thousands of such local initiatives around the country, ranging from community solar to municipal ownership to local microgrids. And in most instances that climate-safe energy is being produced in ways that also produce jobs and increase racial, social, and economic justice—fulfilling the basic principles of the Green New Deal.

SUNLIGHT, JOBS, AND JUSTICE

Solar gardens are sprouting up all over Denver.

On November 3, 2020, Denver voters overwhelmingly approved Ballot Measure 2A, the Climate Protection Fund, to raise approximately $40

The Mueller Austin solar array in Austin, Texas, a series of eighteen- to twenty-foot-tall flower-shaped sculptures that collect solar energy to light the buildings at night. Photo by Larry D. Moore, 2009, Wikimedia commons.

million per year dedicated to climate action. As stated in the ballot measure, its intent is to "fund programs to eliminate greenhouse gas emissions and air pollution and adapt to climate change. Funding should maximize investments in communities of color, under-resourced communities, and communities most vulnerable to climate change."[2]

Community solar gardens use photovoltaic panels to produce electricity from sunlight for an entire neighborhood. Now such solar gardens are dotting sites owned and financed by the City of Denver, including rooftops, parking lots, and vacant lands. The power generated from the solar gardens will be shared between city facilities, income-qualified residents, and publicly accessible electric vehicle charging stations.

In accord with the principles of the Green New Deal, Denver's solar garden program has a strong justice dimension. Since Denver owns the project, the city can set its own standards. Ten percent of the energy generated by the solar gardens is allocated to low-income housing through the Denver Housing Authority. An additional 10 percent will be allocated to low-income households through Energy Outreach Colorado, and will be exempt from subscription fees. A paid workforce training program available to Denver residents will provide 10 percent of the city and county's solar workforce.

The solar gardens are designed to contribute to Denver's "80 × 50 Climate Action Plan" to transition Denver to 100 percent renewable electricity for municipal buildings by 2025; achieve 100 percent community-wide renewable electricity by 2030; and reduce Denver's greenhouse gas emissions 80 percent, as compared to a 2005 baseline, by 2050.[3]

Meanwhile, the Denver Housing Authority and affordable housing developers have launched the CARE Project (Clean Affordable Renewable Energy), including a two-megawatt community solar garden that serves 500 homes throughout the City and County of Denver. Project goals include offering predictable reduced energy costs and renewable energy options to low-income communities and developing a pipeline to employment in the solar industry for underserved communities. Community residents have already had hands-on training and gotten jobs with solar developers in the program. Both the Denver Housing Authority and its residents have saved money on their electric bills—some close to 20 percent per month.[4]

While individual solar gardens are often at small scale, cumulatively they can add up to substantial amounts of electricity. Minnesota's community solar program, started in 2014, now deploys 800 megawatts of operational capacity with more than 12,000 residential customers, as well as commercial and public service entities, including schools, colleges, hospitals, and county and local governments.[5] Community solar employed over 4,000 workers in Minnesota in 2018. Community solar cut global warming emissions by almost a million tons per year and reduced health-threatening sulfur and nitrogen oxide emissions by over 400 tons a year. While so far community solar gardens provide a relatively small proportion of US energy, they can easily multiply to provide a significant part of the climate-safe energy mix—and fix.

California, aiming for 100 percent renewable electricity by 2045, is using another approach to solar energy—the "solar mandate." Since 2014, all new California residential and commercial buildings have been required to have a "solar ready roof." Since 2017, every residential or commercial building below ten stories has been required to have PV solar panels or solar water heaters.[6] The solar mandate legislation articulated the threat of climate change, using San Francisco as an example:

> As a coastal city located on the tip of a peninsula, San Francisco is vulnerable to sea level rise, and human activities releasing greenhouse gases into the atmosphere cause increases in worldwide average temperature, which contribute to melting of glaciers and thermal expansion of ocean water—resulting in rising sea levels. San Francisco is already experiencing the repercussions of excessive CO_2 emissions as rising sea levels threaten the City's shoreline and infrastructure, have caused significant erosion, increased impacts to infrastructure during extreme tides, and have caused the City to expend funds to modify the sewer system.[7]

In 2018, California went further, passing Assembly Bill 178, a unique-to-California mandate that requires solar panels on all new residential buildings of three stories or less.[8]

Over the past decade, local solar energy has grown exponentially city by city. The amount of solar power installed in 2020 in just seven US cities exceeds the amount installed in the entire United States at the end of 2010. Of fifty-seven cities surveyed in one study, almost 90 percent more than doubled their total installed solar PV capacity between 2013 and 2019.[9] With solar energy costs continuing to fall, the opportunities for job-and-justice-promoting solarization are likely to continue to rise.

YOU DON'T NEED A WEATHERMAN . . .

Vineyard Power is a community-owned cooperative with a membership base of nearly 1,400 households and businesses in Martha's Vineyard, Massachusetts. Its mission is to produce electricity from local, renewable resources while advocating for and keeping the benefits within the island community. Its vision is to make the island of Martha's Vineyard 100 percent renewable in domestic electricity, transportation, and home heating by 2040.[10]

In 2015, Vineyard Power Coop formally partnered with Vineyard Wind, an offshore wind development company, through the first community benefits agreement for offshore wind signed in the United States. This partnership is designed to ensure that the benefits of offshore wind remain within the local island community.

Soon thereafter, Vineyard Wind won the rights to develop renewable energy projects in a federal lease area on the outer continental shelf off the southern coast of Massachusetts. Its first project, Vineyard Wind 1, will provide clean, sustainable energy to over 400,000 homes and businesses in Massachusetts at a competitive price as part of the state's effort to achieve net-zero carbon emissions by 2050. Vineyard Wind 1 is scheduled for completion in 2023.

Vineyard Power is working with Vineyard Wind and local, state, and federal agencies to maximize local community benefits, participation, and engagement. The community benefits agreement provides for local jobs, control, and stable electricity prices. Vineyard Wind 1 will generate thousands of jobs through its development, maintenance, and operation phases over the next twenty-five to thirty years, not only in the project itself but also in an operations and maintenance facility and in expanded operations at the local airport.[11] The project includes local job training: Vineyard Power in partnership with Adult and Community Education

Martha's Vineyard and Bristol Community College are providing island-ers with the education and training to become offshore wind technicians and project managers.[12]

Offshore wind projects are developing all along the East Coast, with substantial numbers of good-quality jobs in the offing. In 2020, Virginia passed a law that set a target of developing 5,200 megawatts of offshore wind power by 2034. In Portsmouth, the Spanish wind turbine manufac-turer Siemens Gamesa plans for 310 jobs to make preparations for a new offshore wind farm. Two hundred sixty of them would be in a finishing plant where blades are painted and assembled. In New Jersey, Ørsted of Denmark and EEW of Germany planned to open a factory to build the steel foundations of turbines—called monopiles—that would provide up to 500 jobs; when Orsted pulled out of the deal, New Jersey found the US company Invenergy Energy to replace it.[13] In New York, Marmen of Canada, Welcon of Denmark, and Smulders of Belgium are planning a plant to make steel towers for offshore wind turbines; it will employ up to 350 people.[14] In an era when well-paid, secure jobs are rare, unions and local officials regularly tout the quality of these jobs and their benefit for both workers and the local community.

LOCAL STRATEGIES FOR CLIMATE-SAFE ENERGY

Most US energy production is controlled by so-called "public utilities"—actually, private corporations that often have a monopoly over local elec-tricity supply and use it both to extract high levels of profit and to maintain profitable but climate-destroying fossil fuel energy production.

One alternative is public power. Public power utilities are community-owned, not-for-profit electricity suppliers that provide reliable, low-cost electricity to more than 49 million people. Homes and businesses in 2,000 communities across the United States—large cities like Austin, Nashville, Los Angeles, and Seattle, as well as small towns and the Navajo Nation—get electricity from a public power utility.

Collectively, these utilities serve one in seven electricity customers across the United States and operate in forty-nine states. Like public schools and libraries, public power utilities are owned by the community and run as a division of local government. These utilities are governed by a local city council or an elected or appointed board. Community citizens have a direct voice in utility decisions, including the rates charged and the sources of electricity.[15] In 2019, about 40 percent of power generated by public power came from non-carbon-emitting sources.[16] And many public power utilities are now going greener.

Since the days when Bernie Sanders was its mayor, Burlington, Vermont, has been a precursor of the Green New Deal. Burlington is one of the cities that owns its own electric utility, run by the Burlington Electric Department. In 2014, the department purchased the Winooski One hydroelectric plant, making Burlington the first city in the nation to source 100 percent of its electricity from renewable generation.

The city's recent Net Zero Energy Roadmap aims to realize net zero energy by 2030. That includes making all buildings more efficient and electric, electrification of space and water heating, a district heating system for high-load buildings, and incentives for low- and moderate-income customers. It also includes land-use policies to reduce energy use, powering all municipal vehicles with 100 percent renewable electricity, a 15 percent reduction in vehicle miles traveled, and twenty new electric vehicle charging stations in public locations and multifamily buildings.[17] The city's control of its own electricity makes these goals far easier to achieve.

Another strategy being applied locally to achieve climate-safe energy production is called Community Choice Aggregation (CCA). CCA allows local governments to procure electricity on behalf of their residents, businesses, and the municipalities themselves. It can provide communities more local control over their electricity sources, more green power than is offered by the default utility, and lower electricity prices.

Here's how it works: By buying electricity collectively through their municipality, consumers gain leverage to negotiate with competing suppliers for lower rates and greener power sources. Most CCAs have opt-out provisions, meaning when a community begins a program, customers are given advance notice and have the choice to opt out of the CCA program and continue to receive electricity from their current supplier. Customers who do not opt out are automatically enrolled in the program. CCAs are currently authorized in California, Illinois, Ohio, Massachusetts, New Jersey, New York, and Rhode Island. In 2016, CCAs sold about 8.7 billion kilowatt-hours of green power to about 3.3 million customers.[18]

The town of Swampscott, Massachusetts, launched its aggregation program, Swampscott Community Power, in 2016. The aggregation plan was developed to provide residents and businesses with a green and predictable electric supply. This program is having a measurable and significant impact on Swampscott's carbon footprint. Based on data from the first year of the program, Swampscott was able to reduce its emissions by more than 9,700 tons of carbon dioxide. That's equivalent to removing more than 2,000 passenger vehicles from the road for one year.[19]

Local governments are also using their purchasing power to promote fossil-free electricity. The EPA Green Power program classifies as "Green Power Communities" those that use "renewable energy resources and technologies that provide the highest environmental benefit." That includes solar, wind, geothermal, biogas, eligible biomass, and low-impact small hydroelectric sources. Customers often buy green power for its zero emissions profile and carbon footprint reduction benefits.[20] In 2021, the combined annual green power use of EPA's Top 30 Local Governments amounts to nearly 5 billion kilowatt-hours of green power, which is equivalent to the annual electricity used by 464,000 average American homes.[21] Dallas, Texas, is the most populous city in the United States purchasing 100 percent green power. In 2019, the United States Conference of Mayors presented the city with the 2019 Mayor's Climate Protection Award.[22]

Electrical energy requires not only production but also distribution. That can include local, regional, and national power grids. While improvement of the national grid will require planning and investment by the federal government, local "microgrids" are developing all over the country.

Pam Tau Lee, founder of the Asian Pacific Environmental Network (APEN), recently described the plans for one local microgrid. Boston's Chinatown, she said, is "vulnerable to extreme heat and flooding with the highest level of particulate air pollution in the state." The Chinese Progressive Association is planning for a "community-owned energy microgrid to reduce emissions and bring electric power to those most impacted by environmental injustice." She emphasized the importance of a collective voice to ensure climate issues in these communities "are uplifted and addressed" and that "Green New Deal infrastructure projects provide good-paying union opportunities for community residents."[23]

According to a summary of the project, it will

> improve energy resiliency in Boston's Chinatown neighborhood, which is projected to experience regular flooding, assuring reliable transportation and mobile communications, as well as delivery of essential services like food, water, and energy. The proposal includes eight affordable housing complexes. The project team is strongly committed to modeling a grassroots-driven microgrid project which seeks to address energy justice challenges by engaging politically and economically marginalized communities who are disproportionately affected by high energy costs and the impacts of climate change.

At least fourteen such microgrid projects have received funding in Massachusetts alone.[24]

GREEN POWER TO THE PEOPLE

Protecting the climate requires a rapid transition to 100 percent renewable energy. The original Green New Deal proposal called for 100 percent of national power generation from renewable sources within ten years.[25] That requires rapidly expanding climate-safe sources of energy. As we will see in the next two chapters, climate protection also requires reducing the overall amount of energy needed and a rapid reduction in the use of fossil fuels.

All energy production starts local: solar collectors, windmills, and geothermal installations are located in particular places. In addition, energy policy and regulation in the United States is set less at the national than the local and especially the state level. What federal policy there is has long been driven by the power of private utilities and the fossil fuel industry, reflecting their desire to maximize profits and expand the markets for their products. This impedes a rationally planned transition to climate-safe energy. But—as we have seen above—it also opens enormous opportunities for green energy and Green New Deal from Below programs.

According to a recent study, wind and solar power can meet 85 percent of US electricity needs—and even more if battery storage is added to the equation.[26] The United States now has enough clean energy capacity to power over 50 million homes. Wind power was the number-one choice for utility-scale power generation in 2020, capturing 50 percent of new additions, while solar was number 2 with 26 percent of the market. Wind, solar, and battery storage power combined represented 78 percent of new power growth for the year. In total, they supplied nearly 11 percent of the country's electricity in 2020.[27]

Green New Deal from Below energy production projects are often specifically designed to provide jobs, access, and training to local communities. Renewable energy production normally produces far more jobs than it replaces.[28] According to the 2021 "Clean Energy Workforce Report," there are currently more than 425,000 workers in all fifty states in the wind, solar, and energy storage workforce. Wind technician is the country's fastest growing occupation; solar installer is the third. Clean energy workers make 30 percent more than the national median wage; their unionization rate is significantly above the national average for the private sector. "Build Back Better" policies designed to reach 50–70 percent clean energy generation by 2030 are estimated to create an additional 500,000–600,000 jobs.[29]

While not all renewable energy promotes racial, environmental, and economic justice, a large proportion of such projects include specific social justice objectives and strategies. They replace fossil fuel that causes environmental injustices like coal smoke and drinking water pollution with clean and healthy solar, wind, and other pollution-free energy. Many are specifically designed to provide jobs, access, and training to low-income and discriminated-against groups and communities.

There are many varieties of Green New Deal from Below energy production and many possible options for those who wish to pursue it. The principal energy sources are solar and wind, but there are also others like hydropower, geothermal, ocean waves, and biological sources that are currently less used by Green New Dealers but might play a role in the future. Scale of projects vary from individual rooftops to communities and cities to large utility-scale wind and solar installations. The distribution and utilization of energy produced may be limited to the location where it is produced or make use of a local, regional, or national grid. Production for grids may be centralized in large units or the combined contribution of many small, linked production units. Investment and control may be corporate, nonprofit, governmental, cooperative, or a partnership of different players.

The design and scale of local energy projects at times arouses local opposition. The Copake, New York, town board, for example, recently passed a resolution opposing a proposed 255-acre utility-scale solar farm. The town supervisor said, "The town opposes the project as it is currently proposed" because it is "too big" and "poorly sited."[30]

Nonetheless, powerful forces are pushing Green New Deal from Below power production, including climate protection, environmental justice, economic efficiency, and political advantage. The political process by which these projects came into being varies enormously. Some were the product of progressive coalitions, often including environmentalists, unions, social and racial justice organizations, local community groups, religious congregations, and others. Some were the product of more conventional politicians seeing political advantage in green energy. Some were promoted by economic players taking advantage of economic opportunities. Some were initiated by governmental bureaucrats and experts. But in nearly all cases, underlying them was a groundswell of popular support for the elements of the Green New Deal—protecting the climate while creating jobs and reducing social and racial injustice.

6

NEGAWATTS

Every time you replace an incandescent light bulb with a florescent or LED one, every time you caulk a window to stop heat from escaping, you save energy. Every time a skyscraper installs new heating and cooling equipment, it saves a significant and measurable number of watts. Indeed, the energy that is saved by these and other energy efficiency and energy conservation measures has come to be known as "negawatts."

Energy efficiency and conservation are essential elements of the original Green New Deal resolution. It includes "upgrading every residential and industrial building for state-of-the-art energy efficiency, comfort and safety" and "decarbonizing" manufacturing, agriculture, transportation, and other infrastructure.[1] Spelling out the role of energy efficiency, Sen. Bernie Sanders (I-VT) and Rep. Alexandria Ocasio-Cortez (D-NY), in April 2021, introduced the Green New Deal for Public Housing Act, which aims to strengthen public housing communities, improve living conditions for residents, and create jobs by addressing the housing and climate crises through the retrofitting, rehabilitating, and decarbonizing of the nation's entire public housing stock.[2]

Meanwhile at community, local, and state levels people are already producing "negawatts" through the Green New Deal from Below. Using more efficient home appliances, building houses and workplaces close to public transportation, and insulating buildings are a few examples. Homes, workplaces, stores, and other buildings are among the highest producers of greenhouse gases; this chapter focuses on energy efficiency and conservation that reduce the use of energy in buildings.

North Charleston mayor R. Keith Summey visits with the Sustainability Institute's Energy Conservation Corps at their Green House on East Montague. Photo by Ryan Johnson, 2013, Wikimedia commons.

CARBON-NEUTRAL BY 2030

In June 2019 the city of Ithaca, New York, adopted the Ithaca Green New Deal to address climate change, economic inequality, and racial injustice. It aims for 100 percent renewable electricity for the municipality by 2025 and carbon-neutrality community-wide by 2030—in just eleven years.[3] In response to the COVID pandemic, in 2021 the Ithaca Green New Deal was further defined as a "people-first, socially driven economic strategy, seeking to elevate social capital and to guarantee equity, justice, and sustainable prosperity to all members of the community."[4]

Crucial for the Ithaca Green New Deal is an Efficiency Retrofitting and Thermal Load Electrification program designed to promote energy-efficiency retrofits and eliminate fossil fuel combustion in new and existing residential and commercial buildings. The city set an initial goal of retrofitting 1,000 buildings in the first 1,000 days. Strategies to improve energy performance and eliminate carbon emissions include:

- Envelope intervention to maximize performance and reduce energy loads
- Replacement of low-performance windows
- Installation of energy-recovery ventilation systems

- Efficient and automated LED lighting
- Electrical panel and installation upgrades
- Substitution of electric appliances with highly efficient, smart electric alternatives
- Substitution of natural gas, propane, and fuel oil space heating systems with cold-climate air-source and ground-source heat pumps for space heating and cooling
- Substitution of natural gas and propane water heaters with heat pump water heaters with storage tanks
- Substitution of natural gas and propane cooking stoves with electric induction cooktops
- Substitution of natural gas and propane clothes dryers with electric heat pump dryers
- Load flexibility, grid interacting, advance control systems
- Solar PV and onsite energy storage systems
- Bi-directional electric vehicle charging systems[5]

In addition, Ithaca planned to create 1,000 jobs in the region in those first 1,000 days. The city can require that 80 percent of the workforce be local. It also aims to work with nearby cities to establish a "green workforce corridor" that will create a long-term regional market for energy efficiency and retrofit jobs. A Green Workforce Development Taskforce will lead the training and certification of local skilled workers. It is identifying "community champions" to recruit for job training programs.

Ithaca's Green New Deal operates in a "Justice 50" framework requiring that half of all investment—including workforce development, retrofitting, and transportation—goes into climate justice communities. As an alternative to conventional public consultations, the city is developing a "new model for democratic engagement" based on initiating 1,000 "conversations" about the program with individuals, companies, and institutions. Sustainability director Luis Aguirre-Torres says, "If I were alone in thinking this way, then I would be worried. But you know, there is an army behind me. There's so many people, so many companies, so many organizations working with me to make this happen, that I'm not worried."[6]

The city has already contributed substantially to get the Ithaca Green New Deal off the ground. It is also creating a facility to provide individuals and businesses ten- to fifteen-year, zero- to low-cost financing for energy programs. The city expects to provide $100 million in financing for the first 1,000 residential and 500 commercial retrofitting and electrification projects by borrowing from private equity, leveraging the state and federal government to reduce the cost of capital, and mitigating risk through city financing policies.[7]

LOS ANGELES: SAVING MONEY BY SAVING THE CLIMATE

Chapter 1 described the Los Angeles Green New Deal, which includes programs ranging from renewable energy to electrification of transportation and reduction of vehicle miles traveled, to localization of water supply, to urban redesign. Its most rapid reductions in GHG emissions, however, will come from reducing building energy use. The Los Angeles plan proposes to cut energy use in all types of buildings by 22 percent by 2025, 34 percent by 2035, and 44 percent by 2050.[8]

Los Angeles is currently rated by the US Department of Energy as the #1 Energy Star city. It has 587 "high-performing buildings." In 2020 alone these buildings saved $203 million in energy costs through efficiency savings. Over the past decade, 11,120 gigawatts have been saved in Los Angeles' buildings through electric utility rebates and incentives for energy efficiency, saving Angelenos $1.78 billion on their utility bills.[9]

One part of Los Angeles' Green New Deal is the Comprehensive Affordable Multifamily Retrofits (CAMR) program, launched late in 2021. Its purpose is to help low-income tenants and building owners save money on energy bills, create green jobs, and help meet the goal of the Los Angeles Green New Deal to provide $100 million in energy efficiency programs to renters.

According to Los Angeles Mayor Eric Garcetti, who initiated the city's Green New Deal,

> Tackling the climate crisis is about more than just government action—it's about giving our most vulnerable residents the tools they need to join this fight, reverse generations of environmental inequities, and cut their own energy costs. The CAMR program is an important step on Los Angeles' path to carbon-neutrality—empowering Angelenos who often bear a disproportionate burden of the climate emergency to take advantage of several solutions that will help build a greener, more equitable, and more prosperous city.

More than 3,000 housing units are expected to be enrolled in the program in 2022. To qualify, buildings must have five or more housing units, with at least two-thirds of households at or below 80 percent of the area median income. Incentive amounts will be based on the project's greenhouse gas emissions reductions; projects with larger climate benefits will receive more funding. The largest available incentives will be for retrofit measures that also reduce tenant-paid energy bills. Contractors conducting retrofits through CAMR are required to pay prevailing wages and meet workforce training requirements.

The program's energy and sustainability benefits were worked out through a stakeholder engagement process with the city's Energy Efficiency for All coalition. Blanca de la Cruz, Sustainable Housing program director at the California Housing Partnership, said by specifically supporting multifamily housing serving low-income residents, "the CAMR program will help to fill an important need in Los Angeles while also supporting high-quality jobs for the local workforce. Tenants and housing providers have been eager to see a program like this become available, and many are already lined up to participate."[10]

PUMP IN THE HEAT!

Winters in the state of Maine are long and hard and many of its communities are rural and poor. At the end of 2020, a quasi-state agency called Efficiency Maine and the Nature Conservancy launched a program to help municipalities of 4,000 or fewer residents accelerate heating, ventilation, and air conditioning upgrades and lighting conversions in municipal buildings. Over the next six months sixty municipalities completed 93 heat pump projects that installed 189 heat pumps. Thirty of them also completed forty-seven lighting projects using $113,770 in Efficiency Maine financial incentives that will result in estimated annual energy cost savings of $55,072 and an estimated total annual energy savings of 367,148 kilowatt hours. Community centers, fire stations, police stations, public works facilities like office and bus garages, town halls, libraries, sewer districts, and water districts were eligible.

For the town of Hodgdon (population 1,309), the program helped pay for two lighting projects and five heat pumps the town otherwise wouldn't have been able to afford. Three heat pumps were installed at the fire station and two others make the recreation room at the town's housing project more comfortable for the seniors who regularly gather there. According to James Griffin, town manager of Hodgdon, "Budgets are tight, but the incentives made these projects much more economical for the town. At the fire station we've supplemented an oil heating system and are looking forward to more efficient heating this winter. We also installed new bay lighting at the fire station, as well as improved the lighting in the town offices. Not only is the lighting much brighter, but we already are seeing savings on our electric bills."[11]

HOMELESS AND HEATLESS NO MORE

Mosaic Gardens is a three-story stucco, palm-landscaped complex with forty-six apartments in Pomona, California. It was designed for low-income tenants, with half the units reserved for formerly homeless individuals or households. Linc Housing, the developer, is aiming for Zero Net Energy (ZNE) status, which requires a building to produce as much energy as it consumes averaged over the course of a year. That requires onsite energy generation like a photovoltaic array and high-efficiency measures like top-rated insulation and digital energy monitoring.

Mosaic Gardens utilizes a closed-cell spray foam, which provides superior thermal and sound insulation, as well as air sealing and increased structural strength, thanks to millions of tiny bubbles encased in the material. Each apartment has a smart thermostat, which communicates with all the others in a mesh-network configuration. Other features include:

- Drought-tolerant plants and high-efficiency irrigation system
- Very high efficiency water fixtures and fittings, and low-flow toilets, showers, and faucets
- Energy-efficient LED light fixtures
- EnergySTAR refrigerators, dishwashers, and clothes washers
- A solar PV renewable energy system
- Construction waste reduction

Mosaic Gardens has also focused on engaging tenants and educating them on energy-efficient practices and how to use their devices and appliances to maximize savings.[12]

Facilities in the complex include a community room, a counseling room, laundry facilities, computers with internet access, a large community courtyard, a BBQ area, and a tot lot. A resident services coordinator facilitates educational workshops, after-school tutoring, exercise sessions, financial literacy classes, computer classes, and social events.[13] As a result of all these features, Mosaic Gardens has received a LEED for Homes Platinum rating.

NEGAWATTS ARE EVERYWHERE

These are only a handful of examples among thousands of Green New Deal–type programs at local and state levels that are protecting the climate by reducing greenhouse gases through energy efficiency and conservation while creating jobs and reducing social injustice.

At a state level, Maine, Oregon, Washington, New Mexico, Colorado, California, New Jersey, Illinois, and other states have passed legislation to sharply reduce greenhouse gas emissions while realizing other Green New Deal objectives. In New York State, for example, the Climate Leadership and Community Protection Act targets net zero emissions by 2050. At least a third of the benefits for clean energy and energy efficiency programs in housing, workforce development, pollution reduction, low-income energy assistance, energy, transportation. and economic development are ear-marked for disadvantaged communities.[14]

Many unions are initiating their own energy efficiency and conserva-tion programs. For example, the National Nurses Union and the American Federation of Teachers have advanced energy efficiency and clean energy programs in their workplaces—hospitals and schools. Electrical Workers local 11 in Los Angeles created a Net Zero Plus Electrical Training Institute, the country's largest Net Zero Plus commercial retrofit, to use as a demon-stration and training center for electrical vehicle charging, HVAC, battery storage, microgrids, energy dashboards, lighting, and exterior shading. It aims to "transform commercial markets by employing the newest elec-trical technologies and training the most skilled workforce in the United States."[15]

Negawatts can be captured anywhere—in agriculture, transportation, manufacturing, metropolitan planning, and many other fields. Capturing negawatts through energy efficiency and conservation can achieve the basic Green New Deal objectives of protecting the climate, creating jobs, and rectifying injustices. And there is no need to wait—any individual or group can begin to initiate their own Green New Deal from Below by harvesting their negawatts.

7

FOSSIL FUEL PHASEOUT

The United States needs to cut around 60 percent of its GHG emissions by 2030 to reach zero net emissions by 2050.[1] The world will need to decrease fossil fuel production by roughly 6 percent per year between 2022 and 2030 to reach the Paris Agreement goal of 1.5 C temperature rise. Countries are instead planning and projecting an average annual *increase* of 2 percent, which by 2030 will result in more than double the production of GHG consistent with a pathway to the 1.5 C limit.[2]

The previous two chapters have shown how initiatives from cities, states, and civil society organizations are expanding climate-safe energy production and reducing energy use through energy efficiency and conservation. These are essential aspects of reducing climate-destroying greenhouse gas emissions, but in themselves they will not halt the burning of fossil fuels. That requires action on the supply side—freezing new fossil fuel infrastructure and accelerating the closing of existing production facilities. That is often referred to as a "phaseout" or "managed decline" of fossil fuels.

Such a phaseout of fossil fuel production is necessary to meet the goals of the Green New Deal and President Joe Biden's climate proposals. The original 2018 Green New Deal resolution submitted by Rep. Alexandria Ocasio-Cortez called for a national ten-year mobilization to achieve 100 percent of power generation from renewable sources. Biden's Build Back Better plan sought 100 percent carbon-free electricity by 2035 and net zero greenhouse gas emissions by 2050. These goals cannot be met without sharply reducing the amount of fossil fuel that is extracted from the earth and burned.[3]

While the US government and corporations are failing to effectively reduce the mining and drilling of fossil fuels, hundreds of efforts at a sub-national level are already cutting their extraction. Fifty US cities have already stopped using any but clean and renewable sources of energy. One hundred eighty US cities are committed to 100 percent clean energy.[4] According to a report by the Indigenous Environmental Network and Oil Change International, Indigenous resistance has stopped or delayed greenhouse gas pollution equivalent to at least one-quarter of annual US and Canadian emissions.[5] Such reductions are an essential part of the Green New Deal from Below.[6]

How does supply-side fossil fuel phaseout work? In 2020, two geographers at the University of British Columbia established a global fossil-fuel cuts database of 1,302 "supply-side climate initiatives seeking to constrain fossil fuel production" in 106 countries.[7] They define supply constraints as financial or physical initiatives by public authorities and private actors "constraining the production, transportation, or transformation" of fossil fuels. They identified seven major types of supply-side approaches:

1   *Moratoria and bans*: legislated suspensions or prohibitions on fossil fuel extraction and/or transportation

The Pittsburgh Earth Day Climate Strike, April 22, 2022. Photo by Mark Dixon, Wikimedia commons.

2 *Divestments*: withdrawal or exclusion of funds and assets for fossil
   fuel companies from financial portfolios
3 *Blockades*: physical obstruction or occupation of fossil fuel extraction, transportation, or refining sites
4 *Litigation:* Court cases to disrupt or end fossil fuel extraction
5 *Emission trading schemes*: a system of caps on the maximum level
   of emissions permissible with permits for emissions allowed under
   the cap (They note that emission trading schemes are sometimes
   used by producers to try to maintain production and insulate it
   from demands about more fundamental policy reform.)
6 *Carbon taxes*: taxes imposed on fossil fuel producers in proportion
   to their emissions
7 *Subsidy phaseouts*: cessation of indirect or direct monetary government assistance to fossil fuel companies

Many of these approaches are being applied to phase out fossil fuels by
local and state governments and grassroots activist groups. Although
national and global action will be necessary to phase out fossil fuels completely, in their absence action from below is forming the tip of the climate
protection spear.

AND A CHILD SHALL LEAD THEM

In California, 2.2 million people live within half a mile of an oil or gas
well; another 5 million live within one mile. More than 60 percent of the
25,000 drilling permits issued by the state between 2015 and 2020 were
in majority-Latino communities.

At the age of nine Nalleli Cobo began getting unexplained nosebleeds,
stomach cramps, nausea, headaches, and body spasms. So did other members of her family and others in her low-income, majority Latinx University Park neighborhood. Community-based nonprofessional researchers,
backed by a team of toxicologists from Physicians for Social Responsibility, identified the source of the problems as an oil well thirty feet from
the family home. Cobo and her mother began knocking on doors in the
neighborhood. They helped found the group People Not Pozos (People
Not Wells), which filed complaints with regulators and testified at city
hall and other governmental bodies. After three years of campaigning, the
oil well's owner announced it was shutting the well down. Cobo recalled,
"My nosebleeds stopped, no more headaches or heart palpitations, I didn't
need my inhalers every day. All the kids started to feel better."

There remained more than 1,600 active and idle oil and gas wells in
Los Angeles County, most of them located in communities of color. In
2015, Nalleli Cobo, now a teenager, helped form the South Central Youth

Leadership Coalition in Los Angeles. With other organizations it sued the city of Los Angeles for rubber-stamping oil projects in communities of color. As a result, the city adopted new environmental requirements. The oil industry countersued but lost.

The campaign against oil and gas wells near residential areas has continued to burgeon. In September 2021, the Los Angeles County supervisors voted unanimously to phase out oil and gas drilling and ban new extraction sites in unincorporated areas of the county.[8] In late January 2022 the Los Angeles City Council voted to phase out oil and gas extraction in the city.

The Los Angeles ordinance bans new drilling entirely. It orders an evaluation of how to shut down operating wells across the city. It orders city departments to draft a new policy to ensure the proper plugging and site remediation of closed wells. And it initiates an analysis of economic and job impacts of the shutdown and how to transition oil industry workers to clean energy jobs. City Council President Nury Martinez also introduced a motion to create a new city office to support workers as they transition out of jobs affected by new technology, including those in the oil and gas industry. She stated the city can't "correct the sins of environmental racism" by "taking away jobs from working-class communities."[9]

SHUT IT DOWN!

In 2010 the United States had 530 active coal-fired power plants. Hundreds of local initiatives, many backed by the Sierra Club's Beyond Coal campaign, have led to the completed and planned closing of 353 of them. For example, on December 14, 2021, Ameren Missouri announced its intent to retire its Rush Island coal plant no later than March 2024. Ameren Missouri previously planned to retire Rush Island in 2039, but accelerated the shutdown following Clean Air Act violations and a court order to add modern pollution controls.[10] Similarly, the owners of a coal plant in Rockport, Indiana, announced that it will be fully retired by 2028.[11] But 177 US coal-fired power plants remain in operation.[12]

Many of the closed coal plants are now being repurposed. In New York, the owner of the Cayuga and Somerset coal-fired power plants is considering a $100 million investment that would repurpose the sites into data centers, transforming them "from energy suppliers to energy consumers." Idaho Power announced that it would use transmission lines connected to the retiring North Valmy coal-fired plant in Nevada to connect to a new 120-megawatt solar farm south of Twin Falls, Idaho. Pennsylvania, which has lost fourteen coal plants, is repurposing nine of them for such uses as a medical marijuana farm, a warehouse, and a data center.[13]

KEEP IT IN THE GROUND!

In 2021 the International Energy Agency, the leading advisor to govern-ments on energy policy, reversed its long-established approach and stated that, to meet the Paris Agreement's 1.5 degree C limit for global warming, nations would need to immediately stop approving new oil projects. In short, fossil fuels in the ground need to stay there.

There has been a continuing struggle to shut down the infrastructure that makes possible the burning of fossil fuel. In 2008 the TransCanada Corporation applied for a permit to build the Keystone XL pipeline, which would carry 800,000 barrels of bitumen daily 1,700 miles across the US border to refineries in Texas. A thirteen-year struggle against the pipe-line incorporated life-risking blockades, court cases, and congressional contests. A coalition among farmers, ranchers, Indigenous leaders, and climate activists was met with at least 1,238 arrests. After repeated vacil-lations President Barack Obama declined to give the project a permit, but President Donald Trump reversed that decision. President Joe Biden revoked a permit for the pipeline on his first day in office and in June 2021 the owner finally terminated the project. The struggle not only stopped the pipeline, but also transformed the politics of fossil fuel extraction.

In the year following President Obama's rejection of the KXL pipeline, at least twenty-eight other proposed fossil fuel infrastructure projects in the United States were halted, not only because of unfavorable economic conditions, but of environmental concerns and local resistance.[14] Many had been targets of direct-action campaigns. Other pipeline struggles continue today. The Dakota Access Pipeline, which transports oil from North Dakota to Illinois, is currently being appealed in federal court. And in Minnesota, the Red Lake Band of Chippewa Indians and the White Earth Band of Ojibwe, backed by the Sierra Club, are suing to stop construction of the Line 3 Pipeline, which would carry 760,000 barrels of crude oil a day over and under more than 200 bodies of water.[15]

After initially proclaiming a moratorium on new oil and gas drilling on public lands, President Joe Biden put 80 million acres up for lease for oil extraction in the Gulf of Mexico, the largest such lease sale in US history. Environmental and racial justice groups in the Gulf states launched a last-ditch campaign against the sale based on its climate effects, and the dev-astating impact it would have on coastal residents and the coastal ecology. A coalition of environmental groups, including the Center for Biological Diversity, Healthy Gulf, and Friends of the Earth, sued the Biden admin-istration to stop the lease sale. Rudolph Contreras, a US District Court judge for the District of Columbia, said the lease sale was invalid because the Department of Interior's analysis did not fully take into account the climate impacts of the leases. The decision cancels 1.7 million acres of oil and gas leases. It also lays the groundwork for challenging other fossil fuel extraction projects based on their contribution to global warming.

STOP THE MONEY PIPELINE!

In 2010 a group of college students, many of whom had recently visited the Appalachian coalfields, asked their colleges to divest from coal. Soon universities, foundations, and faith-based organizations were divesting not only from coal but from all fossil fuels. From colleges the movement spread to new sectors, including large insurers, pension funds, philanthropic organizations, and banking institutions. By the end of 2016, institutions and individuals with assets over $5 trillion were divesting from fossil fuels. By 2017, forty-three US cities and states had committed to some form of divestment from fossil fuels, largely in investments of public employee pension funds.[16]

The divestment movement continued to spread through cities and states. In New York State a coalition of more than forty different groups, joined together as #DivestNY, conducted an eight-year campaign for divestment. In February 2021 State Comptroller Tom DiNapoli announced that New York State's Common Retirement Fund, valued at over $226 billion, would decarbonize by 2040. The plan included interim trajectory goals, rigorous reporting, staff hiring, and transparency. New York State became the largest pension fund in the world to take this kind of comprehensive climate action.[17]

In March 2021 New York City's largest pension funds voted to divest from companies related to fossil fuels. The $4 billion divestment is one of the largest in the country and the first time a major city has committed to complete divestment of fossil fuel holdings.

Union leaders representing workers whose pensions are in the funds strongly endorsed the decision. Henry Garrido, executive director, District Council 37, American Federation of State, County and Municipal Employees, AFL-CIO, said, "As NYCERS [members of the New York City Employees' Retirement System] Trustee and Executive Director of District Council 37, New York City's largest municipal union, I am proud to vote today with Mayor de Blasio, Comptroller Stringer, and my fellow NYCERS Trustees in support of divestiture from fossil fuel stocks." Teamsters Local 237 President Gregory Floyd said, "We at Teamsters Local 237 have concluded that, under the current proposal, we can confidently support a vote to divest from fossil fuel holdings in the NYCERS portfolio, and most importantly do so without an adverse effect on the pension fund." United Federation of Teachers President Michael Mulgrew added, "The world economy and our pension investments need to focus on the future, while fossil fuels are the energy sources of the past."[18]

By October 2021, a total of 1,485 institutions representing $39.2 trillion in assets worldwide had begun or committed to a divestment from fossil fuels.[19]

TAKE A WALK ON THE SUPPLY SIDE

These are only a few examples among hundreds of how local, state, and civil society entities are actually cutting the production and burning of fossil fuels. Other examples range from fracking bans to the emission caps established by northeastern states and western states and provinces, to carbon taxes introduced by some states.

Such supply-side strategies are essential to protect the climate by reducing fossil fuel burning. Without such a managed decline in fuel production, reduced consumption of fossil fuels will mean plummeting prices, rebound increases in consumption, and/or huge overcapacity leading to financially devastating stranded assets.

Phaseout strategies need to be combined with managed decline strategies that address the side effects of decreasing or shutting down fossil fuel production and use. They need to ensure that energy needs are met through climate-safe renewable energy and by using energy more efficiently. And they need to provide what is often called a "just transition" for workers and communities that may be affected.

Fossil fuel phaseout can't be fully achieved by action "from below." That will require the power and capacity of governments to make plans for the economy as a whole, develop and select technologies, deploy massive investments, and where necessary enforce managed decline. But the fight to "shut it down," "keep it in the ground," and "stop the money train" have put fossil fuel phaseout on the public agenda and shown how the objectives of the Green New Deal can start to be realized without waiting for national governments to act.[20]

8

TRANSFORMING TRANSPORTATION

The Green New Deal includes programs for housing, healthcare, education, cities, agriculture, manufacturing, and many other aspects of economy and daily life. Many of them are covered by specific federal Green New Deal legislative proposals. All are being implemented in one way or another by the Green New Deal from Below. In this chapter we will take one sector, transportation, as an example of how Green New Dealers are starting to implement such programs from below.

More than a quarter of greenhouse gases emitted in the United States come from transportation—more than from electricity or any other source.[1] Pollution from vehicles causes a significant excess in disease and death in poor communities. Lack of transportation helps keep people in poor communities poor. People are acting at the local and state level to create jobs, reduce greenhouse gas pollution, and equalize access to transportation by expanding and electrifying public transit, electrifying cars and trucks, and making it safer to walk and bike. It's a crucial part of building the Green New Deal from Below.

Proposals for a Green New Deal include many ways to reduce the climate, health, and inequality effects of a greenhouse gas–intensive transportation system. "Transit-oriented development," "smart growth," and other forms of metropolitan planning reduce climate- and health-threatening emissions while providing more equal access to transportation. Switching from private vehicles to public transit reduces greenhouse gas emissions by more than half and substantially reduces the pollution that causes asthma and other devastating health effects in poor communities. Changing from fossil fuel to electric vehicles also greatly reduces emissions. Expanded public transit fights poverty and inequality by providing

Mustafa Salahuddin is the president and business agent of the Amalgamated Transit Union Local 1316 in Bridgeport, Connecticut. Salahuddin posed for this photo in conjunction with a 2022 interview with Labor Network for Sustainability, where he told how the local became part of the company procurement process—leading the company to convert to climate-safe electric buses. Photo courtesy of Taylor Mayes, Connecticut Roundtable on Climate and Jobs.

improved access to good jobs. And expansion of transit itself almost always creates a substantial number of good, often union jobs. Every $1 billion invested in public transit creates more than 50,000 jobs.[2]

Plans for a Green New Deal generally include substantial federal resources to help transform our transportation system.[3] The 2021 bipartisan Infrastructure Investment and Jobs Act provided $20 billion over the next five years for transit projects. But meanwhile, efforts at the community, local, and state level are already greening transportation.[4]

These Green New Deal from Below programs are often characterized by multiple objectives—for example, protecting the global climate, improving local health, providing jobs, and countering inequality. And they often pursue intentional strategies to realize multiple goals, such as "transit-oriented development" that builds housing near public transportation to simultaneously shift travel from cars to public transit and to expand access to jobs and urban amenities for people in low-income communities.

TORE UP A PARKING LOT—PUT UP AFFORDABLE HOUSING

In 1970, Joni Mitchell wrote a song with the oft-quoted line, "Paved paradise to put up a parking lot."[5] In 2022, Chicago tore up a parking lot 400 feet from a transit station and put up an affordable housing complex. That transformation could serve as an emblem of the Green New Deal from Below.

The $40 million, seven-story "transit-oriented development" project, built by a nonprofit developer, will help low-income and working-class residents stay in the gentrifying Logan Square neighborhood. The units are all affordable, with half available for Section 8 voucher holders. "This is exciting news for our community," local Alderman Carlos Ramirez-Rosa wrote. "35th Ward, Logan Square, and Northwest Side neighbors marched, organized, and won this needed affordable housing to address displacement of working-class families from our neighborhoods."

A NIMBY group, Logan Square Neighbors for Responsible Development, whose members and supporters included landlords, real estate agents, architects, and an anti-union libertarian lawyer, opposed the project and filed a nuisance lawsuit to block it. Cook County Circuit judge Neil H. Cohen dismissed the suit, declaring, "The provision of affordable housing for low and moderate income residents of the city is a legitimate government interest. Increasing access to public transportation and encouraging public transportation use for people of all incomes is also a legitimate governmental interest. Building 100 affordable housing units near the CTA's Logan Square Blue Line station is rationally related to these legitimate governmental interests."[6] A local publication titled its story on the project, "Goodbye, Parking Lot, Hello Affordable Housing."

Chicago is not alone. In Atlanta, for example, the Metropolitan Atlanta Rapid Transit Authority (MARTA) is sponsoring the Atlanta Affordable Housing and Transit-Oriented Development initiative promoting mixed-income, transit-oriented development projects located near MARTA's thirty-eight heavy-rail stations, twelve Atlanta streetcar light-rail stops, and new transit investment corridors. The first project, a 250-unit affordable housing community called Skyline Apartments, held its groundbreaking in 2022. Skyline is across the street from the terminus of MARTA's Summerhill Bus Rapid Transit project, which will connect the Southeast

BeltLine to heavy-rail stations and bus routes in South Downtown Atlanta. Yarojin Robinson, managing director in the Urban Investment Group within Goldman Sachs Asset Management, which is making a significant investment in the project, says, "By investing in affordable housing near MARTA's transit offerings, the initiative will help to ensure that Atlanta remains accessible for all residents, regardless of household income. We are committed to partnering with Black-owned and Black-led developers and investing in majority-minority communities."[7]

TRANSITIONING TO TRANSIT

To reduce greenhouse gas pollution it is not sufficient to use more energy-efficient vehicles; it is necessary to reduce the number of miles that vehicles travel. A case in point: Between 1990 and 2017 overall US vehicle fuel efficiency increased 18 percent, largely due to the implementation of CAFE standards. But in the same period there was a 50 percent increase in miles driven. The result was that, despite higher fuel efficiency, the amount of vehicle emissions increased 22 percent.[8]

Shifting from private vehicles to public transportation is one of the most cost-effective ways to reduce greenhouse gas emissions. Yet public transit has been starved for resources for both infrastructure and operations. The 2021 Infrastructure Investment and Jobs Act included significant funding for public transit. But initiative for actually developing public transit lies at the local and state level—and people at the local and state level are taking advantage of that to launch their own Green New Deal–style transit programs.

A group of elected leaders in Kansas and Missouri are seeking funding under the Infrastructure Investment and Jobs Act for a twenty-four-mile regional rapid transit corridor to "enhance mobility, transform communities, and reduce carbon emissions." The proposal will connect Kansas City Kansas; Kansas City, Missouri; and Independence, Missouri, with rapid transit integrated with a wide array of related community development projects. It includes:

- *Zero-emission transportation options*: Electric buses, new and upgraded mobility hubs, expanded KC Streetcar and MAX services, and pedestrian and bicycle infrastructure
- *Affordable housing*: Energy-efficient retrofits, new units and construction, and transit-oriented/connected development
- *Green infrastructure*: Enhanced tree canopy coverage, upgraded stormwater systems, electric vehicle charging stations, and residential solar panels

- *Broadband access*: Implementation of wired and wireless service, increased capacity, and updated equipment
- *Safety and security enhancement*: Shot spotter,[9] license plate readers, Community Improvement Districts, and other public safety technologies
- *Economic development*: Workforce training, access to childcare, and private investment along the corridor
- *Public schools and libraries*: Renewable energy and energy efficiency projects to reduce utility costs[10]

In April 2022 the Kansas City MO Area Transportation Authority received more than $27 million from the Infrastructure Investment and Jobs Act for local transit in the Kansas City region. Announcing the funding, Representative Emanuel Cleaver II of Missouri said, "I see brand-new electric buses, upgraded transit facilities, and, of course, good-paying jobs for workers who will be responsible for building, maintaining, and operating the future of transit in Kansas City. That's going to lead to lower emissions, cleaner air, and stronger communities that will continue to grow in an equitable fashion." He added that it will be "a foundational component of the Bi-State Sustainable Reinvestment Corridor."[11]

Although public transit is often associated with urban areas, it can also be designed for rural ones. Eleven rural counties near Harrisburg, Pennsylvania, have started testing a "Stop Hopper" microtransit service to allow residents to schedule rides on smaller, neighborhood-friendly-sized public transit vehicles. Riders can travel anywhere within the designated zone on a nine-person ADA accessible van for $2; seniors ride free. The program is designed to support small-town economies by connecting local residents with job opportunities and access to food, pharmacies, and other necessities.[12]

Of course, microtransit can sometimes be used to privatize, deunionize, and even dismantle existing transit systems. For example, in Denton County, Texas, microtransit company Via set out to replace all fixed-route bus service (and unionized drivers) with on-demand vehicles driven by independent contractors who are hailed by an app. Denton bus operator and Amalgamated Transit Union member Jim Owen, who had been attending bus company board meetings for eight years, warned his coworkers that the intent was to eliminate all union jobs.

The drivers teamed up with a cross-union group called Denton Worker, formed in 2019 to connect local unionists so they could assist each other in their fights. Its goal, according to UPS part-timer Will Hale, a steward with Teamsters Local 767, was to "find workers who needed to be organized, find issues around unfair labor practices and wage theft, and try to be a touchstone for workers in Denton." The bus drivers and Denton Worker organized a group they called "No Bus Cuts Denton." They began riding the buses to talk to people and discovered the cuts would affect "people who are really fighting for the basics of life, who don't have access to smartphones or banking services." After mass attendance and "call-in filibusters" at transit agency board meetings, No Bus Cuts Denton forced the company to preserve five of the eight fixed-route bus lines. Bus operator Paula Jean Richardson concludes, "We won a battle, but we still have a war going on. We have to keep fighting."[13]

ELECTRIFYING TRANSIT

Mustafa Salahuddin is the president and business agent of the Amalgamated Transit Union Local 1316 in Bridgeport, Connecticut. In 2014 the local began a campaign for improvements in drivers' workstations, including relocating monitors, installing adjustable seatbelts, and correcting blind spots. The company corrected the blind spots and made other union-demanded changes. Then Salahuddin proposed that the union become part of the company's procurement process. When the COO agreed, Salahuddin, an active member of the Connecticut Roundtable on Climate and Jobs as well as a union official, began advocating for low- and no-carbon buses. Salahuddin recalls that he told the company official,

> We're both young. You should want to leave a legacy that you had something to do with renewable energy. It is something to be proud of later on. Your kids can look back on it and say, my dad had something to do with that. I told him climate change, fossil fuels—it's a no-brainer. That diesel with that air that's going through the bus—the drivers and passengers are breathing unhealthy and detrimental air. Sit with the drivers and you'll see. This will stop people from getting sick so much. He said, you're absolutely right. So he purchased about four or five hybrids. Then they ordered five to seven fully electric ones. Now he wants to go fully electric. His goal is to try to do it before the projected year of 2030. I'm really looking forward to the unveiling of our first fully electric buses.[14]

Twenty-five million children ride diesel school buses every school day.[15] In many locations school buses are becoming a first target for electrification. Groups concerned with young people's health, community air pollution, and greenhouse gas climate destruction have been campaigning to replace diesel school buses with electric ones. In 2017, for example, Chispa (Spanish for "spark"), an offshoot of the League of Conservation Voters that aims to create healthier environments in Latinx communities and communities of people of color, launched the "Clean Buses for Healthy

Niños" campaign to eliminate diesel school buses. State governments have begun allocating funds for electric school buses in Illinois, Massachusetts, Ohio, Michigan, California, Maryland, New Jersey, Washington, Arizona, Nevada, and New York.[16] Maryland's Montgomery County Public Schools will replace all its diesel vehicles with electric ones, starting with 326 electric buses over the next four years, the single largest purchase of electric school buses in North America.[17]

Electrification of school buses took a quantum leap forward in April 2022 when the New York State legislature and Gov. Kathy Hochul passed a state budget with a plan to make the state's 50,000 school buses 100 percent electric by 2035. New York is the first state to commit to fully electrifying its school bus fleet. Electrifying school buses in New York City alone will reduce emissions equivalent to taking 650,000 passenger vehicles off the road.[18]

FREE TRANSIT, FREE BIKES FOR KIDS

In March 2022 the Washington State legislature approved "Move Ahead Washington," a $17 billion, sixteen-year transportation package that doubles state support to local transportation agencies. The law makes the biggest investments in sustainable transportation in the state's history, including $1.45 billion for public transit grants. While past funding packages allocated less than 10 percent of their budgets to "multimodal transportation" such as transit, bike, and pedestrian projects, "Move Ahead Washington" allocates 18 percent. Critics point out that the package allocates $4 billion to expanding highway capacity, but most of that is for completing projects already started.

Thirty percent of Americans are unable to drive, either due to the costs of car ownership, age, or disability.[19] In 2021, Disability Rights Washington started a Disability Mobility Initiative to encourage nondrivers to lobby to have their needs included in forthcoming state transportation legislation. The campaign, according to its director Anna Zivarts, "shifted the funding priorities of this package." Transit and active transportation will receive funding from the state's cap-and-invest carbon pricing program.

In order to receive those transit support grants, agencies must adopt a free fare program for riders under eighteen. Young riders will receive an all-access pass to the full transit network in Washington, including Washington State Ferries and Amtrak Cascades. The free transit for kids is intended to help create a culture of transit riding. The package doubles funding for safe routes to school and bicycle and pedestrian projects. It provides bicycle education programs for students at every level—and every kid who participates in the program will be given a free bike and all of the necessary accessories.[20]

CLEANING UP BIG TRUCKS

Medium- and heavy-duty trucks are only a small fraction of all vehicles on the road, but they account for more than 60 percent of tailpipe nitrogen oxide and particulate emissions. California has a special waiver from the EPA that allows it to require that a growing percentage of all medium- and heavy-duty trucks sold be zero-emission. Manufacturers must increase their proportion of zero-emission truck sales to 30–50 percent by 2030 and 40–75 percent by 2035.

Other states are allowed to follow California's rules, and five of them—Oregon, Washington, New York, New Jersey, and Massachusetts—have adopted this California "Advanced Clean Truck rule." Several other states are now considering doing so. Oregon has also adopted the "Heavy-Duty Omnibus rule," which will require new fossil-fueled trucks to be 90 percent cleaner.

In 2020 fifteen governors pledged to make 100 percent of bus and truck sales electric by 2050. The result will be a growing number of electric-powered large pickups, buses, garbage trucks, and tractor-trailers on the road. Paul Miller, executive director of Northeast States for Coordinated Air Use Management, a nonprofit that supports air quality regulators, says the rules could "significantly reduce or eliminate greenhouse gas emissions as well as conventional air pollutants like nitrogen oxides." Vehicle makers, he added, "don't make money on public goods like clean air, so it's not part of their product development plans unless something is in place to require its inclusion."

Though our federal system makes such state initiatives possible, there are limits to what individual states can do. For example, they would have difficulty banning polluting trucks coming in from other states. But as with other tailpipe standards that started in California and spread to other states, the Advanced Clean Truck rule will put enormous pressure on manufacturers to clean up their trucks. Indeed, according to *Bloomberg News*, "The U.S. trucking industry is set to be transformed by a handful of states adopting zero-emission vehicle requirements."[21]

TOWARD ALL-ELECTRIC TRANSPORTATION

In August 2021, New York State passed a law requiring all passenger vehicles sold in the state to be emission-free by 2035. It also requires all medium- and heavy-duty vehicles to be emission-free by 2045 and requires a detailed plan to meet these goals by 2023. Gov. Kathy Hochul said, "New York is implementing the nation's most aggressive plan to reduce the greenhouse gas emissions affecting our climate and to reach our ambitious goals, we must reduce emissions from the transportation sector, currently the largest source of the state's climate pollution." She added, "The new law and regulation mark a critical milestone in our efforts and will further advance the transition to clean electric vehicles, while helping to reduce emissions in communities that have been overburdened by pollution from cars and trucks for decades." New York joined pioneer California, which has ordered all new vehicles sold to have zero-emissions by 2035.[22]

New York State established goals for electrifying transportation but left detailed planning for a 2023 report. So how do you actually do it? In 2021 Seattle approved a "Transportation Electrification Blueprint" that spells out such details. The plan is designed to lower greenhouse gas emissions and air pollution while increasing electric mobility options and creating a pipeline of clean energy jobs and workforce diversity. It is one means of implementing the city's 2019 Green New Deal plan, which requires Seattle to be carbon neutral by 2030.

The Transportation Electrification Blueprint was developed by Seattle's Office of Sustainability and Environment, Department of Transportation, Office of Economic Development, and Seattle City Light. Seattle City Light is a municipally owned power company established as a city department in 1910. In 2005 City Light became the first electric utility in the country to achieve net-zero greenhouse gas emissions by divesting ownership in a coal-fired power plant, investing in renewables, increasing energy efficiency programs, and purchasing offsets for its remaining emissions.[23] The Transportation Electrification Blueprint requires:

- 100 percent of shared mobility, such as carshare services, must have zero emissions
- 90 percent of all personal trips must have zero emissions
- 30 percent of all goods delivery must have zero emissions
- 100 percent of the city's vehicle fleet will be zero-emission
- One or more "Green & Healthy Streets" areas will close streets to cars and deliver goods by electric vehicles
- Electric power infrastructure to enable the transition to electric transportation technologies and vehicles

Seattle City Light is already implementing parts of the blueprint. Sixteen electric vehicle fast chargers have been installed with twenty-five more in the works. Seattle City Light has launched time-of-day rate pilot programs for residential and commercial customers and is working with King County Metro to support the adoption of battery-powered buses and with Washington State Ferries and the Port of Seattle to support electrification.

According to David Logsdon, director of electrification and strategic technology at City Light, the plan "lays out the priorities for City Light's Transportation Electrification efforts, the equity outcomes we intend to achieve via the portfolio, and what initial milestones we will achieve as we invest in the key sectors of public transit; commercial, government, and nonprofit fleets; and personal mobility." The plan "builds on the utility's core mission to achieve a vision of the healthy future that our region depends on—one that is built in concert with our community stakeholders and delivers a grid that is equitable, carbon-neutral, modernized, and future-enabled."[24]

BIKES AND HIKES

Expansion of roads and highways has long been viewed as "American as apple pie." But in April 2022, the San Francisco Board of Supervisors voted 7–4 to close a mile-long section of JFK Drive to vehicles permanently. The street, which had some of the highest injury rates in San Francisco, had been closed early in the COVID pandemic to provide open space for outside activities. When the city considered reopening it to traffic people rallied and marched on the road to keep it vehicle-free. The ordinance permanently closing the road to cars also provided for shuttles for people with mobility issues.[25]

Reducing vehicle traffic is also being accompanied by expanding more environment-friendly alternatives. In February 2022 the Berkeley city council unanimously approved a plan for Telegraph Avenue, the one-way street through the main business district for the University of California campus, that would change a lane for cars and trucks into a dedicated bus lane, with the remaining lane shared by bikes, cars, and trucks. The plan also promised to study a proposal by the student group Telegraph for People to ban private automobiles altogether on Telegraph Avenue.[26]

In Buffalo, New York, federal funding is making possible new projects to expand walking and biking access to the city's waterfront. The centerpiece will be a "skybridge" that will allow people to walk from a railroad terminal to a popular sports arena. An abandoned railroad right-of-way will also be transformed into a 1.5-mile walkway and bikeway, modeled on New York City's Highline, which will create a direct connection between the city's downtown and its waterfront and help ensure equitable access to the waterfront. The plan sets aside $1 million for new bicycle and pedestrian improvements.[27]

Alternatives to private autos are now often being referred to as "mobility." For example, in 2020 the city of Austin, Texas, passed a "Mobility Bond," which raised $460 million for transportation infrastructure projects. Its Local Mobility Program funds bikeways, sidewalks, safe routes to school, vision zero,[28] transit enhancement, urban trails, and neighborhood partnering programs. Its first construction project, authorized in early 2022, will provide pedestrian crossings, transit stops, asphalt speed cushions, pavement markings and signage to enhance safety, and mobility and transit access in neighborhoods throughout Austin. Austin's Assistant City Manager Gina Fiandaca commented, "We heard in 2016, 2018, and 2020 that delivering safety and mobility improvements for Austin is on the top of voters' minds. The community has given us the resources and now it's our job to make sure the improvements happen so all Austinites can get to their destinations safely and sustainably with more mobility options."[29]

A crucial aspect of the Green New Deal is its emphasis on participation in planning and decision-making. It eschews the all-too-familiar approach of tearing down a neighborhood to build a highway without input from those being displaced. Expanded forms of community participation in decision-making are similarly essential for Green New Deal from Below transportation programs. In Culver City, California, for example, population 40,000, in 2021 the city council called for a "bold plan to implement bus and bike mobility lanes now." In response, the city's transportation department developed a plan to redistribute space on streets for a bus lane and a separate bike lane "to encourage mobility in the city while attempting to alleviate traffic congestion."

According to the *Culver City News*, "the project required a great deal of input from the community, so outreach was done in several stages." The project website was discussed at meetings of three different commissions before the full website was launched. A Community Project Advisory Committee was created to further solicit input from various public bodies. The Advisory Committee includes special interest groups, city committees, business associations, and neighborhood associations. Meetings on the project were held in the mobility subcommittee, the Business Roundtable, and several community workshops. The city used both digital and traditional advertising. It documented over 40,000 hits from November to January. Almost 25,000 of those views came from social media, including 11,805 from Facebook and 10,837 from Twitter (now X). "The project has been through four different designs, and 11 project guidelines were created with community input and adhered to throughout the process."[30]

GETTING FROM HERE TO THERE

Getting people and material from one place to another is crucial for any society. Our private vehicle-oriented transportation system leads to enormous inequality, waste, environmental destruction, injury, and death. Our fossil fuel–based transportation systems—local, regional, and national—generate climate change, asthma, and other poisonous health effects.

Even in the most capitalistic society, transportation cannot be left to the market; it takes highways, railroad tracks, traffic regulation, and myriad other forms of action by society. It requires systems, not just individual vehicles. That means public planning, investment, and rights-of-way.

National transportation requires national railroads, highways, planning, and investment—in short, national systems. National Green New Deal proposals include substantial investment in transforming our national transportation system.

But much transportation is not national but local and regional. Transportation infrastructure is always located in specific places. Transportation has enormous effects on the places where it is located. And our federal system puts control of a large part of the transportation system in state and local hands. So there are substantial opportunities for implementing Green New Deal transportation policies from below.

As we have seen, this is actually happening in many places. In some cities, states, and rural areas transit systems are being expanded and encroaching on the domination of private vehicle transportation. Cars, trucks, and buses are being electrified to reduce pollution and protect the climate. Pathways for walking and biking are being expanded, and in some cases bicycles and transit are being made available free to expand access and use. Metropolitan planning is locating housing, workplaces, and amenities close to transit. Such programs serve the immediate needs of local users, protect the climate, create jobs, and lay the groundwork for transforming the transportation system nationally.

Transportation is but one of many sectors in which the Green New Deal from Below is transforming communities, cities, and states. A similar story could be told for housing, healthcare, education, agriculture, manufacturing, and other sectors.

9

PROTECTING WORKERS AND COMMUNITIES—
ON THE GROUND

The Green New Deal–type programs that are needed to fight climate change will produce millions of new jobs. Local and state climate programs are already producing tens of thousands of new jobs. But there are two problems. The new jobs are often low-paid, nonunion, with few benefits and little job security. And workers, families, and communities that lose jobs as a result of the transition away from fossil fuels often face dislocation and hardships that are not assuaged by the increase in jobs in other occupations and locations. This chapter tells what communities around the country are doing "on the ground" to protect workers and local economies from collateral damage during the transition to climate-safe energy.

Harm from fossil fuel shutdowns is not an imaginary threat. Consider: On the last day of September 2022, the San Juan Generating Station in the Navajo Nation burned coal for the last time. It was a victory for protection of the climate, the environment, and Navajo health. But in the five years since the decision to shut the plant was made, nearby Judy Nelson Elementary school lost a quarter of the children because their parents moved elsewhere to look for work. Judy Nelson reading teacher Denise Pierro said, "They've taken the rug out from underneath our feet." Eighty percent of the property taxes that fund Judy Nelson and other schools in the area come from nearby power plants, mines, and associated businesses. To show its concern about the closing's impact on its workers, shortly before the shutdown the company served them green chili cheeseburgers as a "morale booster" alongside a big projection screen that read: "Thank you to all employees at San Juan for your years of dedicated service!"[1]

In many countries welfare state social policies provide dislocated workers and communities economic security and a chance for a new start.

The former Charles R. Huntley Generating Station in Tonawanda, New York, as seen in September 2016. Photo by Ken Lund, Wikimedia commons.

Healthcare, housing, education, and income maintenance programs are often generous enough to protect workers from the most severe hardship. When industrial facilities are shut down, industrial location policies often establish plans and investment for economic redevelopment. These protections are often increased to compensate for economic or environmental policies that adversely affect workers and communities. For example, the European Union is providing more than $30 billion for "just transition" programs and investments to support fossil fuel–producing regions that may be affected by the European "Green Deal" plan to reach net-zero greenhouse gas emissions by 2050.[2]

The United States has long lagged in supplying such protections. It has little tradition of planning for economic transitions. In the face of economic change workers and communities are often just thrown on their own resources—even when those resources are severely limited. The result is often long-term individual and community decline.[3]

It doesn't have to be that way. As the end of World War II approached, there was widespread fear that with the end of war production American workers would be thrust back into the poverty and mass unemployment of the Great Depression. In response the government began to plan for the conversion back to a peacetime economy. And it passed the "GI Bill of Rights," which provided veterans four years of tuition for college or training programs, home mortgages, loans for business ventures, and income maintenance. Some of these programs, notably mortgage loans, were blatantly racially discriminatory. But the GI Bill of Rights saved millions of demobilized veterans from return to Depression conditions and provided the educational and financial start they needed to become the most upwardly mobile generation in modern US history.

Tony Mazzocchi was a World War II veteran who went to college on the GI Bill of Rights and became a leader of the Oil, Chemical, and Atomic Workers (now merged with the Steelworkers).[4] In the early 1990s, following the confirmation of fossil fuel–caused global warming, Mazzocchi revived the GI Bill of Rights idea, initially calling it a "Superfund for workers"—a play on the then-recently established Superfund for toxic cleanup. The Superfund for Workers would provide financial support and an opportunity for higher education for workers displaced by environmental protection policies. That program was soon rebranded with the more positive term "a just transition." The concept gradually gathered support among trade unionists and environmentalists. It also met considerable hostility from other trade unionists; AFL-CIO president Rich Trumka said dismissively, "Just transition is just an invitation to a fancy funeral." Meanwhile, the term "just transition" was adopted by climate justice advocates and others to describe a more general social transformation that went far beyond protecting current fossil fuel workers.[5]

As greenhouse gas reduction policies have begun to come into effect, their impact on workers and communities has become an increasingly pressing reality. This chapter presents examples of Green New Deal–style programs that are under way at a local level to protect workers and communities against undesirable side effects of climate policy.

BRAYTON POINT

Back in 2016 I was asked to give a talk at the University of Massachusetts in Dartmouth about alternative jobs and just transition for the Brayton Point coal-fired power plant in nearby Somerset. Brayton Point was the largest coal plant in New England. It had been named by the EPA as one of Massachusetts's heaviest polluters and there was a campaign to close it. There was also great concern about the plant's 240 workers losing their jobs and other economic impacts like loss of the plant's $12 million annual property tax payment to Somerset. I recounted experiences elsewhere and what strategies might be used to address these concerns, including background from two other New England coal-fired power plants where I had had similar discussions. The community members were extremely pessimistic about either finding new jobs for the plant workers if they were displaced or finding new economic development for Somerset. Plant workers, I was told, would most likely support a conversion to natural gas unless a clean-energy alternative was guaranteed to protect their jobs.

Meanwhile, a coalition of environmental groups commissioned a report on "Reimagining Brayton Point."[6] It proposed converting the plant's 234-acre waterfront site to a "Clean Energy Hub" combining large-scale battery storage, photovoltaics, a food waste digester, and an offshore wind terminal. It concluded that the Clean Energy Hub scenario provided "a vision of the future that would allow for the restoration of some of the town's tax revenues; provide clean, reliable electricity for the region; provide jobs and help advance technological innovation; and reduce pollution and other industrial burdens on the town's waterfront and surrounding communities."

The plant shut down in 2017 but progress toward that vision for a Clean Energy Hub was fitful. Commercial Development Inc. of St. Louis bought the property, started tearing down the plant, and issued plans for a Brayton Point Commerce Center. But with offshore wind development stalled by the Trump administration, it instead leased the property for a polluting scrap metal exporting operation. Residents objected, organized, elected a new town government, and in 2022 won a court order shutting down the operation.

Finally, the vision of a Clean Energy Hub began to come to fruition. In May 2019 grid asset developer Anbaric signed an agreement with Commercial Development to build a 1,200-megawatt, high-voltage, direct-current converter and 400-megawatt battery storage plant at Brayton Point to support the offshore wind industry.[7] And in February 2022 Prysmian Group, an Italian manufacturer of undersea cable, invested $200 million to create a high-tech manufacturing hub to make submarine cables to connect its under-construction wind farms to the mainland power grid. The plant will also have an R&D facility with the first high-voltage test lab in the United States.[8]

On July 20, 2022, President Joe Biden visited Brayton Point to announce new climate initiatives. He said, "On this site, they'll manufacture 248 miles of high-tech, heavy-duty cables. Manufacturing these cables will mean good-paying jobs for 250 workers—as many workers as the old power plant had at its peak."[9]

SPOON RIVER

The Spoon River runs through a rural area in west central Illinois between the Mississippi and Illinois Rivers. A century ago, the region was made famous by Edgar Lee Masters's poetic *Spoon River Anthology*, a once-banned, then best-selling exposé of small-town America. Today the region has a 13 percent poverty rate and an 8 percent unemployment rate. In August 2019 Vistra Energy informed local officials that the region's two coal-fired power plants would be shut down in December of that year. The response by local schools, colleges, unions, and other institutions shows how communities can respond effectively to such shutdowns even within the limits of existing government programs.

The two power plants employed 300 workers, most members of the Steamfitters union (part of United Association or UA) or the International Brotherhood of Electrical Workers (IBEW). They also provided a substantial proportion of the local tax base. Spoon River College, the local community college, received $300,000 annually from the plants' property taxes. The Canton School District received over $1 million annually.

Faced with losing their funding and with little advance notice to plan, the president of Spoon River College and the superintendent of the school district began meeting with other community leaders to develop a response. Spoon River College partnered with the Regional Workforce Investment Board, whose Dislocated Worker Fund is paid for by the federal government but administered by the states. They developed a rapid response program for the 300 power plant workers, who had only sixty to ninety days to find work. Their team met four times with workers on all three shifts to discuss career goals and aspirations. The college used the workers' input to evaluate and redesign their current education and training programs. The coalition held hiring fairs with local employers, open houses at Spoon River College, and programs to connect workers with community resources.

Of the 300 workers laid off in the two power plants, 60 percent were able, under the IBEW contract, to transfer to another power plant in Illinois. Twenty percent enrolled in a community college or university to increase their skills or change to another career. Of those, the largest number took training to get a commercial driver's license for jobs that were readily available locally. Others were trained for diesel locomotive repair, for which workers were needed at the nearby Burlington Northern repair facilities. Some studied advanced manufacturing techniques in welding and computer numerical control, skills that were in demand by Caterpillar and other nearby manufacturers. Five percent of the workers started their own businesses. Most of the remaining 15 percent retired, with the rest moving out of state or remaining unemployed.

Vistra Energy agreed to negotiate over local property tax reductions and accepted a step-down plan to cushion their impacts. This meant, for example, that in the first year of shutdown the community college received 60 percent of its previous year's payments; in the next year 30 percent; and in the third year 15 percent.

The impacts of the Spoon River power plant closings are far from ended. While the property tax step-down will give local institutions some time to adjust, it will not replace their lost revenue in the long run. Even if most plant workers have found new jobs, in the meantime many of their children have dropped out of college or been otherwise adversely affected. And under state law all remaining Illinois coal-fired power plants will be shut down within fourteen years, so that workers who transferred to other plants will again be faced with losing their jobs. But within the limits of existing programs, Spoon River region community action helped ease the transition for workers and other community members.[10]

THE HUNTLEY EXPERIMENT

The Huntley Generating Station sits on the Niagara River thirteen miles from Niagara Falls in the town of Tonawanda, New York, a working-class suburb of Buffalo with a population of 73,000. The station was Tonawanda's largest taxpayer and also its greatest source of air and water pollution. About 70 unionized employees worked at the plant—down from 125.

A downsizing of the plant in 2008–2012 had cost Tonawanda, its school district, and Erie County $6.2 million, leading to the layoff of 140 teachers, the closing of four schools, and a freeze on teachers' pay. Anticipating further cutbacks, in 2013 local labor and environmental groups, including the Clean Air Coalition of Western New York, the Western New York Area Labor Federation, AFL-CIO, and the Kenmore-Tonawanda Teachers Association, formed the Huntley Alliance.

The alliance initially included the IBEW local representing the workers in the Huntley plant, but when a local Sierra Club member organized a protest calling for the plant to be closed Tonawanda political leaders accused the coalition of trying to sabotage the plant and the Huntley union withdrew. The work of the alliance stopped in its tracks.

A study at the start of 2014 made clear that the Huntley plant was not economically viable and would soon be shut down in any case. In 2015 its owner NRG announced the plant would be closed and the next year began decommissioning it. The threat of closure revivified the Huntley Alliance, this time with a greater emphasis on the needs of local workers. The new director of the Clean Air Coalition said, "Always, our key question is, how are we going to take care of our people?" An activist member added, "I was the angry environmentalist" but "I've learned we need to take care of both our workers and our environment."

The union representing Huntley workers declined to join the effort, but the Huntley Alliance pushed ahead with a community outreach program involving a series of public meetings, door-to-door surveys, voter registration drives, and workshops on the economics of the energy industry. According to their surveys, residents' priorities were:

- keeping schools intact
- creating good-paying jobs
- reconnecting the community to the Niagara River waterfront
- expanding the tax base
- protecting utility ratepayers
- improving public health and the environment

The Huntley Alliance then brought together local stakeholders to prepare a sixty-four-page plan titled *Tonawanda Tomorrow* focused on transforming the Huntley plant site into a community asset. The work was supported by a $160,000 grant from the Federal Partnerships for Opportunity and Workforce and Economic Revitalization (POWER) program. In all 1,500 people were involved in the process. A town board member and high school teacher observed, "I have never seen a group of people who were so diverse work together." We had "citizens, businesses, government officials, and environmental activists." It was "kind of magical." In 2017 the town government officially adopted the plan. The plan identified funding sources, set out a timeline, and designated who was responsible for implementation. Town officials convened a team to advise on implementation of the plan but sadly abandoned it after a year.

Meanwhile, Tonawanda was facing imminent loss of tax base for schools and government services. The Huntley Alliance petitioned the New York State Legislature to provide gap funding and went to Albany to testify for it. In 2016 the legislature passed the nation's first Electric Generation Facility Cessation Mitigation Program. Local communities throughout New York that are facing power plant shutdowns can now receive payments, declining annually over a seven-year period, to cover lost tax revenue. State funding comes from the Regional Greenhouse Gas Initiative, which requires payments from polluting utilities throughout the Northeast. The fund has provided $26.1 million in grants to the town of Tonawanda, the

Kenmore-Tonawanda Union Free School District, the City of Dunkirk, Chautauqua County, and the Dunkirk City School District. Tonawanda itself received $1.6 million in 2016–17 and $1.4 million in 2017–18, helping it to maintain essential municipal services.[11]

Liv Yoon, who conducted extensive interviews with Tonawanda residents for her documentary movie *A Tomorrow for Tonawanda*, concluded,

> Partnership and collective action among strange bedfellows—such as labor unions, teachers' unions, and environmental justice organizations—are ultimately what earned the town the attention of politicians and decision-makers. The alliance demonstrated that the aftermath of the industry closure was an issue that impacted the entire town, not just the employees of the plants. Compared to a specific interest group lobbying in isolation, the alliance meant that the politicians had more reason to listen to this broad range of groups (along with increased risk to lose more votes).[12]

MOUNT TOM

Mount Tom Station, perched on a steep hillside alongside the Connecticut River in Holyoke, Massachusetts, was the last coal-fired power plant in Massachusetts. It has become the state's largest solar farm. The Mount Tom story exemplifies a community-centered approach to protecting people from the side effects of transition away from fossil fuel energy—and reaping the benefits of that transition. *CBS News* headlined its account of Mount Tom's transition, "How One Small City Sowed the Seeds for Its Own Green New Deal."[13]

Half of Holyoke's residents were Latinx/Hispanic and 30 percent lived in poverty. Asthma rates from the coal plant were twice the state average—a study found that 28 percent of Holyoke school students had asthma. A campaign to close the plant started in 2010, led by the local resident group Action for a Healthy Holyoke, with support from organizers from Neighbor to Neighbor and the Toxic Action Center.

I met with members of the group in the basement of a rundown public housing project to talk about how to close the plant in a way that would be positive for the impoverished Holyoke community. Residents were worried about the health effects of the plant on their families, but many of them had experienced losing jobs themselves and were deeply aware of the harm to livelihoods that might come from closing the plant. When Action for a Healthy Holyoke members met with state and company officials, they demanded not only closure of the plant but also protections for the plant's workers, including a bridge to retirement, transitional jobs and training, and severance packages. While many Mount Tom workers opposed efforts to close the plant and Action for a Healthy Holyoke was unable to establish an official relation with IBEW Local 445, which represented workers in the plant, a union steward provided an informal liaison between Action for a Healthy Holyoke and the IBEW.

By 2013 it was clear that the Mount Tom plant was going to be shut down, but the impact on workers and the community was still to be determined. IBEW Local 445 demanded to meet with plant officials to provide older workers a "bridge" to retirement benefits, better severance pay, training for new jobs, and transfers within the company. In negotiations with the company IBEW local 445 won nearly all their demands, including:

- Severance packages with two month's pay for each year of service
- Eight months health insurance
- Full retirement packages
- A bridge-to-retirement program
- Full pension at fifty-five for workers within two years of retirement
- $5,000 scholarships for higher education and job training

Workers were reported to be pleased with the agreement. Clarence Kay, who worked at the plant for thirty-two years and helped negotiate the settlement, said the bridge-to-retirement was "a really big thing." Generally speaking, "the company did a pretty good job giving most of us what we needed during such a tough transition." The one demand that they did not win was to have union workers decommission and transition the plant.

The closing of the plant also threatened the community—for one thing, Holyoke had been receiving $315,000 taxes annually from the Mount Tom plant. At first the plant's owner ENGIE North America declined to meet with community activists, but it relented when the activists threatened to hold a press conference outside their offices and city officials pressured them to meet.

As Mount Tom's future dimmed, Holyoke moved proactively to plan for a transition. The city established a Citizens Advisory Group to explore the future of the Mount Tom site. The state provided a $100,000 grant and the city teamed up with the state's Clean Energy Center for a "Mt. Tom Power Plant Reuse Study." More than 200 people participated in the study's activities over eight months. The study used a mix of public input, coupled with expert analysis, to design feasible reuse scenarios. Community outreach activities were held in English and Spanish and included community meetings, mobile workshops, community surveys, and targeted outreach.[14]

The report established the feasibility of using Mount Tom for a large solar array, possibly complemented by anaerobic digestion, agriculture, and public amenities. According to Holyoke mayor Alex Morse, community activists "played a role in being proactive with the visioning of the site. The solar project was already sort of a community-agreed-upon value, a goal that everybody could get behind. And we got ahead of the curve, in that sense, when we started that plan even before the coal plant shut down."[15] After initially standing aloof, the plant's owner, ENGIE North America, partnered with the city-owned utility Holyoke Gas & Energy to provide solar-sourced electricity for the city. Carol Churchill, communications manager at ENGIE North America, said, "We were trying to determine what to put on that site when Mass Clean Energy Center came out with their study." The land was "very conducive to a solar facility" and "Holyoke was looking for non-carbon sources. Everything pointed to solar, so that's what we ended up installing."[16]

By 2017, 17,000 solar panels had been installed and were running on Mount Tom. The next year the company installed three megawatts of battery storage on the site to provide electricity when the sun doesn't shine. Holyoke's city-owned utility company, which also uses hydropower from the Connecticut River, now runs almost completely on clean power. Mayor Alex Morse says, "We have an ambition of being a carbon-neutral community. We get closer and closer with each project like this."[17] The city is continuing to seek job-and-revenue-generating investment for the site, ranging from manufacturing to cannabis production.

DON'T BE ROADKILL!

These examples show what communities and workers can do to protect themselves against the worst effects of energy transition. The results are far from perfect, but they put people in a position to be more than roadkill thrown on the economic scrapheap.

The closing of major infrastructure like a power plant has a wide effect not just on the facilities' employees but on local communities, economies, and governments. Because of this impact there is a need for, and the possibility of, diverse constituencies coming together to address the problem collaboratively. Most of the successful efforts at a local level to protect workers and communities have depended on coalitions that brought together groups who had not customarily worked together.

These efforts have developed in the absence of federal programs to integrate protections for workers and communities into the energy transition we are undergoing—let alone the far greater one we need. They show many of the kinds of actions that can help to keep the burden of climate protection from being dumped on those who are most vulnerable.

These efforts were made necessary in part by the historic failure of American government to provide an adequate social safety net for anyone who is affected by economic change or personal adversity. They similarly reflect the United States' lack of an industrial location policy designed to promote investment in hard-hit communities and regions. These local efforts were rarely able to access federal funding and depended on resources scraped together from inadequate local sources. Recently enacted federal programs like the Inflation Reduction Act, if properly developed, can provide additional resources for future efforts of this kind.

Many of these examples were reactive efforts made in response to the looming emergence of local economic catastrophe. Protection of workers and communities in the face of change requires planning and planning requires time. But in most cases law and public policy give corporations arbitrary power to shut down facilities at will with few requirements for notifying and assisting their workers and communities. In many cases the responses are necessarily making the best of a bad situation. Since economic change is inevitable, public policy should require that facilities whose closing would threaten worker and community wellbeing not only give adequate advance notice, but fund programs *in advance* to provide for an acceptable transition.[18]

These local initiatives provide a sketch for the state and federal programs needed to protect workers and communities while protecting the climate. They represent building blocks for the transition policies that are necessary for a Green New Deal. Indeed, they embody necessary elements of the Green New Deal from Below.

Effective response to the shutdown of plants and other infrastructure takes time. Although the examples in this chapter represent Green New Deal principles, most responded to closings that started before the Green New Deal hit the headlines. They are described here to show strategies that could be included in response to such closings. The next chapter tells how state Green New Deal–type programs are moving proactively to forestall negative side-effects of energy transition.

10

JUST TRANSITION IN THE STATES

"THERE OUGHT TO BE A LAW!"

While the transition to climate-safe energy will create far more jobs than it will eliminate, that is cold comfort for those whose jobs may be threatened—after all, every job is important if it is *your* job. That is why the original Green New Deal resolution guaranteed "wage and benefit parity" for "workers affected by the transition."

Many of the states that are transitioning away from climate-destroying fossil fuels to climate-safe renewable energy are developing policies and programs to protect workers and communities from damaging effects of that transition. While such provisions are still far from adequate, they provide initial experiments that can lay the groundwork for expanded protections at both state and national levels.

WASHINGTON STATE: THE PIONEER

Those who pioneer a new policy don't always succeed, but sometimes they blaze a trail that opens the way for others to follow. That is what happened with the Washington State Initiative 1631, which was narrowly defeated at the polls in 2018 but which has been the inspiration for a string of subsequent legislative successes in other states that have taken it as a model.

In 2008 the State of Washington passed a law requiring greenhouse gas emissions to be reduced to 1990 levels by 2020; 25 percent below 1990 levels by 2035; and 80 percent below 1990 levels by 2050. Numerous proposed laws and ballot initiatives to implement these objectives failed. In 2014 seven leaders representing communities of color, environmentalists, tribes, and labor formed the Alliance for Jobs and Clean Energy. Jeff Johnson, then president of the Washington State Labor Council, AFL-CIO,

A woman holds a Just Transition Now sign at a rally in Minneapolis, Minnesota. Photo by Laurie Shaull, 2020, Wikimedia commons.

and one of the founders of the alliance, says the coalition spent three years "building a climate justice movement based on principles of equity and giving assistance and voice to those most disproportionately impacted by climate disaster."[1]

According to Aiko Schaefer, leader at the time of Front and Centered, an umbrella organization of low-income and community-of-color groups, "Frontline and communities of color came together with workers, environmentalists, public health leaders, and so many others to put our heads together to create what works best for our state." It was "the embodiment of an inclusive democracy."[2] Climate journalist David Roberts described this as a "coalition-first, policy-second approach."

A 2017 report on "A Green New Deal for Washington State" by Robert Pollin, Heidi Garrett-Peltier, and Jeannette Wicks-Lim laid out a program for realizing the climate, justice, and labor goals of the Green New Deal.[3] This became the basis for the Alliance for Jobs and Clean Energy's Initiative 1631.

Initiative 1631 was based on the principle that polluters should pay for the social costs of halting their pollution. The ballot title summarizing the initiative said it would "charge pollution fees on sources of greenhouse gas pollutants" and use the revenue to "reduce pollution, promote clean energy, and address climate impacts" under the oversight of a public board. It charged a fee for each ton of carbon emitted, starting at $15 a ton and increasing $2 every year until the state's greenhouse gas emission target for 2035 was met and its target for 2050 was on track to be met; the fee was projected to generate more than $2 billion over five years.

The revenue from the pollution fees would be used for climate-protecting investments related to transportation, energy efficiency, carbon sequestration in farms and forests, and clean energy, as well as climate adaptation forestry and water conservation projects. A public accountability board with voting representatives from unions, local communities, environmental justice groups, and Indigenous tribes would oversee the distribution of funds. A minimum of 35 percent of all investments would be allocated to benefit pollution-burdened environmental justice communities; 15 percent would assist lower-income populations; and 10 percent of investments would require formal support from a tribal government, with the stipulation that projects on tribal lands receive free prior and informed consent from the tribe. A fifteen-member oversight committee was stipulated whose majority represented communities of color, tribes, environmental groups, public health professionals, and labor. Those most impacted by climate disaster were put in the role of making the decisions about where clean energy investments would be made.

Many of its provisions were designed to ensure just outcomes for the constituencies in the alliance, including:

- Heating and electric assistance to low-income families
- High labor standards: prevailing wages, apprenticeship programs, community workforce agreements with local hire, clean record of employers on labor rights and health and safety
- An exemption for energy-intensive trade: to prevent the "leakage" of pollution and jobs out of state, trade-exposed industries did not have to pay the pollution fee, but were required to reduce their carbon emissions

An unprecedented aspect of Initiative 1631 was its earmarking of funds from the pollution fee to provide support for fossil fuel workers whose livelihoods might be harmed by the transition away from fossil fuel energy. The initiative provided that at least $50 million must be "set aside, replenished annually, and maintained" for a worker-support program for bargaining unit and nonsupervisory fossil fuel workers who are "affected by the transition away from fossil fuels to a clean energy economy." That included a "wage guarantee" to make up the difference for workers forced to accept jobs with lower pay. Worker support could include but was not limited to:

- full wage replacement, health benefits, and pension contributions for every worker within five years of retirement;

- full wage replacement, health benefits, and pension contributions for every worker with at least one year of service for each year of service up to five years of service;
- wage insurance for up to five years for workers reemployed who have more than five years of service;
- up to two years of retraining costs including tuition and related costs, based on in-state community and technical college costs;
- peer counseling services during transition;
- employment placement services, prioritizing employment in the clean energy sector;
- relocation expenses;
- and any other services deemed necessary by the environmental and economic justice panel.[4]

The Alliance for Jobs and Clean Energy built a campaign organization with Climate Justice Stewards in every part of the state. Initial polling on Initiative 1631 was consistently positive.

According to Jeff Johnson, unions representing more than 60 percent of the 450,000 members of the Washington State Labor Council, AFL-CIO, supported Initiative 1631. Some unions, mostly in the building trades, opposed the initiative on the grounds that it would cost their members more money and/or crowd out dollars that might be invested in other projects.

Shortly before the election the Yes campaign had raised a little over $5 million; the No campaign had raised $20 million, overwhelmingly from oil and gas interests. Then began an onslaught of ads attacking 1631. Exxon alone spent over $30 million for anti-initiative television ads in the last days of the campaign. Ultimately Initiative 1631 was defeated 56–44 percent.

Despite this defeat, Initiative 1631 became the inspiration and model for subsequent worker and community coalition efforts, transition programs, and protection measures in Colorado, Illinois, California, and elsewhere.

COLORADO'S OFFICE OF JUST TRANSITION

In 2018, a Democratic bill in the Colorado legislature called for 100 percent renewable energy by 2035. The bill was doomed in the Republican legislature, but it was a wakeup call for Colorado unions. According to Dennis Dougherty, executive director of the Colorado AFL-CIO, which includes 165 unions representing more than 130,000 workers, "It forced the conversation on our end as to what do we need to do to get behind these bills in the future, instead of just blocking them or delaying. It was really the first time we asked ourselves, well what's our game plan?"[5] That year a coalition of community, labor, faith, youth, and environmental groups launched the People's Climate Movement Colorado, affiliated with the national People's Climate Movement. The Colorado AFL-CIO and the Colorado People's Alliance were cochairs. The new coalition held a series of discussions between unions and environmental groups, sometimes guided by a professional facilitator, leading up to a Climate, Jobs, and Justice Summit. At a meeting of the Western States AFL-CIO, Colorado labor leaders learned about the Washington State Initiative 1631 and heard a presentation on Robert Pollin's "A Green New Deal for Washington State" climate jobs report. Colorado unions thereupon commissioned Pollin to conduct a similar study for them.

Democrats won the legislature in the 2018 midterm elections and in 2019 moved to pass a bill to reduce greenhouse gas emissions by at least 90 percent from 2005 levels. That posed the question: What would be the law's impact on workers and communities?

According to the Colorado Mining Association, Colorado is the eleventh largest coal-producing state, with six active coal mines, employing a little over 1,200 mine workers. The National Mining Association estimates that nearly 18,000 people across Colorado are employed directly by the state's mining industry. The proposed climate protection law would clearly have a significant impact on coal industry workers and communities.

Drawing on the experience of Washington Initiative 1631, unions and allies developed—and passed—the Colorado Just Transition law, HB-1314. Responding to fears about the human impact of energy transition, it focused on the needs of coal communities and workers. It instituted an Office of Just Transition and a Just Transition Advisory Committee including unions, corporations, economic development specialists, representatives of affected counties and disproportionately impacted communities, political leaders, and government officers—with a mandate to solicit input for a draft plan for workers and communities.

The law provides a "wage differential benefit" for workers who lose their jobs in a coal mine, coal-fueled electrical power generating plant, or the manufacturing and transportation supply chains of either. The wage differential benefit is defined as "supplemental income" covering all or part of the difference between an individual's previous wages and their wages on their new job or their income during job retraining.

Dougherty said at first unions thought a "just transition" could mean demanding jobs in perpetuity at the same level of pay and benefits that workers are currently earning, but after doing research into the issue and assessing the political realities, they modified their demands. "We hired someone to research every 'just transition' that's been done across the world. We said, okay, well what can we realistically do at the state level that we think is fair while also not coming out and demanding something that's never going to happen?" The answer is embodied in the 2019 Colorado Just Transition law.

The law also provides grants to eligible entities in "coal transition communities" that seek to create a "more diversified, equitable, and vibrant economic future." A "coal transition community" is defined as a municipality, county, or region that has been affected or will be affected by the loss of fifty or more jobs from a coal mine, coal-fueled electrical power generating plant, or the manufacturing and transportation supply chains of either.

At the end of 2020 the Office of Just Transition submitted a Just Transition Action Plan "to help workers continue to thrive by transitioning to good new jobs, and to help communities continue to thrive by expanding and attracting diverse businesses, creating jobs, and replacing lost revenues." The plan required additional funding for implementation.

In March 2022 the Colorado General Assembly passed House Bill 22-1394 to provide an additional $15 million for the Office of Just Transition for coal workers impacted by the shift to clean energy. The Coal Transition Worker Assistance Program received $10 million to provide coal workers and their families funding to cover apprenticeship and retraining programs, childcare services, housing assistance, and other expenses. To support economic development in coal-dependent communities the bill provided $5 million.

The workforce and community grant programs in the original 2019 Colorado Just Transition law were unanimously opposed by Republican legislators, who attacked them as "Orwellian," "egregious," and "offensive." The new bill to help fund these programs passed 51–12 with bipartisan support. Republican Representative Perry Will, who represents several coal-dependent communities in northwest Colorado, voted against the 2019 legislation that established the office, but praised HB-1394 on the floor of the Colorado House. "This is a much-needed bill. I appreciate the $15 million. I know we need more than this, but we're pecking away at it a bite at a time, and this is very important to the communities I represent."

Democratic Representative Dylan Roberts said, "Towns like Hayden, Oak Creek, and Craig will be able to use this just transition funding to invest in projects that diversify rural economies, incentivize new energy jobs, and provide workers with supportive career service. This is the large investment in rural Colorado that our transitioning communities deserve, and I am thrilled this bill is moving forward with strong bipartisan support." House Majority Leader at the time Daneya Esgar said, "This won't be the last time a bill of this nature is going to come before you. We are going to continue to need to help these communities, help these workers, as we transition out of coal."[6]

ILLINOIS: THE DISPLACED ENERGY WORKER BILL OF RIGHTS

In September 2022, after months of difficult negotiations, the Illinois legislature passed the Climate and Equitable Jobs Act (CEJA), incorporating programs laid out by both a labor coalition and a climate justice coalition. The act commits Illinois to zero-carbon electricity by 2045 and a net-zero carbon economy by 2050 while advancing equity, justice, and quality jobs. The CEJA will close all fossil fuel plants by 2045.

The bill's drafters had good reason to be aware of the possible adverse impacts of the energy transition on Illinois fossil fuel workers. In 2019 four communities in central and southern Illinois were devastated when coal plants were closed with little warning. The CEJA accordingly incorporated a bill called the Energy Community Reinvestment Act. According to a fact sheet prepared by the Prairie Rivers Network, which advocated for just transition provisions for workers and communities in the CEJA, the act includes these elements:

- An Energy Transition Workforce Commission will study impacts of plant and mine closures and prepare an Energy Transition Workforce Report with comprehensive recommendations on how to address the impact of the energy transition.
- Energy Transition Community Grants (funded at $40 million per year) will help communities to address economic and social impacts of the energy transition based on diverse community input.
- The Coal to Solar and Energy Storage program establishes renewable energy credits for solar projects and grants for energy storage facilities at former fossil fuel–generating sites.
- The Renewable Energy Development program requires the Illinois Power Agency to optimize financial incentives to clean energy projects located in Energy Transition Community Grant areas.
- The Clean Jobs Workforce Network Program and Clean Energy Contractor Incubator Program create thirteen workforce hubs and thirteen contractor incubators to provide clean jobs training and support for clean energy businesses around the state. Displaced energy workers have priority for placement.[7]
- Displaced Energy Worker Dependent Transition Scholarships provide one-year full-time scholarships to a state-supported college or university for the children of displaced workers who demonstrate need.

The CEJA includes a "Displaced Energy Worker Bill of Rights" to support fossil fuel power plant, coal mine, and nuclear plant workers who lose their jobs due to reduced operations or closures. The Bill of Rights includes advance notice of closures, financial advice, continued health care and retirement packages, full tuition scholarships at Illinois state and community programs, and tax credits to businesses that hire displaced energy workers. Under the Displaced Energy Worker Bill of Rights communities that lose a fossil fuel power plant or coal mine can be designated as Clean Energy Empowerment Zones. They can be eligible for tax base replacement for up to five years for local governments, libraries, schools, and other public services; economic development research assistance; and incentives for clean energy companies to locate and invest. These programs are paid for by an Energy Community Reinvestment Fund, which collects money through a small fee on fossil-fuel pollution and a 6 percent Coal Severance Fee on coal extraction. The fund provides significant funding for the Climate and Equitable Jobs Act community and worker transition programs; for example, $100 million annually can be allocated to tax base replacement.[8]

Illinois programs for worker and community transition are already having an effect. Late in 2019 the Vistra Coal Plant in Havana closed and stopped paying taxes. The Havana Park District lost a third of its funding, cut staff, and shut down its nature center. In April 2022 the Havana Nature Center received the funding necessary to reopen its doors.[9]

CALIFORNIA: "LOOKING AT THE FUTURE"

From the turn of the twenty-first century California has been adopting policies to fight climate change by reducing greenhouse gas emissions. Today California is committed to cut GHG emissions by 50 percent by 2030 and to reach net-zero emissions by 2045.

Roughly 112,000 people are employed in California's fossil fuel–based industries. Forty-five percent of them are people of color (below the state average of 63 percent) and 22 percent are women. While that number accounts for about 1 percent of California's GDP and less than 1 percent of its workforce, pockets of the state are dependent on oil industry revenues. Kern County produces about 70 percent of the state's oil; most of the rest of the state's oil is produced around Los Angeles. In Kern County 15–20 percent of property taxes, which fund local schools, public health, roads, and infrastructure, come from oil and gas producers. California's fifteen refineries are clustered in Los Angeles and Contra Costa Counties. In those counties more than 60 percent of point source emissions come from these refineries.

As California established fossil fuel reduction targets and adopted policies to implement them, the question of what would happen to fossil fuel workers and their communities came to the fore. Organized labor is a powerful force in California and particularly in the Democratic party, which largely controls the state's politics. A powerful group of unions led by the State Building and Construction Trades Council of California—often simply know in California as the "Trades"—has opposed climate protection legislation like a law that would restrict oil drilling near schools and communities. The Trades Council established a formal alliance with the California Business Roundtable and the California Chamber of Commerce to fight climate protection legislation.[10]

Not all unions agreed. Back when Jerry Brown was still governor, California's Steelworkers union began working on a transition plan for their oil and gas workers. In 2019 labor climate activists organized official climate caucuses in the Alameda, Contra Costa, and San Francisco AFL-CIO labor councils. The Alameda Labor Council and the Labor Network for Sustainability cohosted a Labor Convergence on Climate for 150 Bay Area labor leaders, members, and organizers at the hall of IBEW local 595, which discussed in depth how to protect California workers in the transition to a climate-safe economy.

Over the next year a group of unions continued to discuss how to protect workers and communities in the energy transition. They felt the need to move beyond vague rhetoric to concrete plans to protect workers whose jobs might be threatened. Hearing about studies done in other states by University of Massachusetts economist Robert Pollin, they commissioned him to prepare a report on how to achieve California's climate goals in a way that also protected workers.[11]

A crucial force supporting this effort was Steelworkers Local 675, which represents 4,500 workers, about two-thirds of whom work in oil refining and extraction in Los Angeles County. They staff the Chevron refinery in El Segundo; refineries owned by Marathon Petroleum, PBF Energy, and Phillips 66; and the Wilmington oil field of California Resources Corp.[12] David Campbell, secretary-treasurer Local 675, noted that one Bay Area refinery had recently shut down and another was scheduled for closing. "We are reading the handwriting on the wall as to what will happen to these refineries." We're "looking at the future" and "trying to come up with some sort of a game plan."[13]

Such a game plan was embodied in the report Pollin led, titled "A Program for Economic Recovery and Clean Energy Transition in California."[14] The plan, promoted as the California Climate Jobs Plan, would reach California's target of reducing carbon emissions by 50 percent by 2030—and create more than a million jobs. The state would create 418,000 clean energy jobs per year through a program to cut climate pollution in half over the next decade. It would create 626,000 additional jobs per year through investments in related areas such as water infrastructure, leaky gas pipelines, public parks, and roadways.

The plan included specific provisions for workers and communities that might lose jobs in the transition. It proposed "wage insurance" for fossil fuel workers to guarantee new jobs with three years' worth of total pay at the same level as their old fossil fuel employment. It also provided coverage for pension obligations, retraining, and relocation. The cost is estimated at $470 million per year, or 2.1 percent of California's expected GDP. Twenty California unions, including steelworkers, municipal workers, teachers, and three unions representing thousands of oil workers, endorsed the plan.[15]

Elements of the California Climate Jobs Plan are now moving forward on several fronts. The California 2022–23 budget adds $450 million to the Community Economic Resilience Fund, whose goals include fostering "long-term economic resilience in the overall transition to a carbon-neutral economy." The fund emphasizes "inclusive planning to ensure equitable outcomes for each region's disinvested communities," which face "inequitable land use and zoning policies, exclusionary economic development processes, underinvestment, and a lack of meaningful engagement with community residents in planning and policy decisions." Investments that benefit disinvested communities will be a priority for the fund.[16]

The state budget also includes $40 million in a fund for displaced oil and gas workers, a pilot program that may be targeted to workers who will be affected by the shutdown of oil wells or refineries. In 2020 Los Angeles County established a Just Transition Task Force initially focused on capping and cleaning up LA's more than 2,000 idle and abandoned oil wells. The task force mandate includes developing labor standards for well capping. Then-LA Supervisor Mark Ridley-Thomas, who brought the motion for Just Transition for LA, said, "As we transition, we must ensure it is a just transition." We have an opportunity here "to wed our environmental goals with a meaningful workforce agenda."[17]

FROM ECONOMIC INDIVIDUALISM TO SOCIAL PROVISION

So-called "economic individualism" has been a continuing feature of American life. Even when adversity is obviously a product of social causes like depressions and technological changes, US economic policy has generally left working people on their own to cope with the impact on their lives. The main exceptions originated in the Great Depression, where mass misery and its threat to social stability led to the unemployment insurance and social security systems. These have never provided more than a fraction of an adequate livelihood, however. Nor has the United States ever implemented industrial location policies designed to counter the devastating impact of economic change on localities, states, and regions.[18] The few attempts to compensate individuals for the destructive impacts of economic policies on their lives, such as the Trade Adjustment Assistance offered to workers affected by policies promoting globalization, have merely provided a pittance to a small proportion of affected workers.

As a result, protections for workers and communities affected by climate policies have been slow to develop. Such protections have few precedents, and meet virulent opposition from those who advocate economic individualism and oppose social provision of any kind. Some proponents of climate protection policies have maintained that they will produce so many new jobs that it is unnecessary to have specific policies to protect those who may lose theirs, ignoring the barriers that may prevent former fossil fuel workers from gaining access to those new jobs. As federal policy has haltingly moved toward climate protection, it has done little to protect workers and communities from the consequences.

Just as states have stepped into the breach to develop their own greenhouse gas reduction laws and policies, so they have begun to address the unintended negative side effects that may come with those measures—to provide what is sometimes referred to as a "just transition." While they have few precedents to draw on, the examples we have examined from Washington, Colorado, Illinois, and California show that a new approach is possible, and that it is in fact being invented.

These inventions have followed a common pattern. They have been initiated when public opinion supporting state climate protection policies has become irresistible. At that point current and aspiring state political leaders have come to support targets for greenhouse gas reduction and means to reach those targets. But that is soon perceived as threatening workers and communities dependent on the fossil fuel economy. That concern may initially generate opposition to climate protection policies—and particular communities and groups of workers may be held up as "poster children" for the negative effects of climate policies. The result is often perceived as evidence of the purported opposition of "environment vs. jobs," and an aggravation of conflict between environmentalists and organized labor (often gleefully promoted by fossil fuel interests).

But three shifts in mindset have in many cases begun to create an alternative to such a polarization. First, trade unionists begin to recognize that change in energy systems is coming whether they like it or not, and that their members will be vulnerable to that change unless policies are adopted to protect them. Second, climate protection advocates begin to see that there will be massive opposition to the policies they advocate unless they recognize and act on their responsibility to also protect the people and communities their policies may adversely affect. Third, the underlying idea of the Green New Deal—that climate protection offers an opportunity to address inequality and injustice—opens a vista for social change that goes beyond the pursuit of narrow interest group politics. This "new thinking" may initially be based on particular interests, but it may also be encouraged by the development of a broader awareness in unions of the necessity for climate protection; among environmentalists of the necessity for community wellbeing; and among justice advocates of the potential of new coalitions to overcome long-established injustice.

The result has been the development of coalitions among groups that had previously been at odds, lobbing virtual projectiles at each other from separate silos. These coalitions often start with simple exploratory efforts, such as workshops, forums, and other gatherings. The discovery of common ground may lead to an informal or formal coalition, often defined at first more by a sense of common interests than by agreement on specific policies. In many cases the next step has been to commission an expert report laying out how to protect workers and communities while reducing greenhouse gas emissions.[19] That has laid the basis for negotiations—often lasting a year or more—to develop agreement around a specific policy agenda. Then, generally with the help of sympathetic political leaders, specific language is developed that can be included in legislation. That is followed by defining a strategy to pass the legislation and a campaign of public education and a mobilization of public support. Whether they are successful or not, these efforts often redefine the public debate and the frameworks within which public policy is determined; even campaigns that lose can transform the landscape for future possibilities both locally and beyond. If policies are successfully passed into law, the coalitions must turn to ensuring that they are implemented in a way that fulfills their original intentions.

Just transition policies have often combined the needs and objectives of the different coalition members. They include or are included in the most advanced state policies for reducing greenhouse gas emissions. They provide direct help for laid-off fossil fuel workers, such as career guidance, education and training, help finding new jobs, hiring preferences, supplemental payments when new jobs pay less than previous ones, health insurance, pension protection, and retirement benefits. They provide help for communities affected by mine and power plant shutdowns, such as payments to help compensate for lost taxes, support for economic development planning, incentives for employers to locate in affected communities, and investment in economic and infrastructure development. They often require that a substantial proportion of funds be allocated to low-income and otherwise deprived communities.

These policies may have the potential to open the way to longer-term changes in public policy. For example, wage guarantees and supplements could develop into a more robust social provision for the needs of those who, through no fault of their own, have their lives devastated by economic change. Harm-free transition from fossil fuels to clean energy requires extensive planning; community protection policies are making a start in that direction. It also requires public investment since private investment has proven unable to undo the damage of private disinvestment. Programs like the Illinois Energy Community Reinvestment Fund begin to take on public responsibility for developing jobs and taxable enterprises in the communities that need them most. Requirements for participation of diverse segments of local communities in planning and implementing programs could serve as a jumping-off point for broader forms of democratization of economic development.

In an economy that is national and indeed global there are undoubtedly limits on what state policies can accomplish. The Biden administration has made some small initial steps toward addressing the downsides of energy system change, for example, its Interagency Working Group on Coal and Power Plant Communities and Power Plant Revitalization, which is providing assistance to communities affected by mine and power plant closings.[20] The state legislation and programs described in this chapter provide an indication of what is needed at a federal level—and at a much larger scale.

Given our national political deadlock, such a program is not on the immediate federal agenda. But it is an essential part of the long-term agenda often referred to as the Green New Deal. The state and local programs for protecting workers and communities, described in this and the preceding chapter, form an essential part of the Green New Deal from Below.

11

GREEN NEW DEAL JOBS FOR THE FUTURE

Although the Green New Deal is often thought of as a remedy for climate change, a central part of its focus has always been on jobs and economic inequality. The original Green New Deal resolution noted a "4-decade trend of wage stagnation, deindustrialization, and antilabor policies." That had led to "hourly wages overall stagnating since the 1970s"; the "erosion of the earning and bargaining power" of workers; and "inadequate resources for public sector workers to confront the challenges of climate change" at local, state, and federal levels. There was "the greatest income inequality since the 1920s" with a difference of "20 times more wealth between the average white family and the average black family" and a gender earnings gap that results in "women earning approximately 80 percent as much as men."[1]

While the US unemployment rate has gyrated between record highs and record lows over the past two decades, the condition of US jobs has consistently deteriorated. More and more jobs have become low-paid, insecure, and contingent. They are often temporary, part time, dead-end, with few or no benefits. Quality issues are difficult to quantify, but harassment, discrimination, speed-up, arbitrary punishment, and threats of discipline and dismissal are reported by a growing proportion of workers.

The Green New Deal proposed a mobilization plan to create millions of jobs protecting the climate. But it also proposed to use climate mobilization as a vehicle to transform the world of work. It included as part of its mobilization plan:[2]

Quality jobs: high-quality union jobs that pay prevailing wages, hire local workers, and offer training and advancement opportunities

Job guarantee: guaranteeing a job with a family-sustaining wage,
   adequate family and medical leave, paid vacations, and retirement
   security to all people
Worker rights: the right of all workers to organize, unionize, and collectively bargain free of coercion, intimidation, and harassment
Labor standards: labor, workplace health and safety, antidiscrimination, and wage and hour standards across all employers, industries,
   and sectors

Many of these objectives require action by the federal government. In the
absence of national action, Green New Deals and similar initiatives around
the country are making building blocks for them at local and state levels.
This chapter starts with the youth jobs corps that have developed in Green
New Deal cities and others with climate protection programs. These are
providing training and career pathways for young people, especially those
from groups who have been marginalized in the labor market.

The chapter then reviews jobs being created by the Green New Deal
from Below. It evaluates how many jobs are being created by such programs and how many could be created by a fully developed Green New
Deal. It surveys the measures that Green New Deals from Below are taking
to address low wages, lack of opportunities for training and advancement,
de facto exclusion from access to good jobs, and other dimensions of job
quality. The strengthening of unions has always been a central goal of the
Green New Deal, and the chapter reviews the ways that Green New Deals
from Below are making it easier for workers to organize.

A crucial—and controversial—part of the Green New Deal is a "jobs
guarantee" that would ensure a job for every worker who wants one; while
there are so far no fully developed local or state job guarantee programs,
Green New Deals are starting to move in that direction.

Taken together, these initiatives point the way toward correcting the
inequalities, injustices, oppressions, and abuses of the world of work.

CIVILIAN CLIMATE CORPS

One of the most famous agencies of the original New Deal was the Civilian
Conservation Corps (CCC), which provided jobs and training for 3 million
young Americans during the Great Depression of the 1930s. A Civilian
Climate Corps has been a central proposal of the Green New Deal. And
such corps are being developed by the Green New Deal from Below. They
are often located in the poorest neighborhoods and have as an objective,
along with climate protection, the reduction of crime and violence through
youth employment.

The Climate Strike and march in Pittsburgh on September 24, 2021. Photo by Mark Dixon, Wikimedia commons.

When Boston's Green New Deal wanted to establish a youth green jobs corps, they looked to PowerCorpsPHL for a model. PowerCorpsPHL was established in 2013 by Philadelphia city agencies and AmeriCorps, a federal stipended volunteer work program designed to help communities address poverty, the environment, education, and other unmet human needs. More than 600 young people have been through its programs. A new cohort of sixty enter the corps each spring and fall. Sixty percent of them have adult criminal records.[3] To join the corps they must have a GED or high school diploma.

During the first phase of the program, which lasts seventeen weeks, new corps members are paid $10 per hour to engage in work-readiness, career-exploration, and team-building activities, like planting trees. During the second phase, which lasts nineteen to forty-six weeks, graduates of Phase 1 receive training in "industrial academies": The Urban Forestry Academy, the Green Stormwater Infrastructure Academy, and the Solar and Electrical Academy. They are paid $11 per hour and work with mentors from government agencies, nonprofits, and industry.

Attrition is 25 percent in Phase 1 and only 15 percent in Phase 2. Philadelphia's criminal recidivism rate is 45 percent; for PowerCorpsPHL members it is 8 percent. PowerCorpsPHL connects more than 90 percent of its graduates to jobs or higher education—and 92 percent of them succeed. The corps maintains a full-time social worker to help with needs like access to medical care and childcare and provides lifetime support services for all graduates.

Cashmir Woodward, a single mother with a juvenile record, was a low-paid home health aide. She heard about PowerCorpsPHL from a friend and signed up. A staff member helped her get childcare, social security benefits for her son, and expunging of her criminal record. She was trained in green stormwater infrastructure. She says, "I felt like what I was doing before PowerCorpsPHL wasn't enough, and now I can have a real impact on our city and its future. I want other young people, including those with records, to know that PowerCorpsPHL will accept you without judgment and work with you, no matter what."

In April 2019 Mayor Bill de Blasio announced New York City's Green New Deal. It promised investments, legislation, and action to reduce emissions nearly 30 percent by 2030.[4] In 2021 the New York Mayor's Office of Criminal Justice provided a $37 million grant to create a Civilian Climate Corps. The mission of the corps is to help create the workforce needed for the city's climate protection program by providing training and jobs to people in neighborhoods affected by gun violence.[5]

The Civilian Climate Corps recruits workers from low-income neighborhoods with high rates of gun violence. They received $20 per hour during their training. The corps provides one month of classes in workplace etiquette and business communication followed by two months of technical training, including low-voltage electrical work, HVAC installation, and workplace safety training. Most workers then continue with on-site apprenticeships. By 2023, 1,700 people, 80 percent of whom had been unemployed or underemployed, had graduated from the corps's training program. More than 400 participants secured jobs in related fields, and 60 percent had completed the Occupational Safety and Health Administration training, often required for such employment.

One of those graduates is Robert Clark. Perhaps because of a felony conviction for burglary, Clark had been unable to find any but low-paid, dead-end jobs. Then he was recruited to the Civilian Climate Corps where he was paid $20 per hour to learn how to install electric heat pumps, take care of electric vehicle charging stations, and conduct 3D image modeling of buildings due for renewable energy retrofits. He has received a certification for his work with the corps and hopes to go back to school in engineering.

States are also developing climate corps. In 2020, California launched the California Climate Action Corps, the country's first statewide corps of its kind with the mission of empowering Californians to take meaningful action to protect their homes, health, and communities against the impacts of climate change. This initiative engages Californians through a variety of levels and activities, from an hour at home to a full year of service.[6] It includes Youth Jobs Corps in more than twenty-five California cities and counties.[7]

In 2021, Colorado established the Colorado Climate Corps to place AmeriCorps members in fifty-five counties across the state to protect public lands and help low-income communities brace for the climate crisis.[8] In 2022 the Colorado Climate Corps placed the first 633 AmeriCorps members of the Climate Corps on the ground. They focused on wildfire mitigation and water and energy efficiency. The program rapidly expanded to include supporting local governments and nonprofits in planning for and addressing sustainability and climate change issues.[9]

These climate jobs corps are creating models that can be greatly expanded for other cities and states—and for the United States as a whole. They provide a foothold for those who have been marginalized in the labor market. They provide opportunities in communities that have been plagued with high unemployment and resulting crime and violence. And they provide the training and experience necessary for a greatly expanded workforce able to meet the objectives of climate protection and the Green New Deal.

GREEN NEW DEAL JOBS

The shift to a climate-safe economy is happening too slowly, but it is happening. It is happening in part because fossil fuels keep getting more expensive relative to renewable energy. It is happening because many local communities refuse to tolerate the devastation wrought by fossil fuel extraction and burning. And it is happening because of climate protection efforts by governments and civil society.

A frequently asked question is how many jobs will the Green New Deal and the shift to a climate-safe economy produce. Renewable energy and energy efficiency create far more jobs than fossil fuel energy. So the result of this shift is—more jobs.

How to quantify actual and potential job creation is, however, a difficult and uncertain matter. When economists make estimates of the job creation effects of various policies, they generally must rely on unproven—sometimes unprovable—assumptions. They also necessarily disregard unpredictable factors like wars and trade wars, booms and busts, pandemics, regime change, and policy shifts. Results are also affected by the hopes and fears of those who conduct the studies—and those who commission them.

Having personally supervised a number of such studies, I can testify that those conducting the studies are selected in part based on the sponsors' expectations of their results, and that the researchers are well aware of these expectations. I will cite the results of several such studies below, but I encourage readers to treat their conclusions with appropriate skepticism.

There is no question that local and state Green New Deals are creating thousands of jobs. The exact number is almost impossible to calculate, but we have seen examples just in the Green New Deals described in this book:

The Los Angeles Green New Deal plan laid out 445 initiatives estimated to create 300,000 green jobs by 2035 and 400,000 by 2050.

The Ithaca Green New Deal planned to create 1,000 jobs in the region in its first 1,000 days.

The Illinois Climate and Equitable Jobs Act was expected to create thousands of new jobs. The solar industry alone expected to increase its Illinois workforce by almost 50 percent in 2022.

The "California Climate Jobs Plan" proposed by twenty California unions would create more than a million jobs, including 418,000 clean energy jobs per year and 626,000 additional jobs per year through investments in related areas such as water infrastructure, leaky gas pipelines, public parks, and roadways.

According to California Gov. Gavin Newsom, the climate-related laws passed in 2022 will create 4 million jobs.

IBEW 569 members have logged millions of work hours building more than a gigawatt of solar and wind projects, installing rooftop solar and electric vehicle charging stations at homes and businesses, and constructing large energy storage projects. Local 569 brought hundreds of local residents into the IBEW who were able to build renewable energy projects in their local community.

In Portsmouth, Virginia, the Spanish wind turbine manufacturer Siemens Gamesa plans for 310 jobs to make preparations for a new offshore wind farm. Two hundred sixty of them would be in a finishing plant where blades are painted and assembled. In New York, Marmen of Canada, Welcon of Denmark, and Smulders of Belgium are planning a facility to make steel towers for offshore wind turbines; it will employ up to 350 people.

These are part of a much more extensive increase of green jobs throughout the American economy. According to the annual report "Clean Jobs America 2022,"[10] more than 3 million Americans work in clean energy, including renewable energy, energy efficiency, storage, grid modernization, and clean fuels. Jobs building electric vehicles grew by a dramatic 26 percent in 2022. Conversely, fossil fuel jobs fell 4 percent. Clean energy and clean transportation now employ more than 40 percent of all energy workers in America. These numbers are based on US government surveys, not on estimates or projections.

There have been a variety of studies that estimate how many new green jobs will be created by the 2022 Inflation Reduction Act. A study by the Political Economy Research Institute at the University of Massachusetts–Amherst finds that the more than 100 climate, energy, and environmental investments in the Inflation Reduction Act will create more than 9 million good jobs over the next decade—nearly a million a year. That includes 5 million jobs in clean energy, 900,000 in clean manufacturing, 400,000 in clean transportation, 900,000 in efficient buildings, 150,000 in environmental justice, and 600,000 in natural infrastructure.[11]

Another study by the Energy Futures Initiative found the Inflation Reduction Act will create 1.5 million climate and energy security jobs by 2030—seven years from now. Over 100,000 will be in manufacturing, with 60,000 coming from battery production alone. Nearly 600,000 jobs will be created in the construction sector, for example, constructing electrical transmission lines. The electric utility sector will gain 190,000 jobs.[12]

While these two studies illustrate how different economists can come up with different job projections even for policies already defined in legislation, they also indicate that the scale of job creation just from the Inflation Reduction Act is likely to be very substantial.

The Inflation Reduction Act represents only a fragment of what is necessary to eliminate greenhouse gas emissions, let alone realize the full Green New Deal program. Even though specific Green New Deal proposals vary, there is no question that the number of jobs created by a national Green New Deal would be far greater than those created by the Inflation Reduction Act alone. *America's Zero Carbon Action Plan*, to take one plan among many, develops a scenario for the US economy to achieve net-zero CO_2 emissions by 2050. It estimates that this will generate 4.2–4.6 million jobs per year between 2020 and 2050—cutting the average unemployment rate nearly in half.[13] Another study by Stamford professor Mark Jacobson found that transitioning to 100 percent renewable electricity and heat by 2050 would create more than 4.7 million permanent jobs. And these studies don't take into account the other job creation programs that would be included in a full Green New Deal.[14]

MAKING GREEN JOBS BE GOOD JOBS

Simply creating a larger number of jobs does not solve the problem that so many jobs are underpaid, insecure, dangerous, dead-end, and otherwise degraded. Many climate-related jobs, for example, installing solar panels, are often low-paid and insecure with abusive labor practices. The Green

New Deal program has not only proposed to create millions of jobs, but also committed to implement health and safety, antidiscrimination, and wage and hour standards of part of creating an expanded workforce.

A "policy toolkit" from the Blue-Green Alliance lays out a wide range of "State-Based Policies to Build a Cleaner, Safer, More Equitable Economy."[15] They include project labor agreements, prevailing wage and worker benefits, local hire, targeted hire, organizing rights, and apprenticeships.

Local Green New Deals, especially at the state level, have taken the problem of job quality head-on. In this book, we have seen many cases where coalitions, often led by unions, have successfully incorporated job protections and standards into Green New Deal and other climate protection legislation. For example:

The Illinois Climate and Equitable Jobs Act requires prevailing wages for all nonresidential projects. Utility-scale solar and wind projects must establish project labor agreements. State rebates for electric vehicle infrastructure depend on payment of prevailing wages.

Maine's 2019 Green New Deal Act requires construction of grid-scale power generation to employ people from an apprenticeship program. Legislation also required a project labor agreement on the state's first offshore wind project.

Connecticut legislation requires renewable energy developers to partner with approved in-state apprenticeship and pre-apprenticeship programs. It requires prevailing wage for nonresidential utility-scale or grid-connected projects that are assisted by the state.

New York State's 2021 budget included new renewable energy job standards. They require prevailing wage and project labor agreements for construction on renewable-energy projects and labor peace agreements for operations and maintenance work.[16]

MAKING GREEN JOBS BE UNION JOBS

In 1983 the proportion of workers who were members of unions was 20 percent. In 2022 the proportion of wage and salary workers who were members of unions was 10.1 percent.[17] The weakening of organized labor has been a major cause of both the degradation of work and of growing inequality. The Green New Deal has identified the strengthening of the labor movement as a central way to reverse both job degradation and the broader pattern of economic inequality.

In his 2020 presidential campaign Joe Biden promised to "ensure federal contracts only go to employers who sign neutrality agreements committing not to run anti-union campaigns." This promise has never been fulfilled, and the Biden administration has provided massive contracts to Amazon and other notoriously anti-union corporations.

The ability of states and municipalities to require union recognition or even employer neutrality in union elections is severely limited by law. Nonetheless, Green New Deal–type legislation and policy initiatives are making it easier for workers to organize. We have touched on some examples in this book. For example, the 2022 Fast Foods Accountability and Standards Recovery Act gave bargaining rights to California's half-million fast food workers. It established a fast-food council made up of workers, franchise owners, and franchising companies like McDonald's that will negotiate employee wages, hours, and working conditions. And new legislation allows farmworkers—whose unionization efforts are often impeded by geographical dispersion and mobility—to vote to unionize by mail rather than exclusively in person.

Unions are encouraging a wide range of policies to make it easier for workers to organize. For example, IBEW local 569 has proposed that employers and other entities:

- procure power from union-generated sources;
- employ unionized customer service representatives;
- sign project labor agreements on each power generation project;
- sign project labor agreements on energy efficiency projects/programs;
- agree in writing to neutrality in the event employees or subcontractor employees wish to unionize.

Public policy can make a significant contribution to expanding workers' rights and their ability to organize in "green" industries and elsewhere. For example, in 2023 after a three-year organizing struggle, workers who manufacture school buses for Blue Bird in Fort Valley, Georgia, voted to be represented by the Steelworkers union. Blue Bird is the second-largest bus manufacturer in the country. Steelworkers organizing director Maria Somma said, "It's been a long time since a manufacturing site with 1,400 people has been organized, let alone organized in the South, let alone organized with predominantly African American workers, and let alone in the auto industry." (Only 4.4 percent of workers in Georgia are represented by a union.)

The federal Clean School Buses program, which subsidizes Blue Bird's electric bus production, prohibits recipients from using funds to campaign against unions. Enforcement is weak, but the federal policy nonetheless had a deterrent effect. According to Somma, "This is an employer that would have fired workers"—but it didn't. The Clean School Buses program's ban on funding anti-union campaigns "allowed us to calm the employer's union-busting down."[18]

Meanwhile, workers in the "green economy" are organizing themselves and becoming a force for building the Green New Deal from Below. The recently formed Green Workers Alliance is a worker organization made of current and aspiring renewable energy workers demanding more and better green jobs. It is currently focusing organizing the 100,000 workers on utility-scale solar and wind projects.

Matthew Mayers and Lauren Jacobs of the Green Workers Alliance explain its goals: "We need a strong, worker-led movement that supports the Green New Deal and a just transition to a renewable economy." Their work addresses not only those currently employed in the green sector, but also the millions of jobless and underemployed workers who would benefit from such a program. That must include "access to green jobs and paid training for everyone" with an emphasis on "reducing the huge income disparities between white workers and workers of color, especially Black workers."[19]

The Green Workers Alliance has largely focused on clean energy workers in the South and Southeast because their working conditions are the worst in the country. Over the past year they have connected with hundreds of these workers in Facebook groups and listening tours in Texas and Virginia. The alliance has won back lost wages and supported workers being mistreated by temp agencies and other employers. In 2022 it launched a petition drive targeting utility companies Dominion, Duke, and AEP Renewables demanding that they move to 80 percent renewable energy by 2030.[20]

Ohio Green Workers Alliance activist Felicia Allen says,

> We will fight for better wages, better job practices, and fight for the necessary training us renewable workers so desperately need to advance in our careers. We will help lower our carbon footprint for future generations. If we can't lead the change the whole world needs, what message are we sending to our future generations? What will we be leaving them behind when we are gone? What will our legacies say about us if we won't fight for the greater good of our families, and our planet? I believe if there ever was a time to unite and stand for something that affects all of us in some way, that time is now.[21]

GREEN JOBS FOR ALL—THE NEXT FRONTIER?

A centerpiece of the original Green New Deal resolution is a "jobs guarantee," ensuring jobs with a family-sustaining wage, adequate family and medical leave, paid vacations, and retirement security to all who want them. It envisions a federal program somewhat like the original New Deal's Works Progress Administration (WPA) that would provide funds for nonprofit organizations, local governments, and other agencies serving the public to employ anyone who wants a job. In addition to climate protection, workers in the job guarantee program could also provide for a wide range of needs that can help reduce injustice and create a better way of life for all. These range from education to housing to protection and care for the environment. The WPA produced schools, parks, post offices, and other amenities that we still celebrate; a climate-jobs-for-all program could do the same today.[22]

A climate jobs guarantee would provide much of the labor power needed for an emergency mobilization to transition to a fossil-free, climate-safe economy, as well as to meet a wide range of other public purposes. In this it resembles the home front mobilization in World War II, which recruited millions of workers to support the war effort. It would provide work experience and training that will allow its participants to move into higher skilled, higher wage jobs in the private and public sectors.

Senator Cory Booker has introduced a Federal Jobs Guarantee Development Act, a pilot program to guarantee all adults in fifteen high unemployment communities who want to work can have a job that pays a living wage, and provides benefits like health insurance, paid sick leave, and paid family leave.[23]

Could a jobs guarantee program work at a local or state level? So far nobody seems to have tried. There are proposals to create them, however. As part of his 2022 campaign for mayor of Washington, DC, city councilmember Robert C. White Jr. proposed a jobs guarantee that ensures that everyone who wants a job could work. Some jobs would be created by the government, some by industry incentives, and some through government contracts.

White pitched the program as a means both to counter climate change and to address the city's burgeoning crime rate. "This monumental program will drive down violence by giving people a real alternative to crime while addressing one of the most pressing issues of our time, which is climate change. . . . For many people, the streets offer more opportunities than our government does. Violence occurs when people feel that engaging in crime has more benefits than the alternative of living within the bounds of the law. Given a choice between violence and a stable, good-paying job, most people will choose the job." The program would produce up to 10,000 new city positions, a nearly 30 percent increase in the size of the city's current workforce of 33,000. It would cost an estimated $1.5 billion a year, roughly equal to the city's annual budget increases in recent years.[24] White said,

> Working in partnership with our labor unions, we could use apprentice-ships to build skills and technical expertise. One example: crosswalk repainting jobs that would kick off apprenticeships that would lead to traffic engineer positions which focus on pedestrian and bicyclist safety. Another example is tree planting jobs that lead to apprentice-ships for those interested in becoming arborists charged with managing and replacing trees. We could give community members professional training so they could effectively promote energy efficiency, protect our waterways, ensure food justice, and remove environmental hazards. Other jobs could include clearing gutters, installing solar panels and green roofs, housing maintenance, rodent and mosquito abatement, weatherization, installing heat pumps, stormwater infrastructure, urban agriculture, and removing lead pipes.

In April 2023 Philadelphia city council member and mayoral candidate Helen Gym proposed to guarantee a job to every person thirty and under as part of a comprehensive plan to fight violence and crime.[25] Her proposal included paid work for youth both in summer and through the school year. It would prioritize young people in the zip codes most impacted by gun violence, with a goal of increasing youth employment 50 percent during the plan's first summer.

The plan would expand Philadelphia's pioneering PowerCorpsPHL program to provide a pathway to city employment, including work with land care programs to clear vacant lots that increase crime and to increase neighborhood greening as part of the city's tree plan. It would partner with local businesses, institutions, and organizations and provide tax incentives and grants for hiring, training, and mentoring youth. It would ensure that these employers receive technical support around youth mentoring, youth development, and trauma-informed professional supervision. It would partner with the building trades unions and initiate a pilot class of 100 young people completing pre-apprentice and apprentice programs with a guaranteed track to employment by leveraging resources from the Infrastructure Investment and Jobs Act.

While guaranteeing climate jobs for all who want them will surely require federal resources, local and state job guarantee programs may provide a future target for Green New Deals from Below. They could help reduce poverty and unemployment, meet community needs, and create the workforce necessary to protect the climate.

A VISION FOR JOBS

Like many of its proposals, the Green New Deal jobs program combines concrete policies with a vision of social transformation. Job corps that would create a pipeline to good jobs for young people from impoverished and discriminated-against communities could create a pathway to good jobs and incomes for those who have been excluded from them. A massive expansion of jobs to meet climate and social needs could create full employment and strengthen the bargaining power of workers. Elevated standards for wages, job security, health and safety, nondiscrimination, and rights on the job could provide a baseline level of decency and dignity in the workplace. Enforcing the right of workers to organize and engage in collective action on the job would shift the balance of power between workers and employers both in individual workplaces and in society as a whole. A program of jobs for all could eliminate the scourge of unemployment and create an economic sector where workers could dedicate their labor to the public good.

Such measures could also open a vision of a different future for young workers. Maria Brescia-Weiler is an organizer for the Young Workers Project of the Labor Network for Sustainability, which is conducting a Young Workers Listening Project. She says,

> We always ask young workers how they ideally envision their life and work 20 years from now. This question is almost always met by a blank stare, or some kind of sigh or groan and a long pause. But after that long pause, they paint pictures of a beautiful future, where we all have more time off to care for our loved ones and grow sustainable local food, where union construction workers have made public buildings like schools and post offices into community resilience hubs run on green energy, where they have access to safe, clean and reliable public transportation but there's so much affordable housing in their community that they can walk to work. And they truly believe this future is not only possible but absolutely necessary. The key word is always IF—IF we can create a just transition from fossil fuels, led by the workers and community members who are most impacted.[26]

The Green New Deal from Below is laying the foundations for that transformation of the working world.

CONCLUSION

THE GREEN NEW DEAL FROM BELOW
AND THE POLITICS OF THE POSSIBLE

The Green New Deal is happening, and whatever happens is possible. The Green New Deal is not an impossible leftist fantasy, or something that could never win popular support, or a dream that couldn't possibly be realized in practice, or something that would bring disaster if it were realized. The Green New Deal is being created right now by flesh-and-blood people under real-life conditions. It is being created in communities, cities, states, and regions—from below.

Of course, only a limited proportion of US geographies and institutions have fully developed Green New Deals. But efforts to create Green New Deals are ubiquitous; an article in *Popular Science* magazine soon after the first Green New Deal proposal in Congress found that plans and first steps to realize Green New Deals were happening in every state in the union.[1] Today the Green New Deal from Below, dispersed throughout the United States, is transforming the realities where it is—and creating models for broader transformation everywhere.

Green New Deals in cities like Boston and Los Angeles are reducing the greenhouse gases that are destroying our climate. They are creating jobs that protect the climate and training workers to fill them. They are mobilizing city resources to reduce poverty. They are investing in climate-protecting buildings and technologies in low-income neighborhoods. They are expanding cheap or free public transit to reconnect isolated neighborhoods, provide people who lack cars with access to jobs, and reduce greenhouse gas pollution.

In states like Illinois, California, and New York, Green New Deal–style programs are shifting major resources to climate-safe energy development. They are setting targets for greenhouse gas reduction and schedules for

©Hayne Palmour IV / Greenpeace

UAW members joined a global Greenpeace delegation on the ship Arctic Sunrise, on September 8, 2023, shortly before the UAW's "stand up-strike," which demanded and won core elements of a "just transition" to electric vehicle production. The strike was supported by more than one hundred environmental, climate, and climate justice organizations and was by far the largest US strike demanding protections for both workers and the climate. Photo courtesy of Greenpeace.

shutting down fossil fuel–producing and –using facilities—and implementing them. They are reducing fossil fuel use by increasing the energy efficiency of buildings, transportation, agriculture, and other energy users. They are investing in infrastructure to correct historical injustices like polluting facilities concentrated in poor communities. They are creating jobs in the green economy with high labor rights and standards and providing job training, jobs, and job ladders for people who have been marginalized in the labor market.

Unions like the IBEW are promoting programs to expand renewable energy production, building coalitions to support them, training the workers needed to realize them, and monitoring the results to ensure that they produce good union jobs. Unions of educators and nurses are fighting for—and winning—green schools and hospitals.

The Green New Deal from Below is showing that it is possible to challenge the powers that are imposing climate change, inequality, and oppression. That it is possible to formulate realistic alternatives. And that those alternatives can actually be implemented.

Perhaps someone could look at the diverse projects, programs, and initiatives of the Green New Deal from Below and see them as simply scattered, unconnected, one-off phenomena. But that would be like saying, I see the students, the classrooms, and the football field, but where is the university? The Green New Deal from Below is indeed composed of many parts, but that does not prevent it from being a real entity as a whole. This concluding chapter identifies some of the commonalities and connections that make it a whole.

SHIFTING THE SENSE OF WHAT IS POSSIBLE

The Green New Deal transformed America's political imagination. It transgressed the neoliberal, market-only assumptions that dominated public discourse for four decades. It proposed the long-disparaged notion of using government to solve problems. It refused to accept the growing inequality that had reshaped American society. It advocated tackling rather than ignoring the climate emergency. To paraphrase Green New Deal mayor Michelle Wu of Boston, it shifted "the sense of what was possible." It thereby expanded the limits of what was possible.

This transformation flows from the core concepts of the Green New Deal. These core concepts integrate multiple concerns rather than addressing them in separate "silos" or adding them together in "laundry lists." They unite the urgent and universal need for climate protection with the economic and social needs of disadvantaged groups and of working people. They do so by articulating a strategy for rapid greenhouse gas reduction that prioritizes programs that create jobs and reduce injustice. This strategy provides a new way of integrating the interests of previously disconnected or antagonistic constituencies.

The Green New Deal is not just a slogan, a list of demands, or a menu of policies. The Green New Deal provides a framework for moving beyond piecemeal policies to a set of integrated strategies. Like the original New Deal, it makes seemingly antagonistic policies and constituencies complementary by transcending the limitations of established assumptions. It proposes a set of changes in the social framework that meet both the common and the distinct needs of those affected. It thereby constructs a common interest that incorporates the particular interests of different groups. This allows needs and interests that may currently appear incompatible—for example, between jobs and environment—to become compatible or even synergistic.[2]

The Green New Deal integrates such distinct elements in two ways. First, it integrates different kinds of needs and their solutions. Front and center is its integration of the need for climate protection, the need for good jobs, and the need for greater equality. But it integrates other needs as well. For example, it combines policies that attack entrenched forms of discrimination and injustice with ones that increase the power of workers on the job by strengthening their right to organize and engage in concerted action. Legislation in Connecticut and other states exemplifies this by requiring that offshore wind clean energy projects provide both project labor agreements ensuring union wage standards and conditions and community benefit agreements providing access to jobs for communities and demographics often deprived of that access.

Second, the Green New Deal integrates the needs of different constituencies.[3] For example, two separate coalitions backing different bills developed in Illinois to shape climate legislation. One, the Illinois Clean Jobs coalition, was rooted in the environmental movement and local social justice organizations. The other, the Climate Jobs Illinois coalition, was based in the state's labor unions. After considerable tension and extended negotiations, the two united on a common program that included the demands of each—laying the basis for the Climate and Equitable Jobs Act, described by one journalist as a "Green New Deal" for Illinois.

Integrating programs and integrating people go hand in hand. For example, the Green New Deal tames the purported conflict between employment and climate protection. It challenges the "jobs vs. environment" frame. At a local and state level, the Green New Deal from Below has therefore been able to unite often-divided labor, environmental, and climate justice advocates.

INTEGRATING PROGRAMS

The Green New Deal is not a random collection of isolated initiatives; it is a set of synergistic policies determined by a common purpose and exhibiting a common set of characteristics. It relies not on the market, but on action by public institutions and by the people themselves. It establishes Green New Deal policies and programs at community, local, state, and regional levels both for their own sake and as building blocks for a national and even a global Green New Deal. Rather than leaving outcomes to chance or the vagaries of the market, it embraces municipal, metropolitan, state, and regional planning. It mobilizes resources to provide for public needs in ways that also help reverse the rampant inequality of American society. And it pursues climate solutions that eliminate fossil fuel energy rather than using technological or economic fixes to perpetuate it.

All aspects of the Green New Deal from Below are driven by the existential necessity to protect the climate. This requires increasing climate-safe energy production, reducing the need for energy through energy efficiency and conservation, and managed reduction of fossil fuel extraction and burning. Climate protection is generally the pivot around which all the other necessary social transformations turn.

New, climate-safe energy from renewable sources is being created by Green New Deals from Below. For example, the third annual progress report of the Los Angeles Green New Deal found that the city is meeting 43 percent of its energy needs with renewables like wind and solar and will generate 97 percent of its energy with renewables by 2030.

Energy consumption is being reduced. For example, the Ithaca Green New Deal's Efficiency Retrofitting and Thermal Load Electrification program set a goal of retrofitting 1,000 buildings in 1,000 days as part of a plan to get to carbon-neutrality by 2030.

Fossil fuel burning is being reduced and eliminated. Fossil fuel plants, pipelines, and mines are being ratchetted or shut down, such as the closing of 353 of the 530 coal-fired power plants that were active in 2010 and the blocking of the Keystone XL pipeline after a thirteen-year struggle. California, America's largest auto market, is phasing out the sale of gasoline-powered cars over the next thirteen years.

Carbon is being withdrawn from the atmosphere through urban forestry programs in Boston, Philadelphia, and many other cities. Farming, forestry, and "Blue New Deal" ocean farming are contributing to atmospheric restoration.

The Green New Deals from Below are changing energy systems in ways that also rectify past injustices and open new opportunities. That ranges from planting trees in urban hotspots to shutting down polluting power plants in environmental justice communities to electrifying gas-guzzling vehicles or replacing them with public transit in highly polluted areas.

The original Green New Deal program included an expansive social welfare agenda, including education, housing, healthcare, and other social needs. That agenda is being implemented as part of the Green New Deal from Below. In California, for example, the same spurt of legislation that established accelerated climate protection also instituted free nutritious meals for all of the state's 6 million public school students and removed restrictions that had significantly tied up the building of affordable housing.

Workers and communities are being protected against negative side effects of the transition to a just and climate-safe economy. In cities like Somerset, Massachusetts, fossil fuel power plants have been shut down and replaced by nonpolluting, job-creating renewable energy production. In Colorado and Illinois, state programs are providing jobs and new investment for communities that have been hit by the shutdown of coal mines. In cities like Philadelphia and states like California, new green jobs are being created and marginalized workers and communities are being trained to fill them.

A hallmark of these Green New Deal from Below programs is the way they integrate the varied needs of various constituencies. Consider, for example, Washington State's 2022 "Move Ahead Washington" transportation program. It invests $1.45 billion for public transit. This is part of a multimodal transportation program that also includes bike and pedestrian projects, which will reduce accidents. Move Ahead Washington not only reduces greenhouse gases and gives relief to highly polluted communities, but also provides new mobility options for disabled people and other nondrivers. And, in order to encourage a new culture of transportation use, the legislation provides free access to the state's transit, trains, and ferries for riders under eighteen and bicycle education for students—with a free bike for those who participate in the program. Or consider the Denver CARE Project (Clean Affordable Renewable Energy), which has built a community solar garden that reduces energy costs to low-income communities and provides training and jobs in the solar industry for underserved communities—all while reducing the emission of greenhouse gases.

THE GREEN NEW DEAL VERSUS NEOLIBERALISM

The Green New Deal represents a historic shift away from the dominant market-oriented ideology of the past four decades, often referred to as "neoliberalism." It asserts the legitimacy and indeed the necessity of action by institutions representing the public and of collective action by the people themselves.

Neoliberalism has also marked much of the policy of the climate movement itself, which has often advocated so-called market mechanisms like cap-and-trade systems and carbon offsets in effect to bribe the rich and powerful to become climate good guys. The Green New Deal pursues an entirely different climate protection strategy, based on mandatory emissions reductions, managed decline in fossil fuel extraction and burning, public investment, and climate-safe energy alternatives that create jobs and a more just economy.

Of course, the risk remains that the Green New Deal itself can be captured or coopted and made to serve the ends of exploitation and greenwashing. But its basic orientation toward public initiative, investment, and planning in the public interest provides an antidote to the blandishments of green "false flag" operations.

Much of the climate movement itself has presented climate destruction as largely a matter of deleterious individual consumption choices. The fix for climate change, accordingly, has often been posed as a need for individuals to turn off lights, eat less meat, drive electric cars, and otherwise change their consumption habits. This approach has often had a moralistic, self-blaming dynamic while leaving unchallenged the role of production and other broad social structures in climate destruction. The Green New Deal, while recognizing the role of consumption patterns, especially for energy consumption, has put production and other social dimensions front and center.

Green New Deal initiatives come in the context of an emerging struggle between the neoliberal policies that have dominated the United States for forty years and the reemergence of activist government "industrial policy," embodied in Biden administration policies and the 2022 Inflation Reduction Act. From the 1940s until 1980 the United States actually had an active industrial policy, but it was largely shaped and conducted by the military. For example, the substantial movement of US manufacturing to California in the twentieth century was largely promoted by military decisions. And a notorious 1965 Selective Service System memo titled "Channeling" laid out how the military draft and its system of exemptions funneled "manpower" into "endeavors" and "occupations" that are "in the national interest."[4] The current revival of industrial policy was implemented primarily by deals that President Biden made on the one hand with the forces of the Green New Deal and on the other with fossil fuel and other corporate interests, passing the Inflation Reduction Act by paying off conservative fossil fuel Democrats like Sen. Joe Manchin.

The Inflation Reduction Act is providing some support for Green New Deal–type activities and other programs to reduce greenhouse gas emissions. But much of its funding goes for very different purposes. Much is directed toward faux climate protection programs like carbon capture and hydrogen production, which are primarily means to greenwash expanded fossil fuel production. Some may be going to environmentally dangerous projects, notably building a new "fleet" of nuclear power plants. And much of the new American industrial policy is driven by economic nationalism, designed to shift production—especially of "green" products—from other countries to the United States. Such industrial policy programs were justified as part of an economic war against China (accompanied by such other economic nationalist policies as trying to prevent China from acquiring advanced computer chip technology), but in fact they are producing substantial collateral damage to the US's supposed European allies.

The Green New Deal from Below is also engaging in governmental economic activism, but of a very different sort. Its goal is to produce public goods—like a healthy environment, economic security, and justice. Under prevailing circumstances, in which private corporations have a disproportionate share of money and capacity, Green New Deals from Below may at times have to work with them and allow them to make a profit by serving the public good. Its driving purpose is not just corporate profit, however, but environment, jobs, and justice.

Cooperatives, public ownership, and public banks were part of the initial program of the New Deal—and of the Green New Deal. Green New Deals from Below are using them to establish alternatives to dependence on corporate capital to get things done. Green New Deal energy programs include energy coops, community-based energy production, and state and municipally owned power utilities. In a very different sector, the Boston Green New Deal contracts with the worker-owned Roxbury food cooperative to provide free meals each school day for 50,000 Boston students. Connecticut, Illinois, and other states are financing Green New Deal programs with public "green banks."

FROM BELOW OR FROM ABOVE—OR BOTH?

The initial Green New Deal resolution took as its models not only the original New Deal but also the home front mobilization for World War II. A fully developed Green New Deal will need both the kind of federal initiative and strong federal agencies that transformed the American economy during World War II and the popular participation and decentralized creativity represented by the Green New Deal from Below.

The Green New Deal from Below can make a significant difference in reducing greenhouse gas pollution, creating good jobs, and countering injustice. It can help create the support and the building blocks for a national and even a global Green New Deal. But the accumulation of separate initiatives will not automatically culminate in adequate solutions. Green New Deal projects in different localities and different spheres need to hook up to strengthen each other and to generate more extensive projects; to win support from the federal government; and ultimately to make the Green New Deal a national and global reality. A federal Green New Deal is necessary to close the gaps that are difficult to close from below.

Cities and states are limited in their powers and resources. Financially, the federal government can and normally does run budget deficits; cities and states are in most cases constitutionally required to balance their budgets. The federal government can spend trillions of dollars annually and has almost unlimited capacity to borrow trillions more. The federal government owns more than 30 percent of the country's land and has authority to use the power of eminent domain on the rest. It can issue or deny permits for any kind of fossil fuel extraction or infrastructure. The executive, legislative, and judicial branches can regulate almost any kind of economic activity and can determine plans for transportation, energy, and other basic economic systems.

Many of the policies necessary for a Green New Deal require these federal powers. These include establishing financial incentives and disincentives; raising capital; implementing labor strategies; organizing funding for infrastructure such as transmission lines, railways, and pipelines; funding R&D; setting and monitoring energy efficiency standards for buildings, appliances, and equipment; training and retraining professionals and trades people; and setting industrial location policies.[5]

Even with a full federal commitment to the Green New Deal, action "from below" will continue to be essential. Community-based renewables like rooftop solar collectors, energy use reduction like residential weatherization, mobilization of funding like revolving loan funds, and new patterns of consumption like shared bicycles can, with federal support, expand to a still greater role. And they can provide popular support for transition and a means to hold the institutions of transition accountable.

Meanwhile, Green New Deals from Below are taking some initial steps toward coordinating their programs on a larger scale. Programs for energy development and transportation are transcending city and state boundaries, for example in the Northeast's Regional Greenhouse Gas Initiative and the Kansas-Missouri Infrastructure Investment and Jobs Act proposing a regional rapid transit corridor integrated with affordable housing, green infrastructure, and jobs programs. Regional Green New Deals are being fought for, for example, by the Gulf States Green New Deal. As the Green New Deal from Below receives greater recognition there will be increasing opportunities for coalitions of Green New Deal cities and states to take action in common—and to demand that federal politicians and agencies support their doing so.

PLANNING

Many political programs are reactive. One of the key features of the Green New Deal is that it is oriented toward the future. The original Green New Deal proposal was based on a ten-year mobilization to address long-festering problems in a way that would start to put the future of the climate, the economy, and social justice on a secure footing. The activities of the Green New Deal from Below are inevitably piecemeal, but they are shaped by that long-term vision.

Many aspects of the Green New Deal require national planning. The overall development of managed decline of fossil fuel burning with provision for a just transition will depend on national planning. So will the development of an electrical grid that can allocate various forms of renewable energy based on need and availability. Large-scale transportation systems like railroads require national planning. And such large-scale planning and investment requires national resource allocation to determine the quantity, speed, and sequencing of investment. That in turn requires agencies with the capacity for planning and investment.[6]

Meanwhile, Green New Deals from Below are developing their programs on the basis of long-range planning in the public interest. This is most evident in the targets and timetables for greenhouse gas reduction that guide the great majority of Green New Deal programs. In few other areas of American life are there plans based on thirty-year goals with short- and medium-term programs to implement them. The approach to energy planning in cities like Los Angeles and states like Illinois contrasts with the way things are usually done in American politics. Much of US public policy at all levels is based in effect on offering money to private entrepreneurs in the hope that they will somehow do what is necessary for public benefit. The results are often calamitous. Projects are designed to maximize profit rather than the public good. And their results are often at cross-purposes with other social objectives and programs.

A prime example is the history of urban renewal, in which the planning power of cities was devolved to quasi-independent agencies often more responsive to real estate developers than to the people who live in the affected communities. The result was the destruction of urban neighborhoods; the displacement of their residents; the enrichment of developers; the use of public money and legal powers to build luxury housing, commercial towers, sports stadiums, and convention centers, rather than the affordable housing, schools, and hospitals that ordinary residents so desperately needed.

Local Green New Deals offer a radically different approach to urban planning. They aim to put human needs, rather than developer profit, at the center of planning. They often shift control of decision-making, giving representatives of poor and neglected communities a voice and a vote—in the Boston Green New Deal this went as far as shutting down the long-established urban renewal agency and creating a new planning agency within city government. Transportation planning often aims to increase transit and reduce the burden of fossil fuel transportation emissions in low-income neighborhoods. Zoning changes make it easier to build affordable housing. And metropolitan planning seeks to regionally coordinate transportation, housing, and work in a way that reduces greenhouse gas emissions and local pollution while providing deprived people with access to jobs and amenities, good housing, and healthy air to breathe.

Green New Deals plan rather than just passing out loot. Planning for public purposes guides Green New Deal investment. This is most obvious in the case of energy. While conventional energy policies are often based on issuing requests for proposals and seeing who bids, Green New Deal programs have first of all set targets and timetables for the transition away from fossil fuels, then designed concrete programs to realize them, then started to implement those programs. Planning in the public interest is illustrated by the Illinois Climate and Equitable Jobs Act, which channels green energy investment into locations where fossil fuel facilities are being shut down. Public-led rather than developer-led planning helps ensure that investment benefits the communities that need it most, rather than being steered by profit maximization. This is illustrated by programs in California and other states that are requiring 30 percent or more of their investment go to environmental justice communities.

Green New Deal from Below planning is marked by an integration of multiple objectives. For example, Good Food programs in California, Massachusetts, and elsewhere are designed to provide school children healthy food, host communities good jobs, give local farmers a steady market, and support environmentally sound, climate-protecting forms of agriculture. Similarly local green energy programs create local jobs and support environmental justice. Urban projects seek to combine transit, housing, and energy efficiency to meet community needs and simultaneously reduce greenhouse gas pollution.

Planning is also being used to protect workers and communities from unwanted side effects of climate and other Green New Deal policies. For example, the Illinois Climate and Equitable Jobs Act created a Displaced Energy Worker Bill of Rights with extended advance notice of closures and incentives for clean energy facilities to locate and invest where fossil fuel installations have shut down. That's a long way from a neoliberal, laissez-faire approach that, instead of planning, abandons workers and communities to the tender mercies of the market.

While planning is often thought of as a top-down process, Green New Deal planning is highly participatory. Design of the Seattle Green New Deal, for example, involved representatives from more than 200 organizations, including labor unions, advocates from low-income and communities of color, tribal nations, faith leaders, healthcare providers, businesses, environmental advocates, and clean energy experts. Front-line communities hold eight of the nineteen seats on the oversight board that runs the program and allocates city tax money for Green New Deal projects. In Culver City, California, planning for a bus and bike mobility project started with design of a website by three public commissions. A community project advisory committee solicited a wide range of input through meetings, community workshops, and social media—with 40,000 hits on web and social media sites in three months. The project design went through four different designs based on public input before the final plan was determined.

FINDING RESOURCES

It is often asked, how are Green New Deal programs going to be paid for? The money is already coming in from a variety of sources. Some of the funding for Green New Deals comes from what may be called "Robin Hood strategies"—initiatives that take from the haves to provide programs that benefit the have-nots. For example, the Seattle Green New Deal is being paid for by a 2.4 percent "JumpStart Seattle" tax on sala-ries of at least $400,000 at companies with at least $1 billion in annual payroll (think Amazon). California's 2022 climate legislation was paid for by the high tax rate on its wealthiest residents; the top 1 percent of earners paid nearly half of personal income-tax collections.[7] State and municipal policy can also shift budget priorities from the likes of sports stadiums and amenities in wealthy neighborhoods to schools and affordable housing. Green banks can take investors' cash and channel it to Green New Deal–style projects.

Funding can also come from taxes and fees placed on fossil fuel pollut-ers. The program to support Tonawanda and other towns in New York after the closing of the Huntley power plant came from the Regional Green-house Gas Initiative, which requires payments from polluting utilities throughout the Northeast. Had the Washington State just transition initia-tive passed, it would have established a fee on carbon emissions starting at $15 per ton and increasing by $2 per year until the state's greenhouse gas reduction targets were met.

Federal programs like the 2021 American Rescue Plan Act, the 2021 Infrastructure Investment and Jobs Act, and the 2022 Inflation Reduc-tion Act are making substantial sums available that are being captured for use in Green New Deal programs. For example, the city of Boston is using

$350 million in federal funding from the American Rescue Plan Act "to accelerate a Green New Deal for Boston."[8] The Green New Deal Network has developed a program to help local communities and unions access such funds. In April 2023 Sen. Ed Markey and Rep. Alexandria Ocasio Cortez published a Green New Deal implementation guide to use these federal programs to "bring the Green New Deal to life."[9]

Finally, Green New Deal programs are often paid for by the money saved on extracting, purchasing, and burning fossil fuels. Renewable energy is now in many instances substantially cheaper than fossil fuel energy, even when climate and social costs are not counted. Shutting down a coal-fired power plant and replacing it with solar and wind power often now produces not a cost but a savings—witness the hundreds of coal plants that have been shut down by their owners because they were uncompetitive and therefore unprofitable. The Green New Deal energy transition often is paying for itself; one Denver Housing Authority solar garden reduced the electric bills of low-income residents by up to 20 percent. Similarly, insulating schools, public housing, and municipal buildings is likely to significantly lower their energy costs.

COUNTERING FALSE SOLUTIONS

Green New Deals generally pursue the basic strategies laid out by climate science for countering climate change: increase climate-safe energy, reduce energy usage, and rapidly reduce the burning of fossil fuels. These strategies are not only effective; they are cost-effective.

Unfortunately, there are many other purported fixes that have the effect and in some cases the intent of perpetuating rather than ending the burning of fossil fuels. These include various ways of attempting to capture greenhouse gasses after they have been produced; sucking greenhouse gases out of the air after they have been released; adding hydrogen to the fossil fuel mix; and expanding the use of nuclear energy. While there is highly publicized speculation on the potentials of these technologies, overwhelming evidence shows that none of them are as effective or as cost-effective for an emergency response to the climate threat as renewable energy, energy efficiency, and managed decline of fossil fuel burning.[10]

While Green New Deals from Below have rarely pursued such dubious programs, these programs' proponents have often tried to incorporate them in climate legislation and policies, especially at the state level. In California and Illinois, Green New Deal legislation has been amended to slow the phaseout of nuclear power plants. Extension of existing nuclear power plants, coupled with serious efforts to reduce fossil fuel burning, was accepted in these two cases as a means of maintaining existing energy supply during a transition to climate-safe energy.

Capturing carbon, either from smokestacks after burning or by sucking it out of the air, has been a highly touted but unproven method for continuing to burn fossil fuels without aggravating climate change. In California there has been an unresolved struggle over including carbon capture programs in climate legislation—resulting in legislation assigning a state agency to evaluate and set standards for carbon capture subsidies. There are natural forms of carbon capture that have won overwhelming support among Green New Dealers—as well as demonstrable effectiveness in reducing greenhouse gases in the atmosphere. These include reforestation, improved agricultural practices, and cultivation of seaweed. Improving the urban forest has been a special focus of local Green New Deals.

As the Biden administration has promoted the development of "hydrogen hubs" around the country, local climate and Green New Deal advocates are struggling with whether this represents genuine climate protection and whether they should participate in such efforts. In Connecticut, the Connecticut Green Bank initiated exploration of a hydrogen hub, but the labor-climate coalition the Connecticut Roundtable on Climate and Jobs passed a resolution to support hydrogen development only in cases where it was demonstrably not greenwashing, but beneficial for climate protection.

The opponents of the Green New Deal often talk the climate talk without walking the climate walk. It is easy to advocate for new clean energy projects or "clean" fossil fuels while allowing the continuation or expansion of climate-and-health destroying fossil fuel burning. The question of how to relate to such efforts is increasingly pressing for Green New Deals.[11]

Anything but rapid reduction of GHG emissions will continue to accelerate climate destruction. Green New Deals are providing a genuine and effective path for climate protection and restoration. The Green New Deal from Below shows what real climate protection looks like.

INTEGRATING PEOPLES

The Green New Deal is more than a set of policies; it is also a social phenomenon that exhibits many of the traits of a social movement. Historical sociologist Michael Mann describes how new solutions to problems often emerge from multiple locations in the interstices—the nooks and crannies—of existing power structures. The linking of these interstices is frequently the way that isolated, apparently powerless people come to propose and impose alternatives to existing social arrangements. This has sometimes been called the Lilliput strategy.[12] The Lilliput strategy inevitably involves a tension between the need for identity and autonomy among its constituent groups and the need to escape from silos and cooperate on a wider scale. This tension can lead to domination or fragmentation, but it can also drive an interactive process through which the needs and interests of each part are incorporated in the whole and conversely the parts incorporate the needs and interests of the whole as aspects of their own.[13]

This dynamic has been central to the development of the Green New Deal from Below. At the same time that they have recognized the needs and contributions of specific constituencies, Green New Dealers have also forged cooperation among diverse groups across lines that have conventionally divided them. This is particularly striking in the case of organized labor and environmentalists, where these often-opposed groups have joined together in instance after instance around the country. Such coalescence does not have to deny the identities of the distinct elements of the coalition; rather, it adds an additional layer of identity—an identity with the common program and those who need and support it. The care and feeding of such coalitions depend on providing once-antagonistic groups benefits from cooperation and mutual support, such as legislation that includes labor standards, health benefits for environmental justice communities, and reduction in greenhouse gas emissions. Conversely, such coalitions are put at risk by failure to keep the concerns of key constituencies front and center.

While the history of every Green New Deal is different, they typically emerge neither from isolated individuals nor from a unified preexisting organization. They generally develop from a field of quasi-fragmented, quasi-organized groups through a process of integration. Often the groups from which they emerge have complex overlapping, multilevel identities, for example predominantly Black neighborhoods that also include members of other ethnicities or unions with members with varied genders and occupations.

Green New Deal activities have been initiated and led in a variety of ways. Usually they have grown out of a long history of previous struggles, mobilizations, campaigns, research studies, program development, and alliance building that have established relations among different groups. No doubt in some cases those processes would have continued without the emergence of the national Green New Deal, but in many cases participants were galvanized by the national Green New Deal proposals. Narratives of the Boston and Seattle Green New Deals, for example, start with people from diverse constituencies hearing about the occupation of Nancy Pelosi's office and Alexandria Ocasio-Cortez's proposal for a Green New Deal and asking themselves, what would it mean to have a Green New Deal in Boston or Seattle?

This was often followed by small gatherings among groups who had different backgrounds and concerns but who knew each other and had some experience of working together. In Seattle a climate and an environmental justice organization launched the campaign for a Seattle Green New Deal, which was quickly endorsed by over 200 other local organizations. In Somerville, Massachusetts, organized labor had formed a coalition with community and immigrant groups. Environmental activists had started coming to their meetings and the groups had begun to discover common ground, laying the basis for the Somerville Green New Deal. In Illinois, a coalition of environmental groups and frontline communities had worked together for several years, but most of organized labor had not participated and indeed formed a separate coalition of its own; for a considerable time the two groups appeared to be antagonists and this gap was only gradually bridged as they worked out details of major climate-labor-justice legislation.

These nascent coalitions were often defined less by agreement on specific policies than by a sense of common interests. After initial discussions, in several cases they commissioned experts to write reports that would present a strategy to realize their seemingly disparate goals: reducing greenhouse gas emissions while protecting workers and communities and reducing inequality and injustice. Such reports played an important role in unifying Green New Deal groups in Boston, California, Washington, Colorado, and elsewhere. Green New Deal initiatives have also learned from each other. For example, various state just-transition programs have learned from the pioneering efforts in Washington and Colorado; the Boston jobs corps learned from similar efforts in Philadelphia and other cities.

Even after reaching agreement on common goals, Green New Deal coalitions often take significant time and extended discussion to transform those goals into specific policies and legislation. And after the development of tentative policies, these coalitions often put in additional time reaching out to the rank and file of member groups and to constituencies that are not yet part of the coalition. This often allows proposed policies to be tweaked to take into consideration the needs and objectives of varied groups. It also allows extensive education on the proposals, creating a committed base when the time comes for political action to implement them.

At some point these values, objectives, and policies are translated into specific legislation and administrative rules and practices. "Inside the system" politicians, as well as technical legislation experts, often play a significant role at this point. This often involves considerable negotiation and compromise among different groups. It therefore also opens the danger that compromise may morph into sell-out.

Once a specific local or state legislative proposal has been solidified, the next step is usually campaigning for support. This generally starts with the creation of a campaign organization. It utilizes marches, rallies, educational workshops, and door-knocking as well as websites and social media. It may also involve conventional political techniques like advertising.

When legislation or an administrative policy is created, the coalition needs to turn to implementation. There is no guarantee that government officials or agencies will actually carry out legislation or regulations in ways that realize their original intentions; they can easily sit on their hands or put control in the hands of those who have entirely other objectives.[14] The groups within coalitions who are directly connected with impacts on the ground—for example unions and neighborhood organizations—need to monitor the results; coalitions need to support them in pushing back when their objectives are disregarded or betrayed. Green New Deal legislation and policies often include strategies for empowering coalition members to implement their objectives themselves. For example, the Illinois Climate and Equitable Jobs Act established hubs for job training and business development to be led by community organizations. Similarly, legislation in Connecticut and other states provides for project labor agreements and community benefit agreements; unions and community organizations are positioned to take the initiative in negotiating and enforcing such agreements.

Not all campaigns end in victory and not every apparent victory leads to successful implementation. Creating a Green New Deal program is not a once-and-forever thing; it is an ongoing struggle for social transformation. A prime example is the 2016 Illinois climate and jobs legislation, which was touted as a national model but turned out to be highly problematic for both labor and frontline communities. Far from despairing, however, Illinois activists evaluated the weaknesses of their "success," reached out for new input from relevant constituencies, and constructed a new campaign around new legislation that built on but went far beyond the earlier version. Even campaigns that lose can transform the landscape for future possibilities. In Seattle, a proposal to tax businesses to pay for progressive development programs was defeated in 2018 because of its feared impact on small businesses and those who work for them. Two years later a similar proposal was passed after it was modified to place the burden on large businesses like Amazon. In both these instances setbacks led to course correction followed by success.

Even campaigns that succeed can be subject to pushback. In Chicago, real estate interests sued to block the city from building affordable housing near public transit; fortunately, a judge threw out the suit as an infringement on a legitimate government action. In California fossil fuel interests and allies are trying to reverse the decision requiring that oil and gas extraction facilities be set back from residential areas. Such cases evoke the ancient watchword: Eternal vigilance is the price of freedom.

THE GREEN NEW DEAL FROM BELOW AS A POLITICAL STRATEGY

The Green New Deal from Below represents a unique formation, which therefore requires—and has developed—a unique strategy. It is not the same as an electoral campaign, a civil disobedience struggle, a neighborhood organization, a union recognition or contract campaign, or other familiar forms of social action, though it may have similarities to all of them. It is necessary to recognize this uniqueness to avoid being caught up in familiar but inappropriate tactics.[15]

If power were distributed equally in American society there might well be Green New Deals by now in a majority of American cities and states. But in reality, power is concentrated in the hands of a tiny minority—far smaller even than the notorious "1 percent." Under normal circumstances the rest of the people have little influence over the basic decisions that determine their lives. The right to vote is precious, but it confers only limited influence over governments and even less over the corporations that shape economic decisions and in practice largely shape the policies of governments.

Yet ultimately the power of the powerful depends on the rest of us accepting and even enabling them. The withdrawal of our acquiescence and cooperation can render them powerless—as the old labor anthem goes, "Without our brain and muscle not a single wheel can turn."

The problem of strategy is in essence how to organize and mobilize the potential power of the people. One way is to use the power that we have within existing institutional structures. But in a grossly unequal system, voting and other institutionalized forms of action are likely to have only limited impact. From its start, the Green New Deal has combined action within the political system with direct popular action in the streets—and, uninvited, in the halls of power.

THE ANTI–GREEN NEW DEAL FORCES

Those who believe they have an interest in perpetuating the burning of fossil fuels have created powerful obstacles to a Green New Deal. Fossil fuel industries and their allies use their wealth and political clout to resist climate protection policies. They spend millions on deceitful propaganda denying the reality of climate change. They advocate for false solutions that in fact do not reduce the greenhouse emissions that cause climate change. They engage in "greenwashing," promoting policies and activities they falsely claim are "pro-environmental." They conduct environmental blackmail, threatening workers and communities with dire consequences if fossil fuel burning is restricted. They ally with "neoliberal" ideologists who oppose government climate action as impermissible interference with the "free market." They collude with efforts to corrupt and undermine democracy and thereby restrict the power of the people—those who are threatened by climate change—to take effective measures to combat it.

Those who benefit from the inequality of American society also have a powerful incentive to fight the Green New Deal. They fear the redistribution of the good things of the earth from themselves to those less fortunate—whether that takes the form of taxing the rich, ending the super-exploitation of discriminated-against groups, or empowering workers to gain greater freedom on the job and a greater share of the wealth they create.

The antidemocratic control of American politics—the so-called "democracy deficit"—comes about in a variety of ways. Big money—and the freedom to use it to acquire political power—allows those who have it to dominate the political system. Popular political participation is repressed through gerrymandering, voter exclusion, and outright terrorism. US politics is built around individual candidates and officeholders, with little effective accountability of either politicians or parties to their electorates and their promises; electing candidates provides no guarantee of implementing the policies they purported to support.

The national Republican party has made a creed of opposition to climate protection—and of measures to reduce injustice and inequality. With occasional exceptions, this is true of the main forces within the Republican party: the conservative business wing, the proto-fascist right wing, and the politically extremist religious wing. They have made the Green New Deal a scapegoat for everything they find threatening and objectionable.

While a strong wing of the Democratic party supports the Green New Deal, the party leadership has been reluctant either to advocate for the Green New Deal or to attack it directly. Instead, they have generally given some lip service to its aspirations, presented programs designed to coopt its support, and meanwhile kowtowed to corporate and fossil fuel interests, supported expansion of fossil fuel extraction, and acquiesced in a status quo of inequality and injustice. The right wing of the Democratic party, exemplified by Sen. Joe Manchin, has vigorously and often successfully opposed almost every aspect of the Green New Deal program.

STRATEGIC PERSPECTIVES

So far these forces have managed to block the Green New Deal at a national level. The strategy of the Green New Deal from Below is to outflank them. That strategy is often tacit. It is evidenced in the action of Green New Dealers, such as those described throughout this book. It is tacit in part because it has developed as a response to the conditions people are facing as much as from a preexisting theory. And because the Green New Deal from Below has rarely been identified as an entity, neither participants nor observers have had much occasion to address questions about its overall development. In this section we will try to make that tacit strategy explicit.

The Green New Deal from Below does not provide a strategy for total social transformation. That would require transformation of the basic structures of the national and world order, including capitalism and the nation-state system. The Green New Deal from Below can be part of that more extensive process of change, but it cannot subsume it.[16]

Because of the fluidity of the current US political scene, the Green New Deal from Below of necessity presents a fluid strategy. How could it be otherwise in the era of the COVID pandemic; the rise, fall, and possible resurrection of Donald Trump; the wars in Ukraine and Gaza; and the emergence of the Green New Deal itself?

The Green New Deal from Below is, in military terminology, an out-flanking strategy. Blocked in the national arena, Green New Dealers have moved to subnational arenas—hundreds of them. Here they are conducting hundreds of battles. Besides winning immediate benefits, these battles build up the Green New Deal forces and weaken their opponents. Although no one of them is likely to be decisive nationally, cumulatively these battles can shift the balance of forces and open the way toward transformative breakthroughs.

There is still a role in this strategy for national action. It includes concentrating regional and national support for particular local struggles, such as the El Paso climate referendum and the resistance to Gulf oil leases. It also involves national legislative proposals laying out Green New Deal programs for housing, healthcare, transportation, cities, and other aspects of the Green New Deal program. And it involves nationally coordinated demonstrations, tours, and other actions that show support for the Green New Deal and keep it in the public eye.

Despite its shift away from a national focus, the Green New Deal from Below retains many of the core elements of the original Green New Deal strategy. It presents an integrating program based on using climate necessity as the basis for labor and justice transformations. It brings diverse people together around that program. It organizes and mobilizes people to implement it. These elements are not sequential: they are synergistic, depending on each other.

From its inception the Green New Deal has been a fusion of action inside the institutional structure of representative democracy and of popular mobilization for direct action and civil disobedience. Indeed, it was initiated by the confluence of a civilly disobedient occupation of the office of the Democratic party leader of the US House of Representatives and the initial legislative proposal for a Green New Deal presented by a newly elected member of Congress. This is a "pincers strategy" response to the inequality of power and the democracy deficit. Both Sunrise and Alexandra Ocasio-Cortez continue to advocate for—and practice—synthesizing action inside and outside "the system."

The political strategy of the Green New Deal from Below exemplifies this confluence. It aims to capture governmental power—and more broadly institutional power. Legislators, mayors, and governors have been elected under its banner. At the same time it has organized to lead and pressure politicians, institutions, and their leaders. It has organized people to act on their own in civil society—from neighborhoods creating their own solar gardens to unions establishing green training programs to coalitions blocking fossil fuel pipelines. And it has continued to use direct action and civil disobedience when politicians, governments, and corporations won't stop destroying the planet and exacerbating injustice and inequality. While there are inevitably tensions among these various forms of action, institutional and noninstitutional forms of action have been increasingly intertwined in American politics.[17]

While the focus of the Green New Deal and the Green New Deal from Below have been national and subnational, they interface with global arenas in a variety of ways. One origin of the current Green New Deal was in an earlier Global Green New Deal. And today the Green New Deal is not just a local or even a national movement, but a global program being fought for in many countries around the world. Local Green New Deal initiatives are therefore also part of a wider effort to establish a just and sustainable world order. For example, California, Maine, Massachusetts, Oregon, Rhode Island, and Washington are part of the global Under2 Coalition, which brings together over 270 subnational governments—representing 1.75 billion people and 50 percent of the global economy—to pursue climate protection policies.

STRATEGIC OBJECTIVES

The action of Green New Dealers expresses strategic objectives, tacit or explicit, that implement aspects of the Green New Deal, develop the Green New Deal forces, and shift the balance between pro- and anti-Green New Deal forces. Not every action is likely to accomplish all these objectives, but most actions aim to accomplish more than one of them at the same time.

The first set of objectives aim to make concrete changes that accomplish the goals of the Green New Deal. Reducing greenhouse gas emissions is an objective of many actions, ranging from insulating urban housing to shutting down mines and power plants. Reducing injustice and inequality is similarly a goal of actions ranging from ensuring access to climate jobs for those who have been excluded from them to putting low-emission transit in vehicle-polluted neighborhoods. Another objective is improving the position of workers through such means as incorporating labor rights in climate legislation, establishing training and job ladders for climate jobs, and actively supporting the right of workers to organize and exercise their power. Green New Deal projects usually aim to accomplish these purposes synergistically, for example by designing climate-protection policies that also reduce injustice and empower workers on the job.

Green New Deal projects generally embody another set of objectives: educating and inspiring people. They do so through direct educational efforts like workshops, community forums, webinars, educational materials, and making known what has been accomplished elsewhere. Many programs involve basic education on climate, justice, and labor issues.

Campaigns like those for the Washington and Illinois clean energy and jobs acts involved long and extensive educational campaigns. But much of the inspiration and education provided by the Green New Deal takes the form of expanding the limits of what is believed to be possible by showing the power of people when they organize and by constructing exemplary projects that inspire people to believe that more is possible. These exemplary actions produce powerful evidence for the value and feasibility of the Green New Deal. Call it education through action.

Green New Deal initiatives also support a shift in power. They bring into being organized constituencies and coalitions that can serve as political building blocks for more extensive Green New Deal campaigns. Green New Deal projects also create institutional building blocks, ranging from energy systems to transportation networks, that can become part of the economic and social infrastructure of a wider Green New Deal. They help overcome the divisions and contradictions that weaken popular forces by engaging them around projects that embody common interests and a common vision. And they reduce the power of the anti–Green New Deal forces by dividing them, disorienting them, undermining their pillars of support, and even at times converting them.

The fight for the Green New Deal is inevitably entwined with the fight for democracy. Green New Deal initiatives provide models for—and show the benefits of—popular democracy. Green New Deal from Below projects show that people can make concrete gains that benefit their real lives. They thereby contribute to building a base to protect and extend governance of, by, and for the people at every level. They represent a local embodiment of participatory democracy. And they create bastions for reinforcing representative democracy against fascism in the national arena.

The program of the Green New Deal, beneficial as it may be, is not in itself adequate to solve the deeper structural problems of an unjust and self-destructive world order. One of its strategic objectives, therefore, must be to open the way to wider, more radical forms of change.

STRATEGY ON THE GROUND

Green New Dealers seek to realize these objectives in a world that is not of their own making, where powerful forces oppose their efforts. They have developed a multipronged strategy adapted to actually existing power relations.

The federal system of government provides obvious arenas for initiatives "from below." While the power of state, county, and municipal governments is circumscribed by law and by the power of higher jurisdictions, experience shows that in fact the division of powers is flexible and can itself be challenged and changed. Cities and states have often won power over matters that they once seemed excluded from. For example, in the original New Deal era states engaged in such previously excluded programs as bank deposit insurance systems, publicly owned utilities, mortgage moratoriums; and bans on antistrike injunctions.[18] Green New Deal states have similarly expanded their reach into previously federal domains such as regulation of tailpipe emissions and regional energy planning. And even within the established division of powers, Green New Deal states and municipalities have found extensive space for implementing energy, housing, transportation, healthcare, and many other dimensions of the Green New Deal program.

Acting in these arenas requires adapting strategy to the specific realities of the situation. For example, the powers of mayors, city councils, governors, and legislatures vary both constitutionally and in practice; what may seem unimaginable in one location may be achievable in another. Green New Dealers have used not only the institutions of representative democracy but also, where they exist, institutions of direct democracy, for example in the "just transition" initiative in Washington State and several initiatives in California. Federalism and direct democracy provide a certain measure of dual power, in which initiatives can be taken even though they contradict national policy.

But Green New Deal from Below arenas are not limited to those established by governmental jurisdictions. Self-organization in civil society also provides locations in which power is developed and exercised. Unions, neighborhood organizations, ethnic and cultural groups, and other constituencies provide venues in which Green New Deal ideas and programs are incubated. And they also can themselves implement Green New Deal programs like union training programs for green building maintenance, neighborhood-initiated solar gardens, and the plans for a community microgrid in Boston's Chinatown.

Green New Dealers operate within, alongside, and against the institutions and personnel of the political system. They are often active in supporting candidates. They are often members of political parties, usually the Democratic party but occasionally third parties of various kinds. (If Green New Dealers are active anywhere in the Republican party it's a well-kept secret.) In some locations they form an identifiable Green New Deal wing of the Democratic party. Candidates for mayor, governor, state legislator, and city councilor have run on Green New Deal platforms, for example Mayor Michelle Wu in Boston and Governor Jay Inslee in Washington. Pro–Green New Deal politicians have played a powerful role in building support for and implementing Green New Deal programs.

But the relation to elected officials and other political leaders varies. Politicians' motives can range from personal commitment to the purest opportunism. In some cases, such as Mayor Wu in Boston, an elected official played a major role in bringing the coalition together and was widely accepted as the leader of the Green New Deal. In Somerville elected officials participated in forums and other activities developed by the coalition but organized labor remained in the lead. Frequently grassroots groups and coalitions recruit politicians to be advocates and to serve as champions for action in the legislative arena. In California Gov. Gavin Newsom sat on the fence and was largely a target for pressure until at the last minute he endorsed a wide swath of Green New Deal–style legislation; thereafter he backtracked on some of the policies he himself had supported.

The initiative and support for Green New Deal programs often comes less from politicians than from coalitions of civil society organizations outside the formal political system. Even where political leaders have championed a Green New Deal vision, the impetus for actually designing and implementing Green New Deals has often come from forces in civil society. And at times Green New Dealers have had to pressure and even oppose political leaders who put themselves forward as champions of the Green New Deal—for example, self-proclaimed New York Green New Deal governor Andrew Cuomo, whose programs many Green New Dealers found woefully inadequate.

It should come as no surprise that "red," Republican-led cities and states are less than hospitable to Green New Deal policies. But it may be more surprising that Green New Deal–type initiatives are nonetheless happening there—generally initiated by unions and civil society groups not based in the political arena. Some examples have been described in this book. In West Virginia, the United Mine Workers helped initiate an electric battery factory that will employ 350 workers; the union will recruit and train dislocated miners to be the factory's first production workers. The Gulf South for a Green New Deal has organized hubs in Texas, Louisiana, Mississippi, Alabama, and Florida that bring together existing state and local organizations to define state Green New Deal priorities and organize support for action to realize them. There are many other examples as well. Solidly Republican Nebraska, for example, recently adopted net-zero carbon goals across the electricity sector.[19] And in Dallas, a year-long campaign by the youth-led climate organization Sunrise—whose sit-in had kicked off the original Green New Deal—led the city council to let students in grades 6 through 12 ride on the Dallas Area Rapid Transit (DART) for free.[20]

From its inception the Green New Deal has had an ambiguous and multifaceted relationship with the Democratic party. Elements of the Democratic party have supported, opposed, or maintained neutrality on the vision and policy of the Green New Deal. Green New Dealers have variously fought against, won over, and captured Democratic party strongholds. Despite this tactical diversity, however, part of the Green New Deal's overall strategy is to transform the Democratic party both locally and nationally. This involves building a pro–Green New Deal bloc in the Democratic party. And it involves using the Green New Deal as a vehicle for bridging the environmentalist-labor divide in the Democratic party.

Activists involved with the Seattle Green New Deal articulated many of these themes as they reflected on their experience of first winning and then implementing their city's Green New Deal program. Youth leader Syris Valentine said, "This wouldn't have happened without a strong grassroots campaign." And Seattle 350 member Jess Wallach believes their rapid success was due in equal parts to building robust relationships among community partners, maintaining public pressure on city officials, and forging an alliance with a supportive city council member. Taken together, these actions created a strong "inside-outside game."

When once-divided groups reach out to each other, explore common needs and interests, and start cooperating for common objectives they thereby create new forms of social action. That is the process that I have elsewhere called the emergence of "common preservation."[21]

WORKING ON A WORLD

The Green New Deal is driven by a sense of urgency. There is the urgency of the climate emergency. There is also the urgency of people who are suffering and even dying as a result of injustice. The original Green New Deal proposal responded to this urgency by calling for a ten-year mobilization that would reconstruct American society and economy as dramatically as the New Deal and mobilization for World War II.

The Green New Deal arose in a sea of hopelessness and despair. It pointed the way toward viable alternatives to realities that evoked that hopelessness and despair. The Green New Deal from Below provides people a way to start building those alternatives day by day where they live and work.

In the introduction we cited the world historian Arnold Toynbee on how great civilizational changes occur. The existing leadership of existing institutions face new challenges—and fail to change to meet them. But a "creative minority" may arise that proposes and begins to implement new solutions. Those building the Green New Deal are creating such new solutions—from below.

There may be no way to know if those solutions will be good enough or come soon enough. But we can share the experience that songwriter Iris Dement describes in her song "Workin' on a World." She tells how she started waking every morning "filled with sadness, fear, and dread." The world she took for granted was "crashing to the ground." But she got to thinking of the ones who came before and of all the sacrifices they made—sacrifices that opened doors for her that they never got to see.

> Now I'm working on a world I may never see
> I'm joining forces with the warriors of love
> Who came before and will follow you and me
> I get up in the morning knowing I'm privileged just to be
> Working on a world I may never see.

Whether we will see the world of the Green New Deal fully realized, in the Green New Deal from Below we can see that right now we are making a part of that world.

NOTES

Introduction

1. "Ocasio-Cortez Thanks Labour for 'Leading the World' by Adopting a Green New Deal," *Morning Star*, September 25, 2019, https://morningstaronline.co.uk/article/b/ocasio-cortez-thanks-labour-'leading-world'-adopting-green-new-deal.

2. Abel Gustafson et al., "The Green New Deal has Strong Bipartisan Support," Yale Program on Climate Change, December 14, 2018, https://climatecommunication.yale.edu/publications/the-green-new-deal-has-strong-bipartisan-support/. For a list of supporters and opponents see "Green New Deal," *Wikipedia*, https://en.wikipedia.org/wiki/Green_New_Deal.

3. Grace Adcox and Catherine Fraser, "The Green New Deal Is Still Incredibly Popular," Data for Progress, February 6, 2024, https://www.dataforprogress.org/blog/2024/2/6/five-years-after-its-introduction-the-green-new-deal-is-still-incredibly-popular.

4. "The Thrive Agenda," Green New Deal Network, https://www.greennewdealnetwork.org.

5. For background on the evolution of the Green New Deal as a public issue see: John Feffer, "What Remains of the US Green New Deal?" *Foreign Policy in Focus*, May 5, 2022, https://fpif.org/what-remains-of-the-u-s-green-new-deal/; and Aviva Chomsky, "A Brief History of the Green New Deal So Far," *Literary Hub*, https://lithub.com/a-brief-history-of-the-green-new-deal-so-far/.

6. Marcela Mulholland and Saul Levin, "The Green New Deal is Incredibly Popular," *Data for Progress*, March 11, 2022, https://www.dataforprogress.org/blog/2022/3/11/the-green-new-deal-is-incredibly-popular. For more on support for the Green New Deal as of early 2023 see Jeremy Brecher, "Commentary: The Green New Deal: The Current State of Play," Labor Network for Sustainability, February 15, 2023, https://www.labor4sustainability.org/strike/commentary-the-green-new-deal-the-current-state-of-play/.

Chapter 1. The Green New Deal in the Cities

1. "Planning for a Boston Green New Deal and Just Recovery," Office of Boston City Councilor Michelle Wu, August 2020.

2. "Boston Lawmaker, Eying a Mayoral Run, Maps Out a Nordic-Style Climate Haven," *HuffPost*, August 17, 2020, https://www.huffpost.com/entry/boston-climate-michelle-wu_n_5f3715f9c5b6959911e48e07.

3. "Planning for a Boston Green New Deal."

4. Ellen Gerst, "Boston City Council Passes Resolution Supporting Green New Deal," *Boston Magazine*, April 11, 2019, https://www.bostonmagazine.com/news/2019/04/11/city-council-green-new-deal/.

5. Katelyn Weisbrod, "Boston Progressives Expand the Green New Deal to Include Justice Concerns and Pandemic Recovery," *Inside Climate News*, September 28, 2020, https://insideclimatenews.org/news/08092020/boston-progressives-green-new-deal-justice-health-michelle-wu/.

6. "Boston Lawmaker."

7. For more on the "Blue New Deal," see Jeremy Brecher, "The Blue New Deal: Making a Living on a Living Ocean," Labor Network for Sustainability, May 5, 2021, https://www.labor4sustainability.org/strike/the-blue-new-deal-making-a-living-on-a-living-ocean/.

8. "Boston Lawmaker."

9. Ryan O'Donnell, Gustavo Sanchez, and Brian Burton, "Voters Want Michelle Wu to Be the Next Mayor of Boston," *Data for Progress*, October 21, 2021, https://www.dataforprogress.org/blog/2021/10/21/michelle-wu-leads-boston-mayoral-race.

10. John Nichols, "Michelle Wu: Cities Must Lead for the Green New Deal," *The Nation*, December 14, 2021, https://www.thenation.com/article/politics/qa-michelle-wu/.

11. "New Steps to Reduce Vehicle Emissions in Boston," *Boston.gov*, December 13, 2021, https://www.boston.gov/news/new-steps-reduce-vehicle-emissions-boston.

12. "Progress Made toward Electrifying City of Boston Vehicle Fleet," *Boston.gov*, April 6, 2022, https://www.boston.gov/news/progress-made-toward-electrifying-city-boston-vehicle-fleet.

13. "Mayor Wu Signs Ordinance to Divest City Funds from the Fossil Fuel Industry," *Boston.gov*, December 1, 2021, https://www.boston.gov/news/mayor-wu-signs-ordinance-divest-city-funds-fossil-fuel-industry.

14. "Mayor Wu Announces Critical Action to Mitigate Extreme Heat in Environmental Justice Communities," *Boston Orange*, April 22, 2022, https://www.bostonorange.com/2022/04/mayor-wu-announces-critical-actions-to.html.

15. John Lynds, "Wu Announces New Solar-Power Pilot Program in Eastie," *East Boston Times-Free Press*, May 11, 2022, https://eastietimes.com/2022/05/11/wu-announces-new-solar-power-pilot-program-in-eastie/.

16. "Mayor Wu Announces Strategies to Enhance Coastal Resilience in East Boston and Charlestown," *Boston.gov*, August 23, 2022, https://pier5.org/2022/08/23/mayor-wu-announces-strategies-to-enhance-coastal-resilience-in-east-boston-and-charlestown-boston-gov/.

17. "Mayor Wu Unveils First City Budget and $350 Million Federal Spending Plan," *Boston.gov*, April 13, 2022, https://www.boston.gov/news/mayor-wu-unveils-first-city-budget-and-350-million-federal-spending-plan.

18. "Green New Deal for Boston Public Schools Launched," *Boston.gov*, May 12, 2022, https://www.boston.gov/news/green-new-deal-boston-public-schools-launched.

19. "$17 Million BPS Food Service Contract Announced with Roxbury-Based, Black-Owned Business," *Boston.gov*, May 18, 2022, https://www.boston.gov/news/

17-million-bps-food-service-contract-announced-roxbury-based-black-owned-business. For Boston's Good Food Purchasing Program, see https://goodfoodcities.org/portfolio/boston/.

20. "Wu Announces Cabinet for Worker Empowerment," *Beacon Hill Times*, September 8, 2022, https://beaconhilltimes.com/2022/09/08/wu-announces-cabinet-for-worker-empowerment/.

21. "Alex Lawrence Named Chief People Officer; Ashley Groffenberger Appointed Chief Financial Officer," *Boston.gov*, June 13, 2022, https://www.boston.gov/news/alex-lawrence-named-chief-people-officer-ashley-groffenberger-appointed-chief-financial.

22. "Executive Director of Youth Green Jobs Initiative Named," *Boston.gov*, February 14, 2022, https://www.boston.gov/news/executive-director-youth-green-jobs-initiative-named.

23. "Graduation of Boston's Inaugural PowerCorpsBOS Cohort Celebrated," *Boston.gov*, December 23, 2022, https://www.boston.gov/news/graduation-bostons-inaugural-powercorpsbos-cohort-celebrated.

24. Roberto Scalese and Walter Wuthmann, "Wu Sets Sights on Housing, Schools in First State of the City Address," *WBUR*, January 25, 2023, https://www.wbur.org/news/2023/01/25/boston-mayor-michelle-wu-state-of-the-city; and "READ: Boston Mayor Michelle Wu's First State of the City Address," *WBUR*, January 25, 2023.

25. Boston Green New Deal Coalition, https://www.bostongndcoalition.org/.

26. Saraya Wintersmith, "Mayor Wu Says Staffing and Contract Talks Consumed a Lot of Her First Year," *WGBH*, November 16, 2022, https://www.wgbh.org/news/politics/2022/11/16/mayor-wu-says-staffing-and-contract-talks-consumed-a-lot-of-her-first-year.

27. Nichols, "Michelle Wu: Cities Must Lead for the Green New Deal."

28. LA's Green New Deal, *Annual Report*, 2021–2022, https://plan.lamayor.org/sites/default/files/GND_Annual_Report_2022.pdf.

29. "Sustainability," 18, https://plan.lamayor.org/sites/default/files/pLAn_2019_final.pdf.

30. "Sustainability," 24, https://plan.lamayor.org/sites/default/files/pLAn_2019_final.pdf.

31. Elizabeth Fuller, "L.A.s Green New Deal—What It Is and How We're Doing," *Larchmont Buzz-Hancock Park News*, December 8, 2022, https://www.larchmontbuzz.com/featured-stories-larchmont-village/l-a-s-green-new-deal-what-it-is-and-how-were-doing/.

32. LA's Green New Deal, *Annual Report*, 2021–2022.

33. Susan Carpenter, "LA Is Largely on Track to Meet Green New Deal Goals," *Spectrum News*, May 31, 2022, https://spectrumnews1.com/ca/la-west/environment/2022/05/31/la-is-largely-on-track-meeting-green-new-deal-goals.

34. "Mayor Garcetti Signs Series of Environmental Laws on His Last Day in Office," *ABC7 Los Angeles*, December 1, 2022, https://abc7.com/eric-garcetti-mayor-oil-drilling-green-laws/12559725/.

35. "LA Council Bans Gas in New Buildings in 'First Step' toward Electrification," *KFI AM 640*, December 7, 2022, https://kfiam640.iheart.com/content/2022-12-07-la-council-bans-gas-in-new-buildings-in-first-step-toward-electrification/.

36. Syris Valentine, "What Seattle's Green New Deal Reveals about Creating Inclusive, Regenerative, Just Communities," *Grist*, January 27, 2023, https://grist.org/

looking-forward/what-seattles-green-new-deal-reveals-about-creating-inclusive-regenerative-just-communities/.

37. Valentine, "What Seattle's Green New Deal Reveals."

38. "Seattle for a Green New Deal," https://twitter.com/SeattleGND.

39. "Seattle for a Green New Deal," https://350seattle.org/solutions-green-new-deal/.

40. "Climate Agenda for 2024," SeattleClimate.org, https://www.seattleclimate.org/strategies/governments/seattle.

41. Daniel Beekman, "Seattle City Council Passes 'JumpStart' Tax on High Salaries Paid by Big Businesses," *Seattle Times,* July 7, 2020, https://www.seattletimes.com/seattle-news/politics/seattle-city-council-passes-new-jumpstart-tax-on-high-salaries-paid-by-big-businesses/.

42. Seattle Office of Sustainability and Environment, "Green New Deal Oversight Board 2022 and 2023 Budget Recommendations," June 2, 2022, https://drive.google.com/file/d/1AsuaZPIAaD_M4bGPQzOWFvSJoJfLr8xS/view.

43. Jamie Housen, "Mayor Harrell Signs $6.5 Million in 2022 Green New Deal Opportunity Fund," Office of the Mayor, September 22, 2022, https://harrell.seattle.gov/2022/09/22/mayor-harrell-signs-6-5-million-in-2022-green-new-deal-opportunity-fund/.

44. Valentine, "What Seattle's Green New Deal Reveals."

45. "Climate News 2.4.23," *SeattleClimate.org,* https://www.seattleclimate.org/news.

46. C40 Cities, "Building a Climate Movement," https://www.c40.org/awards/building-a-climate-movement/.

47. "City Clean Energy Scorecard," ACEEE, December 2021, https://www.aceee.org/research-report/u2107.

48. "Cities' Clean-Energy Equity Efforts Are Mixed, but Leaders Point the Way Forward," ACEEE, January 13, 2022, https://www.aceee.org/blog-post/2022/01/cities-clean-energy-equity-efforts-are-mixed-leaders-point-way-forward.

Chapter 2. The Green New Deal in the States

1. For reviews of climate policies by state: ClimateXChange, https://climate-xchange.org/mission-impact/; "State Climate Policy Maps," Center for Climate and Energy Solutions, https://www.c2es.org/content/state-climate-policy/; "Policy Databases," United States Climate Alliance, http://www.usclimatealliance.org/state-climate-energy-policies; State and Local Climate Change Resource Center, Columbia Law School Sabin Center for Climate Change Law, https://climate.law.columbia.edu/content/state-and-local-climate-change-resource-center; "Spot for Clean Energy," https://spotforcleanenergy.org.

2. Julian Spector, "Hawaii Has a One-Year Deadline to Ditch Coal," *Canary Media,* October 25, 2021, https://www.canarymedia.com/articles/clean-energy/hawaii-has-a-one-year-deadline-to-ditch-coal.

3. Hallie Golden, "Hawaii to Close Its Only Coal Power Plant in a Step toward Renewable Energy," *Guardian,* August 31, 2022, https://www.theguardian.com/us-news/2022/aug/31/hawaii-close-coal-power-plant-renewable-energy.

4. Julian Spector, "Hawaii's Biggest Solar+Battery Plant Comes Online," *Canary Media,* August 15, 2022, https://www.canarymedia.com/articles/solar/hawaiis-biggest-solar-battery-plant-comes-online-just-in-time.

5. Spector, "Hawaii's Biggest Solar+Battery Plant Comes Online."

6. Julian Spector, "People Power: Hawaii Utility Wants to Pay Households," *Canary Media*, February 14, 2022, https://www.canarymedia.como /articles/batteries/people-power-hawaii-utility-wants-to-pay-households-to-share-clean-energy.

7. Golden, "Hawaii to Close Its Only Coal Power Plant in a Step toward Renewable Energy."

8. Julian Spector, "Hawaii Is About to Get Rid of Coal Power for Good," *Canary Media*, August 22, 2022, https://www.canarymedia.com/articles/fossil-fuels/hawaii -is-about-to-get-rid-of-coal-power-for-good.

9. Spector, "Hawaii Has a One-Year Deadline to Ditch Coal."

10. Julian Spector, "Hawaii Building Huge New Battery, Bidding Farewell to Coal," *Canary Media*, August 18, 2021, https://www.canarymedia.com/articles/energy-storage/hawaii-building-huge-new-battery-bidding-farewell-to-coal.

11. "Hawai'i 2050 Sustainability Plan," Hawaii State Office of Planning, June 2021, 15, https://hawaii2050.hawaii.gov/wp-content/uploads/2021/07/FINAL-Hawaii -2050-Sustainability-Plan-web-1.pdf.

12. H.B. No. 2487, "Relating to a Hawaii Green New Deal," https://www.capitol .hawaii.gov/session2020/bills/HB2487_.HTM.

13. The inside account of organizing for the legislation is based on Sarah Spengeman, "Illinois' Climate and Equitable Jobs Act Is a Roadmap for Climate Justice Policy," *Stamford Social Innovation Review*, March 24, 2022, https://ssir.org/articles/entry/legislating_for_climate_justice_starts_with_listening; and Sarah Spengeman, "A Bigger Tent Delivers Stronger Wins for Climate: The Lesson from Illinois," *Revelator*, January 14, 2022, https://therevelator.org/bigger-tent-climate-illinois/.

14. Kari Lydersen, "Union-backed Bill Calls for Prevailing Wage for Illinois Renewable Projects," *Energy News Network*, April 14, 2021, https://energynews.us/2021/04/14/union-backed-bill-calls-for-prevailing-wage-for-illinois-renewable-projects/.

15. Lydersen, "Union-backed Bill."

16. Liza Featherstone, "Illinois Just Won a Big Green Jobs Victory," *Jacobin*, September 2021, https://jacobin.com/2021/09/illinois-green-new-deal-jobs-labor-nuclear.

17. "Illinois Renewable Energy Growth Surges in the Months after Climate and Equitable Jobs Act Signed," Solar Energy Industries Association press release, February 15, 2022, https://www.seia.org/news/illinois-renewable-energy-growth-surges -months-after-climate-and-equitable-jobs-act-signed.

18. Daniel Farber, "State Governmental Leadership in U.S. Climate Policy," Wilson Center, June 23, 2021, https://www.wilsoncenter.org/article/state-governmental -leadership-us-climate-policy.

19. Unless otherwise noted, this account is based on Brad Plumer, "California Approves a Wave of Aggressive New Climate Measures," *New York Times*, September 1, 2022, https://www.nytimes.com/2022/09/01/climate/california-lawmakers-climate -legislation.html; Kathleen Ronayne, "California Democrats Cap Legislative Year with Climate Wins," *NBC Bay Area*, September 2, 2022, https://www.nbcbayarea.com/news/california/california-climate-wins/2992599/; and Nadia Lopez, "California Approves Big Climate Change Steps—but One Ambitious One Fails," *CalMatters*, September 1, 2022; updated September 16, 2022, https://calmatters.org/environment/2022/09/california-climate-change-legislature/.

20. Emily Pontecorvo, "How a Debate over Carbon Capture Derailed California's Landmark Climate Bill," *Grist*, December 15, 2021, https://grist.org/politics/carbon-capture-why-california-cant-fill-the-net-zero-gap-in-its-climate-strategy/.

21. Common Ground, https://commongroundca.org.

22. Collin Rees, "California Becomes Largest Oil Producer in World to Commit to Total Oil Phaseout, Ban Fracking—but Not Soon Enough," *Oil Change International*, April 23, 2022, http://priceofoil.org/2021/04/23/last-chance-alliance-california-fracking-oil-phase-out/.

23. Dani Anguiano, "California Bans Sales of New Gasoline-Powered Vehicles by 2035 in Milestone Step," *Guardian*, August 25, 2022, https://www.theguardian.com/us-news/2022/aug/24/california-ban-sales-gas-powered-cars-2035.

24. "CEC Adopts Historic California Offshore Wind Goals, Enough to Power Upwards of 25 Million Homes," *HomeNewsroom*, August 10. 2022, https://www.energy.ca.gov/news/2022-08/cec-adopts-historic-california-offshore-wind-goals-enough-power-upwards-25.

25. Julian Spector, "California Is Finally Unlocking Community Solar for the Masses," *Canary Media*, September 8, 2022, https://www.canarymedia.com/articles/solar/california-is-finally-unlocking-community-solar-for-the-masses.

26. "Governor Newsom Signs Sweeping Climate Measures, Ushering in New Era of World-Leading Climate Action," Office of Governor Gavin Newsom, September 16, 2022, https://www.gov.ca.gov/2022/09/16/governor-newsom-signs-sweeping-climate-measures-ushering-in-new-era-of-world-leading-climate-action/. This release includes a list of forty climate-related bills passed by the legislature and signed by the governor in 2022.

27. Romy Varghese, "California Sees Record $97.5 Billion Surplus, Driven by the Rich," *Bloomberg*, May 5, 2022, updated May 13, 2022, https://www.bloomberg.com/news/articles/2022-05-13/california-governor-sees-record-97-5-billion-operating-surplus.

28. Maanvi Singh, "California Governor Caught in Eye of Storm over Climate Budget Cuts," *Guardian*, January 12, 2023, https://www.theguardian.com/us-news/2023/jan/12/california-governor-gavin-newsom-climate-budget-cut.

29. Kelly McCarthy, "California Becomes 1st State to Offer Free Meals at School for Kids," *Good Morning America*, August 12, 2022, https://www.goodmorningamerica.com/food/story/california-1st-state-offer-free-meals-school-kids-88290584.

30. Victoria Namkung, "'The Kids Are Just Happier': Could California's Universal School Meal Program Start a Trend?" *Guardian*, September 26, 2022, https://www.theguardian.com/environment/2022/sep/26/free-school-meals-california-universal.

31. Michael Sainato, "California's Fast-Food Industry Calls for Referendum on New Labor Legislation," *Guardian*, September 18, 2022, https://www.theguardian.com/us-news/2022/sep/18/california-labor-law-fast-food-industry-referendum.

32. Chris Nichols, Nicole Nixon, and Kris Hooks, "Here Are the Major Bills Passed by California Lawmakers in 2022," *capradio.org*, September 1, 2022, https://www.capradio.org/articles/2022/09/01/here-are-the-major-bills-passed-by-california-lawmakers-in-2022/; Ashley Zavala, "Gov. Newsom Signs Bills to Turn Unused Retail Areas into Housing," *KCRA*, September 28, 2022, https://www.kcra.com/article/gov-newsom-to-sign-bills-to-turn-unused-retail-areas-into-housing/41427984#.

33. Nichols, Nixon, and Hooks, "Here Are the Major Bills Passed by California Lawmakers in 2022."

34. Kevin Stark, "California Releases Sweeping New Climate Action Plan to Reach Carbon Neutrality," *KQED*, November 16, 2022, https://www.kqed.org/science/1980792/a-roadmap-to-carbon-neutrality-california-releases-sweeping-new-climate-action-plan.

35. Ellie Cohen and Dan Kammen, "Two Fixes to Bolster California's New Climate Blueprint," *CalMatters*, November 11, 2022, https://calmatters.org/commentary/2022/11/california-climate-air-resources-board-scoping-plan/.

36. "Isaac Bryan Introduces Bill to Achieve Justice40 in California for Historically Underfunded Communities," California Green New Deal Coalition, February 17, 2022, https://greennewdealca.org/news/isaac-bryan-introduces-bill-to-achieve-justice40-in-california-for-historically-underfunded-communities/.

37. Lissa Harris, "In a World of Vague Climate Targets, New York Has a Plan—Almost," *River Newsroom*, November 19, 2021, https://therivernewsroom.com/climate-action-council-draft-scoping-plan/.

38. "Climate Action Council Scoping Plan," *New York State*, January 1, 2022, https://climate.ny.gov/Resources/Draft-Scoping-Plan.

39. Dennis Pillion, "Mississippi Opts to Encourage Solar Panels, as Alabama Fights to Keep Solar Fee," *al.com*, July 16, 2022, https://www.al.com/news/2022/07/mississippi-opts-to-encourage-solar-panels-as-alabama-fights-to-keep-solar-fee.html.

40. Pillion, "Mississippi Opts to Encourage Solar Panels."

41. Kurt Erickson, "As California Moves Ahead on Electric Vehicles, Missouri, Other States Try to Pull Plug," *stltoday.com*, August 25, 2022, https://www.stltoday.com/news/local/govt-and-politics/as-california-moves-ahead-on-electric-vehicles-missouri-other-states-try-to-pull-plug/article_6d990642-156f-57ed-8b51-3563189c4e7b.html.

42. For state New Deal programs, see Jeremy Brecher, "States of Change: What the Green New Deal Can Learn from the New Deal in the States," Labor Network for Sustainability, November 9, 2020, https://www.labor4sustainability.org/files/LNSpdf_States_nov2020.pdf.

43. David Roberts, "Illinois' Brilliant New Climate, Jobs, and Justice Bill," *Volts,* September 22, 2021, https://www.volts.wtf/p/illinois-brilliant-new-climate-jobs.

44. Daniel Farber, "State Governmental Leadership in U.S. Climate Policy," Wilson Center, June 23, 2021, https://www.wilsoncenter.org/article/state-governmental-leadership-us-climate-policy. For US Climate Alliance see http://www.usclimatealliance.org. For Under2 Coalition see https://www.theclimategroup.org/under2-coalition.

Chapter 3. Unions Making a Green New Deal

1. For contemporary labor climate coalitions, see Todd E. Vachon, *Clean Air and Good Jobs: U.S. Labor and the Struggle for Climate Justice* (Philadelphia: Temple University Press, 2023). For older studies of labor climate coalitions, see Brian Mayer, *Blue-Green Coalitions: Fighting for Safe Workplaces and Healthy Communities* (Ithaca, NY: Cornell University Press, 2009); and Brian Obach, *Labor and the Environmental Movement: The Quest for Common Ground* (Cambridge, MA: MIT Press, 2004). For social movements and coalition more generally see Nella Van Dyke and Holly J. McCammon, *Strategic Alliances: Coalition Building and Social Movements* (Minneapolis: University of Minnesota Press, 2010).

2. "Energy Startup to Bring Electric Battery Factory to W.Va.," *AP*, March 17, 2022, https://umwa.org/news-media/news/energy-startup-to-bring-electric-battery-factory-to-w-va/.

3. "IBEW 569 Position on Reaching 100% Renewable Energy," IBEW Local 569, https://ibew569.org/news/ibew-569-position-reaching-100-renewable-energy.

4. "Energy Independence," IBEW Local 569, https://www.ibew569.org/energy-independence.

5. Interview with Micah Mitrosky, Labor Network for Sustainability, June 2017, https://www.labor4sustainability.org/uncategorized/san-diego-areas-local-569-is-helping-to-lead-the-transition-to-a-low-carbon-economy/.

6. "IBEW 569 Position on Decarbonization & Electrification," IBEW Local 569, https://www.ibew569.org/news/news-ibew-569-position-decarbonization-electrification/.

7. "IBEW 569 Position on Reaching 100% Renewable Energy."

8. "IBEW 569 Position on Decarbonization & Electrification."

9. Mitrosky interview.

10. "IBEW 569 Position on Reaching 100% Renewable Energy."

11. Renewable Energy Certificates allow a company to meet its minimum renewable electricity requirements by purchasing the certificates rather than by increasing its renewable energy or reducing its fossil fuel use.

12. Terry O'Sullivan, "LIUNA on the Green New Deal," LIUNA, https://www.liuna.org/news/story/liuna-on-the-green-new-deal.

13. "Great Projects," LIUNA, https://www.liuna.org/great-projects.

14. Jeremy Brecher, "First U.S. Union-Authorized Climate Strike?" Labor Network for Sustainability, February 29, 2020, https://www.labor4sustainability.org/strike/first-u-s-union-authorized-climate-strike/.

15. "SEIU Local 26 Janitorial Bargaining Update #3," http://www.seiu26.org/files/2019/11/C_Janitorial_Bargaining_3_14Nov2019.pdf.

16. "First Union-backed Strike to Protect the Climate Wins Contract," Labor Network for Sustainability, February 29, 2020, https://www.labor4sustainability.org/articles/first-union-backed-strike-to-protect-the-climate-wins-contract/.

17. "Commercial Janitorial SEIU Local 26 Janitors Timeline," https://www.seiu26.org/commercial-janitorial.

18. Catherine Carlock, "The Green Line Is Coming to Somerville. Big Changes Are Coming Too," *Boston Globe*, March 2, 2022.

19. Based on "Remarks of Brian Doherty at Summerville Stands Together Unity Breakfast," December 20, 2021, *YouTube*, https://www.youtube.com/watch?v=U5NN-xKdMLQ.

20. "Somerville Stands Together," https://somervillestandstogether.com. For more on the origins of SST, see Jim Clark, "Coalition Calls on City to Support Good Jobs, Affordable Housing, Contracts," *Somerville Times*, May 2, 2018, https://www.thesomervilletimes.com/archives/83486; and "Somerville Stands Together for Good Jobs, Affordable Housing," *Somerville Times*, July 25, 2018, https://www.thesomervilletimes.com/archives/85387.

21. Union Square Neighborhood Council, "USNC Community Benefits Agreement Term Sheet," August 13, 2019.

22. "Somerville Climate Further Forward Plan," Somerville Stands Together, June 21, 2021.

23. "A Green New Deal for Somerville—Getting the City 'Shovel Ready' for State and Federal Support to Meet Climate and Equity Goals. A Position Statement of Somerville Stands Together," June 2021.

24. "A Green New Deal for Somerville."

25. "Resolution in Support of the Green New Deal, Student Climate Strikes, and a Climate Action Plan for Rutgers University," Rutgers AAUP-AFT, March 10, 2020, https://rutgersaaup.org/green-new-deal-support/.

26. "Resolution in Support of Green New Deal," American Federation of Teachers, 2020, https://www.aft.org/resolution/support-green-new-deal.

27. Aristide Economopoulos, "Hundreds March during Climate Strike at Rutgers in New Brunswick," *NJAdvance Media for NJ.com*, September 20, 2019, https://www .nj.com/news/g66l-2019/09/51ca3476e81266/hundreds-march-during-climate-strike -at-rutgers-in-new-brunswick-photos.html.

28. "'Years in the Making': Rutgers Union Celebrates Fossil Fuel Divestment," Rutgers AAUP-AFT, March 9, 2021, https://rutgersaaup.org/years-in-the-making -rutgers-union-celebrates-fossil-fuel-divestment/.

29. "Divest from Fossil Fuels and Reinvest in Workers and Communities," AFT Resolution, July 16, 2022, https://www.aft.org/resolution/divest-fossil-fuels-and-reinvest -workers-and-communities#:~:text=RESOLVED%2C%20that%20AFT%27s%20Climate %20Justice,corporations%20and%20reinvest%20them%20in.

30. "Rutgers AAUP-AFT Freedom School series," *YouTube*, https://www.youtube .com/results?search_query=rutgers+aft+freedom+school.

31. "Senate Bill 999: The Climate and Community Investment Act!" Connecticut Roundtable on Climate and Jobs, https://ctclimateandjobs.org/campaigns/sb999/.

32. David Roberts, "New York Just Passed the Most Ambitious Climate Target in the Country," *Vox*, July 22, 2019, https://www.vox.com/energy-and-environment/ 2019/6/20/18691058/new-york-green-new-deal-climate-change-cuomo.

33. Climate Jobs New York, "Statement on New York's Historic Renewable Energy Job Standards," April 6, 2021, https://www.climatejobsny.org/news/2021/4/6/ cjnys-statement-on-new-yorks-historic-renewable-energy-job-standards.

34. J. Mijin Cha, Hunter Moskowitz, Matt Phillips, and Lara Skinner, *Maine Climate Jobs Report*, ILR Worker Institute, March 2022, https://www.mainelaborclimate.org/ our-report.

35. Cha, Moskowitz, Phillips, and Skinner, *Maine Climate Jobs Report*.

36. Michael Sainato, "Labor and Environmental Movements Team Up and Win Big in Illinois," *Real News*, September 28, 2021, https://therealnews.com/labor-and -environmentalist-movements-team-up-and-win-big-in-illinois%EF%BB%BF.

37. Jeremy Brecher, *Climate Solidarity: Workers vs. Warming*, Labor Network for Sustainability, 2017, 42, https://labor4sustainability.org/wp-content/uploads/2017/06/ Climate-Solidarity.pdf. For background see Scott L. Cummings, *Blue and Green: The Drive for Justice at America's Port* (Cambridge, MA: MIT Press, 2018)

38. Nancy Romer, "Setting a Climate Justice Agenda for CUNY," CUNY Urban Food Policy Institute, July 20, 2022, https://cunyurbanfoodpolicy.org/news/2022/2/1/ setting-a-climate-justice-agenda-for-cuny/.

39. Jeremy Brecher, *Climate Solidarity: Workers vs. Warming*, Labor Network for Sustainability, https://www.labor4sustainability.org/wp-content/uploads/2017/06/ Climate-Solidarity.pdf, 42.

40. "The Clean Economy Revolution Will Be Unionized," Center for American Progress, July 7, 2021, https://www.americanprogress.org/article/clean -economy-revolution-will-unionized/.

41. "Mike Fishman," Climate Jobs National Resource Center, https://www.cjnrc.org/ our-team/mike-fishman/.

42. "UWUA Urges Large-Scale Investment in Transmission Infrastructure before House Energy and Commerce Committee," UWUA, June 30, 2021, https://uwua.net/ news/uwua-urges-large-scale-investment-in-transmission-infrastructure-before -house-energy-and-commerce-committee/.

Chapter 4. Climate Justice from Below

1. "Recognizing the Duty of the Federal Government to Create a Green New Deal," H. Res. 109, 116th Congress, 1st session, https://www.congress.gov/116/bills/hres109/BILLS-116hres109ih.pdf.

2. "A Just Transition Doesn't Have to Be Top-Down," *Grist FIX Solutions Lab*, May 4, 2021.

3. For a contemporary account see Katherine Goldstein, "Occupy Sandy: Hurricane Relief Being Led by Occupy Wall Street," *Slate*, November 4, 2012, https://slate.com/news-and-politics/2012/11/occupy-sandy-hurricane-relief-being-led-by-occupy-wall-street.html.

4. "Climate Justice—Uprose," https://www.uprose.org/climate-justice#.

5. Caspar Gajewski, "The South Brooklyn Marine Terminal Will Bring Jobs to Sunset Park," blog, March 29, 2023, https://blogs.baruch.cuny.edu/locke2023/?p=545.

6. Iris Crawford, "Can Kelp Farming Bring Back Shinnecock Bay?" *nexus media news*, November 15, 2022, https://nexusmedianews.com/can-kelp-farm-save-shinnecock-bay/.

7. Bren Smith, *Eat Like a Fish: My Adventures Farming the Ocean to Fight Climate Change* (New York: Knopf, 2019). See also Jeremy Brecher, "The Blue New Deal," Labor Network for Sustainability, May 5, 2021, https://www.labor4sustainability.org/strike/the-blue-new-deal-making-a-living-on-a-living-ocean/.

8. Teresa Tomassoni, "A Sisterhood of the Sea," *American Indian*, Spring 2023, https://www.americanindianmagazine.org/Shinnecock-kelp-farmers.

9. "Gulf South for a Green New Deal Policy Platform," Gulf Coast Center for Law and Policy, 2019, https://www.gcclp.org/services-products. The creation of the Gulf South for a Green New Deal Policy Platform was a six-month process anchored by the Gulf Coast Center for Law & Policy, https://www.gcclp.org, which was subsequently renamed Taproot Earth, https://taproot.earth. A Southern Communities for a Green New Deal grew out of the Gulf South for a Green New Deal with the goal of extending its approach to other states throughout the South, https://www.scen-us.org/scgnd.

10. "Gulf South for a Green New Deal 2022 Overview and Action Plan," https://www.gulfsouth4gnd.org/post/read-the-gs4gnd-action-plan-for-2022-and-beyond-here.

11. Gulf South for a Green New Deal, March 16, 2022, https://www.facebook.com/hashtag/floridagreennewdeal.

Chapter 5. Climate-Safe Energy Production

1. Alexandria Ocasio-Cortez, "A Green New Deal: Draft Text for Proposed Addendum to House Rules for 116th Congress of the United States," https://biotech.law.lsu.edu/blog/FINAL-Select-Committee-for-a-Green-New-Deal-1-1.pdf. Energy discussions use a plethora of terms like "renewable," "green," "clean," "fossil-free," "low-carbon," "net-zero," and the like. This chapter uses whatever terms are being applied to the various projects, targets, and standards it describes. Whatever the metric, all the projects described involve actual reductions in greenhouse gas emissions.

2. Denver, Office of Climate Action, Sustainability, and Resiliency, "Climate Protection Fund Five-Year Plan," https://denvergov.org/files/assets/public/climate-action/cpf_fiveyearplan_final.pdf.

3. John Farrell and Maria McCoy, "Why Minnesota's Community Solar Program Is the Best," Institute for Local Self-Reliance, November 29, 2021, https://ilsr.org/mnnesotas-community-solar-program/.

4. "DHA Wins Top Prize in DOE's Solar Energy Competition," *Our Colorado,* October 17, 2018, https://www.thedenverchannel.com/news/our-colorado/denver-housing-authority-wins-top-prize-in-dept-of-energys-solar-in-your-community-challenge.

5. Farrell and McCoy, "Why Minnesota's Community Solar Program Is the Best."

6. Michelle Lewis, "California Energy Commission Mandates Solar for New Buildings from 2023," *Electrek*, August 12, 2021, https://electrek.co/2021/08/12/california-energy-commission-mandates-solar-for-new-buildings-from-2023/.

7. Camila Domonoske, "San Francisco Requires New Buildings to Install Solar Panels," *Two-Way*, NPR, April 20, 2016, https://www.npr.org/sections/thetwo-way/2016/04/20/474969107/san-francisco-requires-new-buildings-to-install-solar-panels.

8. Lewis, "California Energy Commission Mandates Solar for New Buildings from 2023."

9. "Shining Cities 2020," *Environment America*, https://environmentamerica.org/feature/ame/shining-cities-2020.

10. Vineyard Power, http://vineyardpower.com.

11. George Brennan, "A 'Momentous Day' for Vineyard Wind," *Martha's Vineyard Times*, November 18, 2021, https://www.mvtimes.com/2021/11/18/momentous-day-vineyard-wind/.

12. Vineyard Power, "Offshore Wind Power," http://vineyardpower.com/offshore-wind.

13. Susan Phillips, "New Jersey Takes an 'Educated Leap into the Future' as state Approves 2 New Offshore Wind Projects." *WHYY*, January 24, 2024, https://whyy.org/articles/new-jersey-board-public-utilities-offshore-wind-farms-invenergy-energy-attentive-energy/.

14. Dan Gearino, "Inside Clean Energy: Who's Ahead in the Race for Offshore Wind Jobs in the US?" *Inside Climate News*, October 28, 2021, https://insideclimatenews.org/news/28102021/inside-clean-energy-wind-energy-jobs-virginia/.

15. "Public Power," American Public Power Association, https://www.publicpower.org/public-power.

16. "Public Power."

17. Peter Maloney, "Burlington Electric to Help Meet Net Zero Energy Goal," American Public Power Association, September 16, 2019, https://www.publicpower.org/periodical/article/burlington-electric-help-meet-net-zero-energy-goal.

18. Michelle Lewis, "EGEB: Local Areas Are Buying Electricity in Bulk for Residents," *Electrek*, February 19, 2020, https://electrek.co/2020/02/19/egeb-towns-cities-community-choice-aggregation-electricity-bulk-notpla/.

19. "Swampscott, MA Community," EPA, https://www.epa.gov/greenpower/green-power-communities#SwampscottMACommunity.

20. "Frequently Asked Questions," Green Power Partnership, EPA, https://www.epa.gov/greenpower/green-power-partnership-frequently-asked-questions.

21. "Green Power Partnership Top 30 Local Government," EPA, https://www.epa.gov/greenpower/green-power-partnership-top-30-local-government.

22. "Green Power Partnership Top 30 Local Government."

23. Judy Asman, "Rooted in Legacy," Labor Network for Sustainability, https://www.labor4sustainability.org/articles/renowned-labor-and-environmental-justice-leader-calls-for-place-based-just-transition-to-empower-aapi-communities/.

24. Sarah Rubenoff, "Details on the 14 Massachusetts Community Microgrid Projects That Won Funding," *Microgrid Knowledge*, February 23, 2018, https://microgridknowledge.com/community-microgrid-projects-massachusetts/.

25. Ocasio-Cortez, "A Green New Deal."

26. K. Holt, "Wind and Solar Could Meet 85 Percent of Current US Electricity Needs," *Engadget*, November 8, 2021, https://www.engadget.com/wind-solar-energy-needs-study-172901659.html.

27. "Clean Power Annual, 2020," American Clean Power Association, https://cleanpower.org/wp-content/uploads/2021/07/ACP-CPA-2020-Public.pdf.

28. Robert Pollin, James Heintz, and Heidi Garrett-Peltier, "Clean Energy Investments for the U.S. Economy," Political Economy Research Institute University of Massachusetts–Amherst, March 16, 2010, https://peri.umass.edu/fileadmin/pdf/conference_papers/Surdna/Pollin-Heintz-Garrett-Peltier_paper_for_Surdna_Conf-3-16-10.pdf.

29. "Clean Energy Workforce Report Summary," American Clean Power Association, 2021, https://cleanpower.org/wp-content/uploads/2021/06/Summary-Clean-Energy-Workforce-Report.pdf.

30. Dave Lucas, "Residents, Town Officials Discuss Copake Solar Facility," *WAMC*, November 30, 2021, https://www.wamc.org/capital-region-news/2021-11-30/residents-town-officials-discuss-copake-solar-facility.

Chapter 6. Negawatts

1. Alexandria Ocasio-Cortez, "A Green New Deal," press release, April 20, 2021, https://ocasio-cortez.house.gov/media/press-releases/ocasio-cortez-markey-reintroduce-green-new-deal-resolution-0.

2. Bernie Sanders, "Sanders and Ocasio-Cortez Rollout Green New Deal for Public Housing Act," press release, April 19, 2021, https://www.sanders.senate.gov/press-releases/news-sanders-and-ocasio-cortez-rollout-green-new-deal-for-public-housing-act/.

3. City of Ithaca, "Ithaca Green New Deal," https://www.cityofithaca.org/DocumentCenter/View/11054/IGND-Summary-02–11–2020.

4. City of Ithaca, "Efficiency Retrofitting and Thermal Load Electrification Program: Request for Proposals," 2021, http://www.cityofithaca.org/DocumentCenter/View/13214/City-of-Ithaca-Retrofitting-Electrification-RFP.

5. City of Ithaca, "Efficiency Retrofitting."

6. "Ithaca Races against the Clock to Decarbonize All Buildings by 2030," Episode 144 of Local Energy Rules, Institute for Local Self-Reliance, https://ilsr.org/ithaca-new-york-building-decarbonization-ler144/.

7. City of Ithaca, "Efficiency Retrofitting." For a critical view of BlocPower, one of the Ithaca Green New Deal's principal contractors, questioning many of its claims, see Lee Harris, "Energy Insufficiency," *American Prospect*, September 6, 2023, https://prospect.org/environment/2023-09-06-energy-insufficiency-blocpower/.

8. "Sustainability," 11, 55, https://plan.lamayor.org/sites/default/files/pLAn_2019_final.pdf.

9. "Sustainability."

10. "Mayor Garcetti Announces New Energy Efficiency and Building Decarbonization Investments for Low Income Angelinos," City of Los Angeles, October 29, 2021, https://www.lamayor.org/mayor-garcetti-announces-new-energy-efficiency-and-building-decarbonization-investments-low-income.

11. Efficiency Maine, "Sixty Municipalities Use Funding from Efficiency Maine and The Nature Conservancy to Upgrade Lighting and Heating Systems," *EE Online*, August 18, 2021, https://electricenergyonline.com/article/energy/category/climate-change/82/913797/sixty-municipalities-use-funding-from-efficiency-maine-and-the-nature-conservancy-to-upgrade-lighting-and-heating-systems-.html.

12. "Mosaic Gardens: Low-Income, Multifamily Housing Leading in the Energy Transition," Active Efficiency Collaborative, https://activeefficiency.org/project/mosaic-gardens-low-income-multifamily-housing-leading-energy-transition/.

13. "Mosaic Gardens at Pomona," Linc Housing, https://www.linchousing.org/signature-properties/mosaic-gardens-at-pomona.

14. David Roberts, "New York Passes the Country's Most Ambitious Climate Target," *Vox*, June 20, 2019, https://www.vox.com/energy-and-environment/2019/6/20/18691058/new-york-green-new-deal-climate-change-cuomo.

15. "'We Have to Have an Eye toward the Future': LA's IBEW Local 11 Spearheads a Transition to Clean Energy," *Making a Living on a Living Planet*, https://www.labor4sustainability.org/uncategorized/we-have-to-have-an-eye-toward-the-future/.

Chapter 7. Fossil Fuel Phaseout

1. Climate Tracker, Josh Lederman, "Biden's Over-Under for Paris Climate Goal: 50 Percent," *NBC News*, March 19, 2021, https://www.nbcnews.com/politics/joe-biden/bidens-paris-climate-goal-50-percent-rcna454.

2. Swedish Environmental Institute, International Institute for Sustainable Development, ODI, E3G, and UN Environmental Programme, "The Production Gap Report: 2020 Special Report," http://productiongap.org/2020report.

3. For a detailed analysis of the necessity for supply-side reductions as a part of climate protection see Oil Change International, *The Sky's Limit*, September 2016, chapter 4, https://priceofoil.org/2016/09/22/the-skys-limit-report/.

4. Sierra Club, "Ready for 100?' https://www.sierraclub.org/ready-for-100/about-our-program.

5. Indigenous Environmental Network and Oil Change International, "Indigenous Resistance against Carbon," August 2021, https://www.ienearth.org/wp-content/uploads/2021/09/Indigenous-Resistance-Against-Carbon-2021.pdf.

6. Jeremy Brecher, "The Green New Deal—From Below," Labor Network for Sustainability, October 22, 2021, https://www.labor4sustainability.org/strike/the-green-new-deal-from-below/.

7. Nicolas Gaulin and Philippe Le Billon, "Climate Change and Fossil Fuel Production Cuts: Assessing Global Supply-Side Constraints and Policy Implications," *Climate Policy*, February 14, 2020, https://doi.org/10.1080/14693062.2020.1725409.

8. Nina Lakhani, "Nalleli Cobo: The Young Activist Who Led Her LA Neighbourhood against Big Oil," *Guardian*, November 10, 2021, https://www.theguardian.com/society/2021/nov/10/nalleli-cobo-the-young-activist-who-led-her-la-neighbourhood-against-big-oil.

9. Gabrielle Canon, "Los Angeles City Council Votes to Ban New Urban Oil and Gas Drilling in Historic Move," *Guardian*, January 26, 2022, https://www.the

guardian.com/us-news/2022/jan/26/los-angeles-vote-phase-out-oil-and-gas
-drilling; and Dakota Smith, "L.A. City Council Takes Steps to Phase Out Oil Drilling," *Los Angeles Times,* January 26, 2022, https://www.latimes.com/california/
story/2022-01-26/l-a-city-council-moves-to-phase-out-oil-and-gas-drilling.

10. Sierra Club, "ACC Approves Major Expansion of Gas-Fired Power Plant without Allowing Any Public Comment," November 29, 2023, https://coal.sierraclub.org/
press-releases?page=1.

11. Sierra Club, "The Sierra Club's Beyond Coal Campaign Marks 350th Coal Plant
Set for Retirement," December 15, 2021, https://www.sierraclub.org/articles/2021/12/
sierra-club-s-beyond-coal-campaign-marks-350th-coal-plant-set-for-retirement?_
ga=2.138220339.2018989559.1643391125-734552592.1641400575.

12. Sierra Club, "America, Let's Move Beyond Coal and Gas," https://coal.sierraclub
.org.

13. Karl Cates and Seth Feaster, "IEEFA Update: Out-to-Pasture Coal Plants Are
Being Repurposed into New Economic Endeavors," Institute for Energy Economics
and Financial Analysis, June 7, 2019, https://ieefa.org/ieefa-update-out-to-pasture
-coal-plants-are-being-repurposed-into-new-economic-endeavors/.

14. Zahra Hirji, "It's Not Just Dakota Access. Many Other Fossil Fuel Projects
Delayed or Canceled, Too," *Inside Climate News,* December 5, 2016, https://inside
climatenews.org/news/06052016/fossil-fuel-projects-cancellations-keystone-xl
-pipeline-oil-coal-natural-gas-climate-change-activists.

15. James Steinbauer, "In a Major Victory, Keystone XL Pipeline Canceled," *Sierra,*
June 10, 2021, https://www.sierraclub.org/sierra/major-victory-keystone-xl-pipeline
-canceled.

16. "Should Your Union's Pension Fund Divest from Fossil Fuels?" Labor Network
for Sustainability, 2019, https://labor4sustainability.org/wp-content/uploads/2019/03/
Divest-Invest-Guide-2019.pdf.

17. "New York State Divests Pension Funds from Fossil Fuels," Labor Network
for Sustainability, February 16, 2021, https://www.labor4sustainability.org/articles/
new-york-state-divests-pension-funds-from-fossil-fuels/.

18. "New York City Pension Funds Ditching Fossil Fuels," Labor Network for
Sustainability, March 16, 2021, https://www.labor4sustainability.org/articles/new
-york-city-pension-funds-ditching-fossil-fuels/. For an account of the New York
City divestment movement see Nancy Romer, "How New York City Won Divestment from Fossil Fuels," *Portside,* March 2, 2018, https://portside.org/2018-03-02/
how-new-york-city-won-divestment-fossil-fuels.

19. "1485 Institutions with Assets over $39.2 Trillion Have Committed to Divest
from Fossil Fuels." *Stand.earth,* October 26, 2021, https://stand.earth/insights/1485
-institutions-with-assets-over-39-2-trillion-have-committed-to-divest-from-fossil-fuels/.

20. Laurence L. Delina, *Strategies for Rapid Climate Mitigation: Wartime
Mobilisation as a Model for Action?* (London and New York: Routledge, 2016),
chapter 6: "Legislations, Control, Oversight," https://www.routledge.com/Strate-
gies-for-Rapid-Climate-Mitigation-Wartime-mobilisation-as-a-model/Delina/p/
book/9780815364542.

Chapter 8. Transforming Transportation

1. EPA, "Sources of Greenhouse Gas Emissions," November 16, 2023, https://www
.epa.gov/ghgemissions/sources-greenhouse-gas-emissions.

2. "Economic Impact of Public Transportation Investment," American Public Transportation Association, February 2020, https://www.apta.com/research-technical-resources/research-reports/economic-impact-of-public-transportation-investment/.

3. For a detailed presentation of Green New Deal transportation policy see "A Green New Deal for City and Suburban Transportation," *Data for Progress*, March 2020, https://t4america.org/wp-content/uploads/2020/03/20.03_GND-Transit_use_v4.pdf.

4. Jeremy Brecher, "The Green New Deal—From Below," Labor Network for Sustainability, October 22, 2021, https://www.labor4sustainability.org/strike/the-green-new-deal-from-below/.

5. Joni Mitchell, "Big Yellow Taxi," *YouTube*, https://www.youtube.com/watch?v=94bdMSCdw20.

6. "Goodbye Parking Lot, Hello Affordable Housing: Logan TOD Construction Starts Next Month," *Streetsblog*, August 18, 2020, https://chi.streetsblog.org/2020/08/18/goodbye-parking-lot-hello-affordable-housing-construction-on-logan-tod-starts-next-month/; Jack Crawford, "Affordable Housing Development Emmett Street Apartments Wraps Up in Logan Square," *Chicago YIMBY*, November 27, 2021, https://chicagoyimby.com/2021/11/affordable-housing-development-emmett-street-apartments-wraps-up-in-logan-square.html.

For an account of how the project was won, see Carlos Ramirez-Rosa, "How a Socialist City Councilor Won 100% Affordable Housing in a Gentrifying Chicago Neighborhood," *Jacobin*, November 5, 2022, https://jacobinmag.com/2021/05/socialist-city-councilor-100-percent-affordable-housing-chicago-carlos-ramirez-rosa.

7. "MARTA, Goldman Sachs Announce $100 Million Increase to Atlanta Affordable Housing TOD Initiative," *Mass Transit*, March 23, 2022, https://www.masstransitmag.com/technology/facilities/press-release/21261484/metropolitan-atlanta-rapid-transit-authority-marta-marta-goldman-sachs-announce-100-million-increase-to-atlanta-affordable-housing-tod-initiative.

8. "A Green New Deal for City and Suburban Transportation," *Transit Center*, 5, https://transitcenter.org/wp-content/uploads/2020/03/20.03_GND-Transit_use_v4.pdf.

9. "Shot spotter" is a gunshot detection system. For a report critical of shot spotter, see "The Chicago Police Department's Use of Shotspotter Technology," City of Chicago Office of Inspector General, August 24, 2021, https://igchicago.org/wp-content/uploads/2021/08/Chicago-Police-Departments-Use-of-ShotSpotter-Technology.pdf.

10. Mischa Wanek-Libman, "Kansas-Missouri Bi-state Sustainable Reinvestment Corridor Project Proposed," *Mass Transit*, February 22, 2022, https://www.masstransitmag.com/bus/infrastructure/article/21257692/kansasmissouri-bistate-sustainable-reinvestment-corridor-project-proposed.

11. "Congressman Cleaver Announces $27 Million from Bipartisan Infrastructure Law for Kansas City Transit," *Northeast News*, April 7, 2022, http://northeastnews.net/pages/congressman-cleaver-announces-27-million-from-bipartisan-infrastructure-law-for-kansas-city-transit/.

12. Christopher Benson, "Public Transit Service expanding in Valley Counties," *Daily Item*, March 17, 2022, https://www.dailyitem.com/news/public-transit-service-expanding-in-valley-counties/article_adef15a2-a580-11ec-9fe0-738f5eb41ffd.html.

13. Joe DeManuelle-Hall, "Texas Union Activists Fight 'Microtransit' Privatization," *Labor Notes*, March 8, 2022, https://www.labornotes.org/blogs/2022/03/texas-union-activists-fight-microtransit-privatization.

14. "Amalgamated Transit Union Bus Drivers Steer Procurement to Electric Buses," *Making a Living on a Living Planet*, November 13, 2019, https://www.labor4sustainability

.org/articles/amalgamated-transit-union-bus-drivers-steer-procurement-to-electric -busses/.

15. "Clean Buses for Healthy Ninos," CHISPA, League of Conservation Voters, https://chispalcv.org/clean-buses-for-healthy-ninos/.

16. "Clean Buses for Healthy Ninos."

17. Leighton Schneider, "Maryland School District Replacing Diesel School Buses with Electric," *ABC News*, March 7, 2021, https://abcnews.go.com/Technology/ maryland-school-district-replacing-diesel-school-buses-electric/story?id=76286416.

18. Michelle Lewis, "New York State Commits to 100% Electric School Buses by 2035," *Electrek*, April 8, 2022, https://electrek.co/2022/04/08/new-york-state -governor-100-electric-school-buses-2035/.

19. "A Green New Deal for City and Suburban Transportation," 7.

20. Ryan Packer, "Welcome to the Move Ahead Washington Era," *Urbanist*, March 13, 2022, https://www.theurbanist.org/2022/03/13/welcome-to-the-move-ahead -washington-era/.

21. Laura Bliss, "Six States Adopt Clean Truck Rule," *Bloomberg News*, January 6, 2022, https://www.ttnews.com/articles/six-states-adopt-clean-truck-rule.

22. Zack Burdryk, "Hochul Signs Law Requiring Zero-Emission Passenger Vehicles by 2035," *The Hill*, September 8, 2021, https://thehill.com/policy/energy -environment/571385-hochul-signs-law-requiring-zero-emission-passenger-vehicles -by-2035.

23. Seattle City Light, https://www.seattle.gov/city-light/about-us/history.

24. Peter Maloney, "Seattle City Light, Agencies Release Clean Transportation Electrification Plan," American Public Power Association, March 24, 2021, https:// www.publicpower.org/periodical/article/seattle-city-light-agencies-release-clean -transportation-electrification-plan; "Seattle's Clean Transportation Electrification Blueprint," City of Seattle, March 2021, https://www.seattle.gov/documents/Departments/ OSE/ClimateDocs/TE/TE%20Blueprint%20-%20March%202021.pdf.

25. "San Francisco Officials Vote to Keep JFK Drive Car-Free," *NBC Bay Area*, April 27, 2022, https://www.nbcbayarea.com/news/local/san-francisco/officials-expected -to-vote-on-whether-jfk-drive-in-sf-should-remain-car-free/2874687/.

26. Anna Armstrong, "Berkeley Reimagines Telegraph Avenue Streetscape as Car-Free Zone," *Daily Californian*, February 1, 2022, https://www.dailycal.org/2022/01/26/ berkeley-reimagines-telegraph-avenue-streetscape-as-car-free-zone/.

27. Robert J. McCarthy, "New Federal Money to Connect DL&W to KeyBank Center; Aid Other 'Green' Projects," *Buffalo News*, May 1, 2022, https://buffalonews.com/ news/local/new-federal-money-to-connect-dl-w-to-keybank-center-aid-other-green -projects/article_5317d9bc-a3ae-11ec-ade2-6b6a2c1178ca.html.

28. "Vision zero" is "a strategy to eliminate all traffic fatalities and severe injuries, while increasing safe, healthy, equitable mobility for all." Vision Zero Network, https:// visionzeronetwork.org.

29. "Austin City Council Awards First 2020 Mobility Bond Construction Contract," *Mass Transit*, March 25, 2022, https://www.masstransitmag.com/alt-mobility/ shared-mobility/article/21261779/austin-city-council-awards-first-2020-mobility -bond-construction-contract.

30. Christian May-Suzuki, "Moving Forward: Culver City Accepts Mobility Lane Project," *Culver City News*, February 11, 2021, https://www.culvercitynews.org/ moving-forward-culver-city-accepts-mobility-lane-project/.

Chapter 9. Protecting Workers and Communities—On the Ground

1. Susan Montoya Brian, "US Shift Away from Coal Hits Tribal Community in New Mexico," *AP News*, October 2, 2022, https://apnews.com/article/business-new-mexico-climate-and-environment-a8235ae76179ee10004f26b0a72fb689.

2. "European Union's Just Transition Mechanism: Transnational Funding and Support for a Just Transition," World Resources Institute, April 21, 2021, https://www.wri.org/update/european-unions-just-transition-mechanism-transnational-funding-and-support-just-transition. For analysis of the many issues surrounding "just transition," see Dimitris Stevis, *Just Transitions: Promise and Contestation* (Cambridge: Cambridge University Press, 2023) and references therein, https://www.cambridge.org/core/elements/abs/just-transitions/AE1A61FF8C637A72C13DC3F43113DC64.

3. J. Mijin Cha, Vivian Price, Dimitris Stevis, and Todd E. Vachon with Maria Brescia-Weiler, "Workers and Communities in Transition: Report of the Just Transition Listening Project," Labor Network for Sustainability, 2021, https://www.labor4sustainability.org/files/JTLP_report2021.pdf. For the long-term, sometimes multigenerational, impacts of local economic affliction, see Howard Botwinick, *Persistent Inequalities: Wage Disparity under Capitalist Competition* (Chicago: Haymarket Books, 2018), https://www.haymarketbooks.org/books/1200-persistent-inequalities.

4. Les Leopold, *The Man Who Hated Work and Loved Labor: The Life and Times of Tony Mazzocchi* (White River Junction, VT: Chelsea Green, 2007).

5. "Just Transition: Just What Is It?" Labor Network for Sustainability and the Grassroots Policy Project, https://www.labor4sustainability.org/uncategorized/just-transition-just-what-is-it/; and Jeremy Brecher, "How to Protect Workers While Protecting the Climate," Labor Network for Sustainability, July 15, 2021, https://www.labor4sustainability.org/just-transition/how-to-protect-workers-while-protecting-the-climate/. For links to other LNS materials on "just transition": https://www.labor4sustainability.org/just-transition/.

6. Sarah Jackson et al., "Reimagining Brayton Point," Synapse Energy Economics, March 3, 2016, https://www.synapse-energy.com/sites/default/files/Reimagining_Brayton_Point_15-076.pdf.

7. "Massachusetts Site Completes Offshore Wind Port Upgrades," *Renewable Energy News*, April 2, 2020, https://renews.biz/59470/massachusetts-site-completes-offshore-wind-port-upgrades/.

8. "President Biden Picks Brayton Point Site for Major Climate Change Speech," *Prysmian Group*, https://www.prysmiangroup.com/en/insight/projects/president-biden-picks-brayton-point-site-for-major-climate-change-speech.

9. "Remarks by President Biden on Actions to Tackle the Climate Crisis," *White House*, July 20, 2022, https://www.whitehouse.gov/briefing-room/speeches-remarks/2022/07/20/remarks-by-president-biden-on-actions-to-tackle-the-climate-crisis/.

10. Based on presentation by Curt Oldfield, president of Spoon River College, to "Where to Start? Webinar for Energy Communities Starting a Transformation," November 2021, https://energycommunities.gov/wp-content/uploads/2021/11/IWG-Where-to-Start_-Slides-for-Nov-3_FINAL.pdf. Oldfield presentation starts at 53 minutes.

11. Unless otherwise noted, information in the section comes from "Creating the First National Model for 'Gap Funding' in New York," Just Transition Fund, https://justtransitionfund.org/resources/tonawanda-ny/; and Richard Lipsitz and Rebecca Newberry, "Huntley, a Case Study: Building Strategic Alliances for Real Change," Labor

Network for Sustainability, 2016, https://www.labor4sustainability.org/wp-content/uploads/2016/09/The-Huntley-Experiment.pdf.

12. Liv Yoon, "Short Film Captures the Story of a Just Energy Transition in Tonawanda, NY," *State of the Planet*, October 10, 2022, https://news.climate.columbia.edu/2022/10/10/short-film-captures-the-story-of-a-just-energy-transition-in-tonawanda-ny/.

13. Rachel Layne, "How One Small City Sowed the Seeds for Its Own Green New Deal," *CBS News*, March 8, 2019, https://www.cbsnews.com/news/climate-change-how-one-small-city-sowed-the-seeds-for-its-own-green-new-deal/.

14. *Mt. Tom Power Plant Reuse Study*, Massachusetts Clean Energy Center, November 2015, https://files.masscec.com/research/MtTomReuseStudyENGLISH.pdf.

15. Adele Peters, "How a Holyoke, MA, Coal Plant Became a Solar Farm," *Fast Company*, January 3, 2019, https://www.fastcompany.com/90286009/this-old-coal-plant-is-now-a-solar-farm-thanks-to-pressure-from-local-activists.

16. Kristin Palpini, "From Coal to Sol! Holyoke's Mt. Tom Generating Plant Is Making the Switch to Solar, but Its Dirty Past Lurks," *Valley Advocate*, October 31, 2016. https://valleyadvocate.com/2016/10/31/from-coal-to-sol/. This article also includes a vivid description of an "intense" meeting between the owners of Mount Tom station and sixty community members and environmental activists.

17. Chris Teale, "A New Lease on Life for Holyoke, MA's Former Coal-Fired Power Plant," *Smart Cities Dive*, January 22, 2019, https://www.smartcitiesdive.com/news/holyoke-coal-fired-power-plant/546447/.

18. Arjun Makhijani, "Beyond a Band-Aid: A Discussion Paper on Protecting Workers and Communities in the Great Energy Transition," Institute for Energy and Environmental Research and Labor Network for Sustainability, 2016, https://labor4sustainability.org/files/pdf_06142016_final.pdf.

Chapter 10. Just Transition in the States

1. C. J. Polychroniou, "Oil Companies Spent Millions to Defeat Green New Deal in Washington State," *Rozenberg Quarterly*, https://rozenbergquarterly.com/oil-companies-spent-millions-to-defeat-green-new-deal-in-washington-state/.

2. David Roberts, "Washington I-1631 Results: Price on Carbon Emissions Fails to Pass," *Vox*, November 6, 2018, https://www.vox.com/energy-and-environment/2018/9/28/17899804/washington-1631-results-carbon-fee-green-new-deal. For more on the climate justice work of the coalition, see Sasha Abramsky, "This Washington State Ballot Measure Fights for Both Jobs and Climate Justice," *The Nation*, July 20, 2018, https://www.thenation.com/article/archive/green-new-deal-evergreen-state/. For Front and Centered, see https://frontandcentered.org.

3. Robert Pollin, Heidi Garrett-Peltier, and Jeannette Wicks-Lim, "A Green New Deal for Washington State: Climate Stabilization, Good Jobs, and Just Transition," Political Economy Research Institute (PERI), December 2017, https://peri.umass.edu/component/k2/item/1033-a-green-new-deal-for-washington-state.

4. "Initiative Measure No. 1631," *Washington Secretary of State*, March 13, 2018, https://www.sos.wa.gov/sites/default/files/2022-05/Voters%2520Pamphlet%25202018.pdf?uid=649c67302d5a6.

5. Rachel M. Cohen, "The Just Transition for Coal Workers Can Start Now. Colorado Is Showing How," *In These Times*, July 24, 2019, https://inthesetimes.com/working/entry/21975/colorado-just-transition-labor-coal-mine-workers-peoples-climate-movement.

6. Chase Woodruff, "As Coal Burning Goes Away in Colorado, Money for Coal Workers Goes Up," *Colorado Newsline*, April 30, 2022, https://coloradonewsline.com/2022/04/30/just-transition-colorado-coal-workers-rural-communities-advanced/.

7. "Energy Community Reinvestment Act Fact—CEJA," *Prairie Rivers Network*, https://docs.google.com/document/d/1q23G-pfUqrNInX7tGl9Nr9ooyHcOeFxOVQ9NGYNV9iE/edit.

8. "The Clean Energy Jobs Act," Illinois Clean Jobs Coalition, http://ilcleanjobs.org/wp-content/uploads/2021/03/JustTransition.pdf.

9. "Reinvesting in Illinois' Energy Communities," *Prairie Rivers Network*, May 23, 2022, https://prairierivers.org/front-page/2022/05/reinvesting-in-illinois-energy-communities/.

10. Emily Pontecorvo, "How a Debate over Carbon Capture Derailed California's Landmark Climate Bill," *Grist*, December 15, 2021, https://grist.org/politics/carbon-capture-why-california-cant-fill-the-net-zero-gap-in-its-climate-strategy/.

11. The Labor Network for Sustainability and San Francisco Jobs with Justice helped coordinate the study.

12. Sammy Roth, "Why a California Oil Workers Union Is Getting Behind Clean Energy," *Los Angeles Times,* June 10, 2021, https://www.latimes.com/environment/newsletter/2021-06-10/why-a-california-oil-workers-union-is-getting-behind-clean-energy-boiling-point.

13. Jesse Bedayn, "'Just Transition' Bill for Oil Workers Pits Unions against Unions," *Cal Matters*, February 17, 2022, updated March 4, 2022, https://calmatters.org/california-divide/2022/02/just-transition-bill-for-oil-industry-workers-exposes-labor-rift/.

14. Robert Pollin, Jeannette Wicks-Lim, Shouvik Chakraborty, Caitlin Kline, and Gregor Semieniuk, "A Program for Economic Recovery and Clean Energy Transition in California," PERI, June 2021, https://peri.umass.edu/publication/item/1466-a-program-for-economic-recovery-and-clean-energy-transition-in-california. See also "Twenty Unions Stand By a California Climate Jobs Plan," *Making a Living on a Living Planet*, July/August 2021, https://labor4sustainability.ourpowerbase.net/civicrm/mailing/view?reset=1&id=675. For a list of unions endorsing the California Climate Jobs Plan, see https://www.californiaclimatejobsplan.com.

15. Roth, "Why a California Oil Workers Union Is Getting Behind Clean Energy."

16. "Community Economic Resilience Fund Program Program Year 2022–24," California Grants Portal, https://www.grants.ca.gov/grants/community-economic-resilience-fund-program-program-year-2022–24/.

17. Monica Embrey, "Los Angeles County Forms Just-Transition Taskforce to Clean Up Old Oil Wells," Sierra Club, September 29, 2020, https://www.sierraclub.org/articles/2020/09/los-angeles-county-forms-just-transition-taskforce-clean-old-oil-wells.

18. J. Mijin Cha, Vivian Price, Dimitris Stevis, and Todd E. Vachon, "Just Transition Listening Project," Labor Network for Sustainability, 2021, https://www.labor4sustainability.org/jtlp-2021/.

19. Three of the four cases in this chapter included reports by economist Dr. Robert Pollin and the Political Economy Research Institute (PERI) at the University of Massachusetts–Amherst.

20. For a review of the Interagency Working Group's activities so far, see "Interagency Working Group (IWG) on Coal and Power Plant Communities and Economic Revitalization," *Congressional Research Service*, October 24, 2022, https://crsreports.congress.gov/product/pdf/IF/IF12238.

Chapter 11. Green New Deal Jobs for the Future

1. "Recognizing the Duty of the Federal Government to Create a Green New Deal," H-Res. 109, https://www.congress.gov/bill/116th-congress/house-resolution/109/text.

2. "Recognizing the Duty of the Federal Government to Create a Green New Deal," S. Res., https://www.markey.senate.gov/imo/media/doc/gnd_resolution_-_042023.pdf.

3. Jessica Blatt Press, "Nurturing Tomorrow's Workforce," *Philadelphia Citizen*, February 11, 2020, https://thephiladelphiacitizen.org/powercorpsphl-philadelphia/.

4. "Action on Global Warming: NYC's Green New Deal," City of New York, April 22, 2019, https://www.nyc.gov/office-of-the-mayor/news/209-19/action-global-warming-nyc-s-green-new-deal#/0.

5. Michelle Ma, "This New York Program Has Trained 1,700 Workers for Green Jobs," *Fast Company*, January 11, 2023, https://www.fastcompany.com/90833282/this-new-york-program-has-trained-1700-workers-for-green-jobs-and-its-only-getting-started. For a critical view of the program's contractor, BlocPower, questioning many of its claims, see Lee Harris, "Energy Insufficiency," *American Prospect*, September 6, 2023, https://prospect.org/environment/2023-09-06-energy-insufficiency-blocpower/.

6. "California Climate Action Corps," California Volunteers, Office of the Governor, https://www.californiavolunteers.ca.gov/about-california-climate-action-corps/.

7. "Youth Jobs Corps," California Volunteers, Office of the Governor, https://www.californiavolunteers.ca.gov/californiansforall-youth-jobs-corps/.

8. Sam Brasch, "As Colorado Announces Its Own Climate Corps, Democrats Push for a Far More Expansive National Version," *CPR News*, September 11, 2021, https://www.cpr.org/2021/09/11/colorado-climate-corps-democrats-national-version/.

9. *Serve Colorado 2022 Annual Report*, AmeriCorps, https://drive.google.com/file/d/1Xz-UTkG3UmdDDoYUc4uejKqrqg5rUcq8/view.

10. "Clean Jobs America 2022," E2, https://e2.org/reports/clean-jobs-america-2022/.

11. BlueGreen Alliance, "9 Million Good Jobs from Climate Action," https://www.bluegreenalliance.org/wp-content/uploads/2022/08/BGA-IRA-Jobs-Factsheet-8422_Final.pdf.

12. David Foster, Alex Maranville, and Sam F. Savitz et al., "Jobs, Emissions, and Economic Growth—What the Inflation Reduction Act Means for Working Families," EFI Foundation, January 2023, https://energyfuturesinitiative.org/reports/jobs-emissions-and-economic-growth-what-the-inflation-reduction-act-means-for-working-families-jobs-emissions-and-economic-growth/.

13. The Zero Carbon Consortium, *America's Zero Carbon Action Plan*, 2020, chapter 3, 51, https://irp-cdn.multiscreensite.com/6f2c9f57/files/uploaded/zero-carbon-action-plan-exec-summary.pdf.

14. Mark Z. Jacobson, Anna-Katharina von Krauland, Stephen J. Coughlin, Frances C. Palmer, and Miles M. Smith, "Zero Air Pollution and Zero Carbon from All Energy at Low Cost and without Blackouts in Variable Weather throughout the U.S. with 100% Wind-Water-Solar and Storage," *Renewable Energy*, December 1, 2021, https://web.stanford.edu/group/efmh/jacobson/Articles/I/21-USStates-PDFs/21-USStatesPaper.pdf.

15. Blue-Green Alliance, "State-Based Policies to Build a Cleaner, Safer, More Equitable Economy," https://www.bluegreenalliance.org/wp-content/uploads/2020/07/StatePolicyToolkit_Report2020_vFINAL.pdf.

16. Climate Jobs New York, "Statement on New York's Historic Renewable Energy Job Standards," April 6, 2021, https://www.climatejobsny.org/news/2021/4/6/cjnys-statement-on-new-yorks-historic-renewable-energy-job-standards.

17. US Bureau of Labor Statistics, "Union Members Summary," January 19, 2023, https://www.bls.gov/news.release/union2.nr0.htm.

18. Luis Feliz Leon, "Union Win at Bus Factory Electrifies Georgia," *Labor Notes*, May 16, 2023, https://labornotes.org/2023/05/union-win-bus-factory-electrifies-georgia.

19. Matthew Mayers and Lauren Jacobs, "Organizing for the Economy We Want," *Forge*, September 8, 2020, https://forgeorganizing.org/article/organizing-economy-we-want.

20. Lauren Kaori Gurley, "Shifting America to Solar Power Is a Grueling Low-Paid Job," *Vice*, June 27, 2022, https://www.vice.com/en/contributor/lauren-kaori-gurley.

21. Green Workers Alliance, https://www.greenworkers.org/news.

22. For background on climate jobs guarantee programs see Jeremy Brecher, "Climate Jobs for All: Building Block for the Green New Deal," Labor Network for Sustainability, December 2018, https://www.labor4sustainability.org/wp-content/uploads/2018/11/LNSpdf_dec2018.pdf.

23. "Sen. Booker, Reps. Watson Coleman and Omar Introduce Bicameral Bill to Create Federal Jobs Guarantee Program," press release, September 12, 2019, https://www.booker.senate.gov/news/press/sen-booker-reps-watson-coleman-and-omar-introduce-bicameral-bill-to-create-federal-jobs-guarantee-program. Other proposals for a federal jobs guarantee have been introduced subsequently.

24. Martin Austermuhle, "Robert White Pledges to Tackle Public Safety with Massive Green Jobs Program," *DCist/WAMU*, April 22, 2022, https://dcist.com/story/22/04/22/robert-white-green-jobs-program/; and Robert C. White Jr., "WHITE: My Jobs Guarantee Program Would Reduce Violent Crime and Foster Greater Hope," *Washington Informer*, June 15, 2022, https://www.washingtoninformer.com/white-my-jobs-guarantee-program-would-reduce-violent-crime-and-foster-greater-hope/.

25. Helen Gym, "A Community Safety Plan to Restore the Village to Philadelphia," https://helengym.com/safety/.

26. Maria Brescia-Weiler, "Young Workers Face the Climate Future," *Making a Living on a Living Planet*, April 2023, https://labor4sustainability.ourpowerbase.net/civicrm/mailing/view?reset=1&id=806.

Conclusion

1. April Reese, "What a Green New Deal Would Look Like in Every State," *Popular Science*, February 27, 2020, https://www.popsci.com/story/environment/green-new-deal-state-by-state/.

2. This interpretation draws on the concept of the "historic bloc" outlined by the Italian thinker Antonio Gramsci. Gramsci's historic bloc establishes "a synthesis of the aspirations and identities of different groups in a global project which exceeds them all." Such a synthesis becomes possible, notwithstanding current antagonisms, if the parameters of what is considered possible are expanded. Perry Anderson, "Problems of Socialist Strategy," in *Toward Socialism*, ed. Perry Anderson and Robin Blackburn (Ithaca, NY: Cornell University Press, 1965), 243. For a more recent explication of Gramsci's concept of "historical bloc" and a review of recent interpretations, see

Panagiotis Sotiris, "Gramsci and the Challenges for the Left: The Historical Bloc as a Strategic Concept," *Science and Society* 82, no. 1 (January 2018).

3. For a perspective on such coalitions, see Fred Rose, *Coalitions across the Class Divide: Lessons from the Labor, Peace, and Environmental Movements* (Ithaca, NY: Cornell University Press, 2000).

4. Edward Hasbrouck, "The 'Channeling' Memo from the Selective Service," https://hasbrouck.org/draft/channeling.html.

5. Delina and Diesendorf, cited in Jeremy Brecher, Ron Blackwell, and Joe Uehlein, "If Not Now, When: A Labor Movement Plan to Address Climate Change," *New Labor Forum*, 2014, https://www.labor4sustainability.org/wp-content/uploads/2014/09/NLF541793_REV1.pdf. See also Jeremy Brecher, "18 Strategies for a Green New Deal: How to Make the Climate Mobilization Work," Labor Network for Sustainability, 2019, https://www.labor4sustainability.org/wp-content/uploads/2019/02/18Strategies.pdf.

6. Laurence L. Delina, *Strategies for Rapid Climate Mitigation: Wartime Mobilization as a Model for Action?* (London and New York: Routledge, 2016).

7. Romy Varghese, "California Sees Record $97.5 Billion Surplus, Driven by the Rich," *Bloomberg*, May 5, 2022, updated May 13, 2022, https://www.bloomberg.com/news/articles/2022-05-13/california-governor-sees-record-97-5-billion-operating-surplus.

8. "Mayor Wu Unveils First City Budget and $350 Million Federal Spending Plan," *Boston.gov*, April 13, 2022, https://www.boston.gov/news/mayor-wu-unveils-first-city-budget-and-350-million-federal-spending-plan.

9. *Delivering a Green New Deal*, https://www.markey.senate.gov/imo/media/doc/delivering_a_green_new_deal.pdf.

10. *Hoodwinked in the Hothouse: Resist False Solutions to Climate Change*, 3rd ed., 2021, https://climatefalsesolutions.org/wp-content/uploads/HOODWINKED_Third Edition_On-Screen_version.pdf.

11. For proposed criteria for selecting climate strategies for Green New Deal and other programs, see "Recommendations," in Jeremy Brecher, "Can Carbon Capture Save Our Climate—and Our Jobs?" Labor Network for Sustainability, https://www.labor4sustainability.org/files/LNS_CarbonCapture_06082021.pdf.

12. Michael Mann, *The Sources of Social Power*, 4 vols. (Cambridge: Cambridge University Press, 1986–2013). There is vast literature on social and political networks. Classic studies include Margaret E. Keck and Kathryn Sikkink, *Activists Beyond Borders: Advocacy Networks in International Politics* (Ithaca, NY: Cornell University Press, 1998).

13. David Sink, "Transorganizational Development in Urban Policy Coalitions," *Human Relations* 44, no. 11 (1991), https://journals.sagepub.com/doi/10.1177/001872679104401103.

14. Eric M. Patashnik, *Reforms at Risk: What Happens after Major Policy Changes Are Enacted?* (Princeton, NJ: Princeton University Press, 2008).

15. For classic discussions of social movement action, see Doug McAdam, Sidney Tarrow, and Charles Tilly, *Dynamics of Contention* (New York: Cambridge University Press, 2001); and Sidney Tarrow, *Power in Movement: Social Movements and Contentious Politics* (Cambridge: Cambridge University Press, 2011).

16. For proposals for such a process, see Jeremy Brecher, *Save the Humans? Common Preservation in Action* (Boulder, CO: Paradigm Publishers, 2012).

17. This intertwining is discussed in Jeremy Brecher, *Strike!: 50th Anniversary Edition* (Oakland, CA: PM Press, 2020), 502–3.

18. For state New Deal programs, see Jeremy Brecher, "States of Change: What the Green New Deal Can Learn from the New Deal in the States," Labor Network for Sustainability, November 9, 2020, https://www.labor4sustainability.org/files/LNSpdf_States_nov2020.pdf.

19. John Matson, "Reality Check: Red-State Voters Want Clean Energy Too. Just Ask Nebraska," *RMI*, February 17, 2022, https://rmi.org/reality-check-red-state-voters-want-clean-energy-too-just-ask-nebraska/.

20. Matthew Miles Goodrich, "Dallas Climate Activists Won a Major Investment in Green Transit. We Can All Learn from Their Fight," *In These Times*, October 4, 2023, https://inthesetimes.com/article/dallas-climate-activists-won-investment-green-transit-mass-organizing-green-new-deal-public-schools-buses.

21. Jeremy Brecher, *Common Preservation in a Time of Mutual Destruction* (Oakland, CA: PM Press, 2021), https://pmpress.org/index.php?l=product_detail&p=1095.

INDEX

JEREMY BRECHER is a cofounder and senior strategic advisor for the Labor Network for Sustainability. His books include *Strike!*, *Save the Humans? Common Preservation in Action*, and *Climate Insurgency: A Strategy for Survival*.

The University of Illinois Press
is a founding member of the
Association of University Presses.

———————————————————

Composed in 10.5/13 Mercury Text G1
with Myriad Pro display
by Lisa Connery
at the University of Illinois Press
Manufactured by Sheridan Books, Inc.

University of Illinois Press
1325 South Oak Street
Champaign, IL 61820–6903
www.press.uillinois.edu